The Films of Clint Eastwood

The Films of
CLINT EASTWOOD

Critical Perspectives

EDITED BY MATT WANAT AND LEONARD ENGEL

University of New Mexico Press ■ Albuquerque

© 2018 by the University of New Mexico Press
All rights reserved. Published 2018
Printed in the United States of America

Library of Congress Cataloging-in-Publication Data
Names: Wanat, Matt, 1973– editor. | Engel, Leonard, 1936– editor.
Title: The Films of Clint Eastwood: Critical Perspectives /
edited by Matt Wanat and Leonard Engel.
Description: Albuquerque: University of New Mexico Press, 2018. |
Includes filmography. | Includes bibliographical references and index. |
Identifiers: LCCN 2017049040 (print) | LCCN 2017053329 (e-book) |
ISBN 9780826359537 (e-book) | ISBN 9780826359520 (cloth: alk. paper)
Subjects: LCSH: Eastwood, Clint, 1930-—Criticism and interpretation.
Classification: LCC PN2287.E37 (e-book) | LCC PN2287.E37 F55 2018 (print) |
DDC 792.02/8092—dc23
LC record available at https://lccn.loc.gov/2017049040

Cover photographs: (top) *The Good, the Bad, and the Ugly* (1966);
(middle) *The Eiger Sanction* (1975);
(bottom) *Gran Torino* (2008)
Designed by Felicia Cedillos
Composed in Adobe Garamond Pro 10.5/14

Once again, to Toby
Tobias Rafael Engel (1993–2012)

Contents

Acknowledgements

Like Walt Whitman, Clint Eastwood is "large," and he contains "multitudes"—directing, acting, composing, sometimes all three in one film, in addition to heading his own studio, Malpaso, and producing films of such variety, depth, and complexity that it is easy to forget he once had bit parts in movies called *Revenge of the Creature* and *Tarantula* (both 1955). Then, almost overnight, he reached stardom in the 1960s in a series of Spaghetti Westerns directed by Sergio Leone. His career, to refute F. Scott Fitzgerald's purported claim that there are "no second acts in American lives," has been a series of highly successful second acts; he is still going very strong, and on May 31, 2018 he will be 88. His work has had a lasting effect on us and has been an inspiration for this collection of essays. This project has been a labor of love, and we are grateful to a number of people who have helped bring it to fruition. First, our thanks to the contributors; they are as enthralled with Clint's films as we are and have shown it through their fine work and dedication.

Len Engel gives special thanks to Professors Patricia Comitini, Chair of English, and Robert Smart, Dean of the College of Arts & Sciences, at Quinnipiac for their support and encouragement. Many thanks to Quinnipiac's fine library staff who have been very helpful, particularly Janet Valeski, Robert Young, and June DeGennaro. Thanks, also, to our patient and very helpful editor Elise McHugh. Finally, a heartfelt thanks to my wife, Moira, for her love, understanding, and support, especially during the many hours of watching Eastwood's films, which have touched, many times, the very core of what it means to be human.

Matt Wanat would like to thank Jane Wells and the kids, his mother and the rest of his loving family, Judy Carey Nevin and the staff of the Hannah V. McCauley Library at Ohio University Lancaster, Amber Landis, Scott Minar, Patrick Munhall, and Ohio University Lancaster Dean Jim Smith.

Introduction

Matt Wanat and Leonard Engel

C lint Eastwood is indefatigable. He just keeps making one film after another, sometimes acting, but mostly directing. Since our last collection of essays on his films appeared in 2012, he has starred in *Trouble with the Curve* (2012) and has directed *Jersey Boys* (2014), *American Sniper* (2014), and *Sully* (2016). Eastwood's films have often ignited controversy, and this is particularly true of *American Sniper*, which has raised the ire of many but has also had advocates and, in some cases, champions. Based on the memoir by Chris Kyle, the Navy SEAL who had the most sniper kills during the Iraq War, the film renders a vivid yet agonizing portrayal of Kyle while also offering a devastating and personal picture of the horrors of the war itself.

About half the chapters in this volume discuss *American Sniper* while the others address films not touched on in the first two collections (2007 and 2012). The chapters vary by topic, with attention to issues ranging from aging, race, and gender, to generic uses of Western conventions and myth, to the subtleties of what contributor Dennis Rothermel calls quieter moments in Eastwood's work or what John M. Gourlie identifies as Eastwood's interest in inspiration. Though Eastwood is not generally considered a stylist, Landon Lutrick in this collection is attentive to Eastwood's style as it might complicate our assumptions about the actor and director's vision. Indeed, if the bulk of these essays have an overriding concern, it is that the contributors persistently seek to understand a filmmaker at once straightforward and nuanced, sometimes contradictory, who is often inclined toward complex subjects delivered in story-and-character-driven narratives without obvious directorial didacticism or reflexivity but intertwined with an acting and directorial iconography laden with cultural meanings, as Craig Rinne's essay in this collection meticulously shows.

In their interest in what Eastwood *means*, these essays are often unapologetically attentive to auteur elements though in diverse ways, suggesting that Eastwood's age, gender, race, American iconography, and overall image pervade thematic elements of his films yet fail to account for the sum of Eastwood's vision, which is multifaceted and embedded in contradictory generic and social conventions for dealing with issues ranging from domestic societal conflict and cooperation, to war.

When contemplating the idiosyncrasies of Eastwood's *meaning*—this is to say, of what his films intend, but also of what his iconography means within the context of his work overall—it might be instructive to consider Eastwood's preoccupations and the specific nature of his complexity and ability to stir controversy alongside another complicated and controversial filmmaker. For example, regarding the controversy surrounding *American Sniper*, one is tempted to recall a short film within a longer feature film that, were it not released five years prior to *American Sniper*, might without anachronism effectively function as a parody thereof. We are thinking here of *Stolz der Nation*, Eli Roth's short film within the film *Inglourious Basterds* (Quentin Tarantino, 2009).[1] Like *American Sniper*, Roth and Tarantino's *Stolz der Nation* takes as its subject a sniper, in this case a Nazi sniper whose biopic serves as a pro-Reich propaganda film for an in-film special screening attended by Adolf Hitler (played by Martin Wuttke). The screening within Tarantino's movie serves as the setting for the attempted and eventual assassination of Hitler, planned separately by a holocaust survivor named Shosanna (Mélanie Laurent) and a Jewish American special ops unit led by Lieutenant Aldo Raine (Brad Pitt). More importantly for comparative purposes, *Stolz der Nation* functions as an absurd parody of the outrageous demands of propaganda and as a reflexive device encouraging the viewer to consider the implications of Tarantino's film as well, but these are complicated points worth considering separately.

We say "parody" because *Stolz der Nation* is treated absurdly. Before the Nazis at the special screening are burned alive like the Nazis in *The Dirty Dozen* (Robert Aldrich, 1967), they leer blood-lustfully at the screen like the monstrous *Snow White* revelers in *Gremlins* (Joe Dante, 1984)—the gremlins, incidentally, also being burned in a movie theater, while watching one of Hitler's favorite films, no less—and the leering of Tarantino's Nazis, as much as suggesting any specific allusion direct or indirect, invites the viewer to see the utter ridiculousness of a film celebrating the heroism of a man who kills others from a tower. But beyond Roth and Tarantino's parody of propaganda, and the social satire implied therein, the viewer is also invited to consider the violence in Tarantino's own film, which asks us not only to watch but also to enjoy the burning alive of Hitler and his high-ranking officers. Indeed, the violent demise of the Nazis at the end of *Ingiourious Basterds* is exhilarating, yet the film-within-the-film invites a self-reflexive reading of Tarantino's larger film, suggesting that the morality or ethics of filming violence, and more significantly of mediating events as horrific as the holocaust, is at least partly contingent on who gets to tell and consume the story. Much of the controversy surrounding Tarantino's film—including general indictments of Tarantino's violence and more specific outrage over the possibility that *Inglourious Basterds* somehow makes light of the holocaust—seems to miss the point that American films have been mediating the war and the holocaust for entertainment since the 1940s. For instance, in Spielberg's *Raiders of the Lost Ark* (1981), a considerably less controversial film, Yahweh makes the Nazis' heads melt and explode to the delight of blockbuster-hungry hordes.

Here we discuss Tarantino, a director at least as controversial as Eastwood but in many ways nothing like the elder filmmaker, not to digress but rather, first, to show the potential audacity of Eastwood's making a serious film about the potential heroism of a sniper—subject matter rendered as self-consciously absurd propaganda by Roth and Tarantino—and, second, to use comparison to articulate the specific idiosyncrasies of Eastwood's style and their bearing on the *American Sniper* controversy. Fittingly, in his collection *Quentin Tarantino's* Inglourious Basterds: *A Manipulation of Metacinema* (2012), editor Robert von Dassanowsky begins to define the metacinematic qualities of Tarantino's cinema with Stanley Kubrick's line: "We're not interested in photographing the reality. We're interested in photographing the photograph of the reality" (qtd. in Dassanowsky vii), adding later in his introduction that "Tarantino is the fantasist doubling as Greek chorus" (viii). In other words, Dassanowsky rightly notes that Tarantino is fundamentally a metafictional filmmaker, a director making movies about movies and ostensibly about his own moviemaking processes and their consequences, with Tarantino drawing attention not only via allusion to the position of his own films within a filmic history but also, self-referentially, to the ethical stakes of his own filmmaking. Eastwood is, of course, nothing like this.

Opposite Tarantino's allusion-laden, explicitly stylized, arguably formally self-reflexive cinema is Eastwood's relative austerity—films made under budget, minimally stylized, with virtually everything driven by the building blocks of film narrative: action and character. This is not to say that there are no intertextual implications in Eastwood's work. The Eastwood iconography, both across films and within filmmaking history, informs much of our understanding of Eastwood's movies and has informed readings of his work alert to the intersection of his films' narratives and his branding through self-directing and Malpaso Productions, as Paul Smith, in his excellent book *Clint Eastwood: A Cultural Production* (1993), pointed out early in the body of critical work on Eastwood. And as Glenda Pritchett and others in this collection note, an understanding of genre and generic revision also informs our viewing of the movies of Clint Eastwood, an actor and director constantly re-invoking the American and Italian Western—in fact, basically re-adapting *Shane* (1953) in the film *Pale Rider* (1985)—but often also, as Pritchett notes, applying Western tropes and myth in more subtle ways. Nevertheless, though Eastwood's self- and generic legacy informs viewing, he is not primarily, or at least not obviously, a formally self-reflexive filmmaker so much as he is a storyteller.

Though as capable of social controversy as Tarantino is, going back at least as far as accusations about reactionary politics in *Dirty Harry* (Don Siegel, 1971), Eastwood's controversy and complexity reside in a combination of his public image with the events and psychological reactions of characters within his stories. There is in Eastwood's cinema—compared with the metacinema of someone like Tarantino—little or no, or at least far less, explicit blurring of the intradiegetic and extradiegetic, or, stated less academically, there is little blurring of the lines separating what happens within film narrative from the systems and processes responsible for the making of the film. No doubt Eastwood himself would hate the words "intradiegetic" and "extradiegetic," and likewise he would hate the concept of "metacinema." Such concepts run counter to his self-image and his major preoccupations as a filmmaker. On the one hand, this tendency of East-wood to avoid stylistic or self-reflexive devices leads to a greater sense of straightforward clarity. On the other, however, it leads many to want a clearer sense of what Eastwood's movies are trying to do.

Consider, for example, the aforementioned controversy surrounding the film *Dirty Harry*, a film Don Siegel directed in close collaboration with the actor Eastwood. *Dirty Harry* is replete with visual elements aligning the belea-guered detective Callahan (Eastwood) with the psychotic serial sniper Scorpio (Andy Robinson), not least of which is a scene that has Eastwood's character, with a big-game rifle, sniping the sniper, the predator becoming the prey, as Mike Smrtic and Matt Wanat argued in the previous East-wood collection. Not only is *Dirty Harry*'s sniping motif, as contributor Brett Westbrook and our friend Tim Dansdill have noted, one of many in Eastwood's work that predates *American Sniper*, but it is likely that if such a doppelgänger device of visualized (and voyeuristic) violence were in a film by, say, Alfred Hitchcock instead of Don Siegel, critics would trample one another proclaiming the film's self-consciousness about the limits of Harry Callahan's heroic morality, a likelihood for which Wanat argued in Engel's 2007 Eastwood collection. With Eastwood, however, we tend not to notice elements of formal and generic self-consciousness, even when they are present. This is partly by virtue of Eastwood's direct, plainspoken on-screen and off-screen image and partly by virtue of the stylistic mini-malism he learned from Siegel, a master of noir shadow but one not pri-marily inclined toward fabulation.

In other words, Eastwood's films rarely announce their own ironies, formal structures, or generic conventions, nor do they, to borrow again from Dassanowsky's description of Tarantino, play Greek chorus to themselves. That said, it is hard to describe a film like *American Sniper*—which is, as some of our contributors suggest, many types of war movie at once, and perhaps equally hard to describe a film like *Mystic River* (2003), with its Fritz Lang's *M*-like treatment of victimization through both predatory sexual vio-lence and vigilantism—as lacking complexity. It is just that Eastwood's films' complexity lies in the varying points of view of the characters and in the director's tendency to include competing values rather than in the layer-ing of stylistic expression or self-referential commentary.

Our goal for this collection of essays is to bring multiple critical voices to bear, some descriptively critical and others prescriptively so, on the diver-sity of values and ideas in Eastwood's more recent and less examined cinematic works. Along these lines, our chapters fall roughly into two broad categories: those dealing with his critically underrepresented films and those dealing with *American Sniper*.

In chapter 1, "*The Eiger Sanction*: Midlife and Midcareer on Eastwood's Vertical Frontier," Mark Maynard argues that Eastwood's 1975 adaptation of Trevanian's 1972 novel depicts the director and actor addressing shifting midlife and midcareer roles that are echoed in Eastwood's later, more mature work—films such as *The Outlaw Josey Wales* (1976), *Firefox* (1982), and *Heartbreak Ridge* (1986)—in which he both acts and directs. *The Eiger Sanction* captures the cold war mentality of global imperialism that was deeply entrenched by 1975, and Eastwood's character Jonathan Hemlock stands in stark contrast with the gunfighter loners of *High Plains Drifter* (1973) and Sergio Leone's Westerns. He is a sophisticated college professor and art collector returning to his former life as an assassin. *The Eiger Sanction*, mired in tonal inconsistency, racism, and homophobia, falls short of dealing with aging as effectively as Eastwood does in *Unforgiven* (1992) and *Gran Torino* (2008) yet hints at the technical skill and wit that would come to define the director's later work.

Our second chapter, Edward Lamberti's "Forced into Heroism: Clint Eastwood's Reluctant Protagonists in *The Eiger Sanction*, *The Gauntlet*, and *Firefox*," addresses films (1975, 1977, and 1982, respectively) generally neglected by critics and audiences more interested in *The Outlaw Josey Wales*, the *Dirty Harry* sequels, and the hugely successful comedies *Every Which Way but Loose* (1978) and *Any Which Way You Can* (1980). More than star vehicles, *The Eiger Sanction*, *The Gauntlet* (1977), and *Firefox* exemplify Eastwood's development as storyteller director, demonstrating two recurring qualities of his work: (1) the Eastwood character as a loner who needs to learn *how* to become a hero, and (2) plots based on a mission affording highly dramatic spectacle. The result is a tension between crowd-pleasing storytelling and the solitary nature of Eastwood's performance, revealing the subtle complexities in otherwise accessible and entertaining films.

In the third chapter, "Why Are We Stuck in Low-Earth Orbit?: Sexagenarian *Space Cowboys* and the Failing Body of Their American Dream," W. D. Phillips reads the titular quotation about Eastwood in relation to the dramatic scenarios within which he places his protagonists. A number of films made by Eastwood over the last thirty years have sought to *save* an America in decline, in addition to saving the aging protagonists he portrays within them, and they present a nostalgic view of the mid-century America of Eastwood's youth. These characters tend either to push for a return to American greatness or to right some of the wrongs wrought in the intervening years. Set inside NASA at the end of the millennium, *Space Cowboys* (2000) exemplifies this trend in Eastwood's work by depicting the old men of the original generation of astronauts and their efforts to return America to its previous position of power in the newly internationalized space program. In addition to *Space Cowboys*, Phillips also considers the nostalgic perspective in *Gran Torino* (2008—American auto power and working-class suburbs); *Absolute Power* (1997—American politics and politicians); *Heartbreak Ridge* (1986—American military power and discipline); and *Unforgiven* (1992—the American Western as a genre of meaning and import). The aging American male cannot return the country to its former status, Eastwood emphasizes, yet he has undeniable integrity in his struggle to stamp his identity on events in his path, which Eastwood powerfully and compellingly dramatizes.

In chapter 4, "Empowering the Victim: Eastwood as a Director of Women," Raymond Foery points to Eastwood's reputation as a "man's man," both as an actor in various action films and as a director of movies wherein Eastwood has developed a reputation for being able to probe the inner angst of the male hero. But often overlooked has been Eastwood's remarkably sensitive direction of women. Indeed, Foery claims, the first scholar to pay considerable attention to this aspect of his work was Drucilla Cornell, whose *Clint Eastwood and Issues of American Masculinity* (2009) broke new ground in a field that had lain fallow for decades. Her examination of gender designation is poignantly articulated in her claim that Eastwood's films "show us what it means to be a good man . . . but what a struggle it is to even make an attempt" (Cornell 189–90). Foery argues that in a select body of his work Eastwood explores what it means to be a woman, not merely a victim. According to Foery, Eastwood's nuanced directing of women over the past two decades demonstrates his interest in this theme. Beginning with *The Bridges of Madison County* (1995) and continuing up to the present with such works as *Midnight in the Garden of Good and Evil* (1997), *Million Dollar Baby* (2004), *Changeling* (2008), *Hereafter* (2010), and *American Sniper* (2014), Eastwood has honed his skills as a director with a special sensitivity to the female character.

Chapter 5, "Manufactured in America: Clint Eastwood, Chrysler's *Halftime in America*, and the Republican National Convention," by Craig Rinne, also offers a view of Eastwood that has not been part of his popular reputation. The years between *Gran Torino* (2008) and *American Sniper* (2014), Rinne argues, were less flashy for Eastwood as a filmmaker. The films from *Invictus* (2009) to *Trouble with the Curve* (2012), which neither reaped commercial success nor inspired reviewers, were capped by his infamous speech at the 2012 Republican National Convention. However, in the midst of this quieter period lies hidden a rare gem, a powerful, well received, and widely discussed short film, viewed by over one hundred million people simultaneously (by far Eastwood's largest audience ever)—*Halftime in America*, a two-minute Chrysler commercial that aired during Super Bowl XLVI in February 2012. Written by American poet Matthew Dickman and directed by David Gordon Green, the commercial features Eastwood through a voice-over narration, with glimpses of him in a montage of Americana images—shots that are lit in his distinctive chiaroscuro, film noir, directorial style. As the short film suggests, Americans are concerned over events in the preceding years, but Eastwood's fatherly persona strives to reassure and inspire; his experience over the decades is America's, and he is still here and moving forward. *Halftime in America* could easily be retitled *Clint Eastwood Is America*.

John Streamas in chapter 6, "The Real War That Got into the Movies: Eastwood and Spielberg in the Pacific," compares three of Eastwood's recent films—the Iwo Jima films, *Flags of Our Fathers* and *Letters from Iwo Jima* (both films from 2006), and the Korean war-vet film *Gran Torino*—to the work of Steven Spielberg, with special attention to stereotypes that still govern mainstream American moviemaking. Even though it is based on actual documents written by Japanese soldiers, Eastwood's *Letters from Iwo Jima*, at first glance, could be accused of white appropriation. Streamas argues, however, that Eastwood's Iwo Jima films and *Gran Torino* rise above the common stereotypes perpetuated by most American films of those wars, and that even when Eastwood succumbs to stereotypes, as he does with the white savior in *Gran Torino*, Eastwood recognizes a need for Asian visibility. Streamas claims that Eastwood at least recognizes and engages the most troubling aspect of the Pacific wars better than Spielberg—in fact, far better than any other mainstream U. S. filmmaker except Terrence Malick.

In chapter 7, "Captain of My Soul: Inspiration in Eastwood's Films," John M. Gourlie suggests that a key element of Eastwood's storytelling is "inspiration," in *Hereafter* (2010) and other films. The point is most clear in *Invictus* (2009), but *The Bridges of Madison County* (1995) and *Gran Torino*

(2008) closely consider inspiration as well. These Eastwood films, like the sermons by the priest in *Gran Torino*, explicitly raise the question of the meaning of life. To demonstrate this, Gourlie groups the movies in pairs. *Hereafter* and *The Bridges of Madison County* deal with love—especially in the personal realm of dealing with those who love you. *Gran Torino* and *Invictus* deal with love as well but do so in a broader context of social and racial politics—how to deal with those who, because of racism, do not love. Whatever their differences, each film places love at the center of life's meaning.

The centrality of the hero to cultural mythologies provides an entrance point for Glenda Pritchett in chapter 8, "Cultural Hero-Systems in *Shane*, *Gran Torino*, and *American Sniper*." Pritchett notes that the myths of the American West and Western hero have created a hero-system in the arts that persists in more recent cinematic endeavors belying their genesis in classic Western achievements, such as George Stevens's 1953 film *Shane*, based on Jack Schaefer's 1949 novel. Just as Akira Kurosawa's *Sanjuro* (1962) can be described as an "Eastern 'Western,'" indebted to *Shane*, Pritchett argues that *Gran Torino* and *American Sniper*—two of Eastwood's most successful recent films with contemporary settings—use key elements of the Western myth portrayed in *Shane*, showcasing how Eastwood has pressed the conventions of the Western into the service of twenty-first-century demands.

In chapter 9, "'Life Takers and Heart Breakers': Moral Injury in Clint Eastwood's War Films," Kathleen Brown and Brett Westbrook discuss seven Eastwood war films. With Eastwood as either actor, director, or producer (or some combination), these films include *Where Eagles Dare* (1968), *Kelly's Heroes* (1970), *Heartbreak Ridge* (1986), *Flags of Our Fathers* and *Letters from Iwo Jima*, *Gran Torino*, and *American Sniper*. *Where Eagles Dare* and *Kelly's Heroes* fall short of exploring the physical and psychological brutality of war. The remaining Eastwood war films, however, show what happens to men who manage to "overcome and neutralize [their] earlier resistance to violence." In these movies, the wartime experiences of the major characters have left them damaged in ways best described as "moral injury."

David Buchanan in chapter 10, "Another Fistful: The *American Sniper* Franchise and Clint Eastwood's Post-9/11 American War Film as Neo-Western," focuses on *American Sniper* and "the-book-to-movie manipulations" that Eastwood and Jason Hall, the screenwriter, make in their portrayal of Chris Kyle as a Navy SEAL sniper. Buchanan asks whether the ends justify the actions Kyle took as a sniper. Additionally, Buchanan reveals and considers the facts

Kyle manipulated while constructing his narrative. Most striking, however, is Eastwood and Hall's imposition of formulaic devices into Kyle's narrative, particularly insofar as *American Sniper* follows the narrative arc of Sergio Leone Westerns that made Eastwood famous. In the end, the movie shows us how easy it is to pander to an audience's desire for conventional Western tropes and the contrived scapegoats they create. Buchanan argues that we should feel uncomfortable with Kyle's existence and death and representation, not only because of what he did or how he spoke of what he did, but because we needed him to exist at all.

In chapter 11, "The Legend: Situating *American Sniper* in Clint Eastwood's Canon," Landon Lutrick argues that although the film's scenes depicting sniper shootings follow formulaic Western shootouts, they are critically rendered by the way Eastwood directs them. Alternately high and low camera angles emphasize Americans' loss of power, as part of a cinematic experience steeped in chaos rather than in the law and order that would normally resolve a Western shootout. Lutrick claims that *American Sniper* represents a significant development in Eastwood's style, bringing together two veins of his work (identified by David Sterritt in *The Cinema of Clint Eastwood*, 2014): the mythic movie that focuses on individual lives rooted and revered in the American unconscious; and the history movie that revises the grand narratives of the past.

Chapter 12, "With Some Trepidation, I Suggested That We See *American Sniper* Together," is a poignant, personal reflection by Dennis Rothermel. "With some trepidation," Rothermel writes, he invited a friend to see *American Sniper* with him. Part of Rothermel's trepidation stems from common misunderstandings of Eastwood's values, which because of his directing style often speak softly from a distance. What Eastwood has to say is in the showing rather than in the telling, and Eastwood does his best work in *American Sniper* in the quiet scenes between deployments. After the screening, Rothermel's friend called the movie "an anti-war film," a claim with which Rothermel agreed, though Rothermel found himself adding that *American Sniper* avoids both politics and glamor in ways that might confuse viewers conditioned to think of war films in "pro-" and "anti-" terms. *American Sniper*, Rothermel argues, neither justifies the American military activity in Iraq nor condemns it. Rather, it shows the experience of soldiers, Kyle in particular, in war for what it is—and this is what an anti-war war movie can do, specifically if the goal is not to glamorize that experience. Eastwood—an opponent of every American foreign war, beginning with Korea—has created a film that challenges this fantasy of warfare viscerally, at times shockingly.

Chapter 13, *"American Sniper* and the Critics:: A Note on the Art of Interpretation,"* by Leonard Engel, briefly surveys the tumultuous reception greeting *American Sniper* when it appeared in 2014. It recalls, Engel claims, the commentary (often sharply divergent) that earlier Eastwood films provoked: *High Plains Drifter, Pale Rider, Unforgiven, Million Dollar Baby, Mystic River*, and even *J. Edgar*—all of which had reviewers in various stages of apoplexy. However, none of their reviews exploded with the volatility of the remarks about *Sniper*—mostly concerning patriotism, or lack of it, and whether the film is pro-war or anti-war. Is there a path through this thicket of controversy, this dizzying maze of diverse criticism? Is it possible to assemble a reasonable approach to *American Sniper*—to engage the film as a "fictionalized biopic to be debated"? He thinks there is, but viewers have to be very attentive to the small but crucial details Eastwood reveals.

In addition to the essays in this collection, we conclude with an afterword by Drucilla Cornell—whose *Clint Eastwood and Issues of American Masculinity* (2009) has transformed readings of an actor and director who is important to discussions of filmed gender and sexuality—after a remarkable interview with longtime Eastwood editor Joel Cox, conducted and written by fellow film editor and scholar Paul Seydor. Cornell's afterword, in addition to offering many insights into the complicated and often surprising implications of Eastwood's gender politics, reinforces the aforementioned point in our introduction that understanding Eastwood often involves careful considerations of story and character. Seydor's interview with Joel Cox, we believe, will stand with the most important scholarship on Eastwood and his films. These essays bring to bear multiple critical approaches to a director whose mysteries lie partly in the minimalism of his process; thus, we find it fitting to follow such a collection of essays with Seydor's interview, a conversation between film editors that at once probes the details of Eastwood's and Cox's filmmaking processes and pays tribute to the still underrated art of film editing and the truth that, whatever the burden of acting and directorial iconography on our understanding of Eastwood films, Eastwood's movies are, like all movies, part of an ongoing process of collaboration.

Note

1. As our contributor Landon Lutrick points out, the similarities between *Inglourious Basterds's* interior film *Stolz der Nation* and *American Sniper* have not escaped

informal reviewers on Internet Movie Database. As one reviewer identified as Raoul Duke puts it, after comparing Eastwood to Tarantino's Goebbels (Sylvester Groth), "A big irony this movie is, and as such it shows" the extent of the American film industry's attempt "to brainwash its own people." 13 May 2016, www. imdb.com/title/tt2179136/reviews. See also Dennis Rothermel's comments on *Stolz der Nation*, available in his chapter in this collection.

Works Cited

American Sniper. Directed by Clint Eastwood, performance by Bradley Cooper, Warner Bros., 2014.

Cornell, Drucilla. *Clint Eastwood and Issues of American Masculinity*. Fordham UP, 2009.

Dirty Harry. Directed by Don Siegel, performances by Clint Eastwood and Andy Robinson, Warner Bros., 1971.

The Eiger Sanction. Directed by Clint Eastwood, performance by Eastwood, Universal, 1975.

Inglourious Basterds. Directed by Quentin Tarantino, performances by Brad Pitt and Mélanie Laurent, Universal / Weinstein Company / A Band Apart, 2009.

Raiders of the Lost Ark. Directed by Steven Spielberg, performances by Harrison Ford, Karen Allen, and Paul Freeman, Paramount, 1981.

Smith, Paul. *Clint Eastwood: A Cultural Production*. Minnesota UP, 1993.

Sterritt, David. *The Cinema of Clint Eastwood: Chronicles of America*. Columbia UP, 2014.

Stolz der Nation. Directed by Eli Roth, performance by Daniel Brühl, A Band Apart / Studio Babelsberg / Visiona Romantica / Universal, 2009.

Von Dassanowsky, Robert. *Quentin Tarantino's* Inglourious Basterds: *A Manipulation of Metacinema*. Bloomsbury Press, 2012.

1

The Eiger Sanction

Midlife and Midcareer on Eastwood's Vertical Frontier

Mark Maynard

*T*he Eiger Sanction* marks a turning point for Clint Eastwood as the actor/director begins to come to terms with aging in a midcareer film that focuses on a mature, urbane protagonist and explores themes of physical aging, masculinity, retirement, and the midlife concerns of a man who worries that he may lose his purpose. The 1975 film, an adaptation of the 1972 Trevanian[1] novel of the same name, moves from the frontier imperialism of Eastwood's hyper-masculine Westerns to a more sophisticated materialism exhibited by the film's protagonist, Jonathan Hemlock, a worldly art collector, college professor, and reluctant international assassin. Playing Hemlock as a sophisticated and intelligent character, Eastwood subtly parodies the frontier codes and ideologies of violence that defined his early career. The evolution of Eastwood's on-screen and off-screen self-identity is evident throughout *The Eiger Sanction*. The Man with No Name, with his desire for solitude and revenge, has grown into a middle-aged anti-hero who is as concerned with his own declining physical abilities and income tax liabilities as he is with avenging a friend's death. *The Eiger Sanction* offers Eastwood a chance to examine the identity crisis of an aging, rugged, masculine individualist against the moral ambiguities and declining global popularity of America during the Vietnam era.

The Eiger Sanction is a faithful adaptation of Trevanian's popular novel. The book alternates between a taut international thriller and a send up of Ian Fleming's James Bond novels plus the films they inspired. This material is ideal for allowing Eastwood to evolve his familiar on-screen persona into a more urbane, intellectual one that still retains his solitary inclinations and refusal to play by external rules imposed on him by society. Several Eastwood films released just prior *to The Eiger Sanction*—including *Dirty Harry* (1971), *High Plains Drifter* (1973), and *Magnum Force* (1973)—feature protagonists motivated by justice or retribution. In *The Eiger Sanction*, however, Hemlock is a materialist motivated by acquisition and self-indulgence. He is a former counterintelligence assassin called out of retirement by his previous employer, the covert American spy agency CII, helmed by the reclusive Dragon.[2] The early part of the film follows a standard "one more job" narrative as the refractory Hemlock—now content to teach art history to flirty co-eds while collecting priceless paintings on the black market to display in the secret gallery of his home—is pressured by CII to avenge the assassination of one of their agents, code-named Wormwood, who was brutally killed in Zurich, Switzerland. Hemlock is reluctant to return to his assassin ways, but Dragon is able to press him into service with the promise of a black market Pissarro, a guarantee that the IRS won't investigate the provenance of Hemlock's art collection, and, most importantly for Hemlock, a promise to double his usual fees for performing an assassination (or "sanction" in the euphemistic vernacular of CII). Hemlock is committing to a contract kill in order to build a retirement nest egg.

Many of Hemlock's Eastwood-suited traits—a cool aloofness; an unromantic, animal libido; and a predilection for fisticuffs—are present in Trevanian's novel. Many scenes and characters are lifted nearly verbatim from the book, including dialogue and mannerisms that so suit Eastwood it feels at times as if the novel were written with the actor in mind. This fits the pattern of Eastwood claiming the protagonists of novels and screenplays for himself and adapting them to fit his particular (and evolving) on-screen persona by imbuing these iconic roles with an intertextual version of the familiar Eastwood character—quiet, strong, and bent on justice.[3] In Hemlock, Eastwood incorporates an awareness of his own aging—and many of Hemlock's traits mirror Eastwood's personal growth at the time as an actor, a director, and the head of his own production company, Malpaso, which,

Eastwood biographer Richard Schickel explains, is "run like a small free-standing business, with its sole proprietor enjoying astonishing autonomy" (369). The role of Hemlock was originally offered to Paul Newman, who declined, claiming that the film and the role were too violent for his own carefully curated on-screen persona (McGilligan 241).

There are three distinct themes in *The Eiger Sanction* that reflect Eastwood's conscious efforts to adapt his on-screen character to his own sense of self as a middle-aged man advancing along a career line from actor to director to curator of his on-screen identity and legacy as head of Malpaso. First, Eastwood explores a shifting concept of right and wrong in which a sense of justice and ethical behavior comes into doubt in the moral ambiguity of post–World War II America. Hemlock neither adheres to the moral code of his government as espoused by the CII organization nor intentionally defies or circumvents those codes, as does Harry Callahan. Instead, Hemlock's moral code is internal, self-defined, and personal. Hemlock seeks only to satisfy himself as he realizes the futility of trying to somehow improve society or impose justice on it through his own actions.

Next, *The Eiger Sanction* functions to redefine Eastwood's narrow definition of ideal masculinity in order to acknowledge the physical vulnerabilities of aging and the importance for a man to mitigate the ravages of time on his mental and physical well-being. Eastwood emphasizes traits in the film that are critically important to achieving and maintaining his masculine ideal: a willingness to stay fit through an ascetic dedication to training, a confident self-reliance, and an unwavering dedication to understanding and avoiding deviant behavior.

Finally, the looming physical presence of the North Face of the Eiger becomes a metaphorical device that allows Eastwood the director to acknowledge the closing of the American West as a frontier, and the need for rugged individuals like Hemlock (and his predecessor the Man with No Name) to transfer their goals of conquest in the name of manifest destiny to a personal endeavor of acquisition based on material needs of self-worth and Hemlock's own ego-driven climber's dream of claiming a first ascent.

Eastwood's Hemlock has an elaborate and well-defined moral code that he adheres to throughout the film, and by which the character judges others from his perch of moral superiority, but this code is not founded in the frontier imperialism of manifest destiny. Rather, Hemlock understands that America's divine providence and mantle of exceptionalism are nothing more than a Machiavellian attitude toward the nation's imperial desires, allowing the United States government to develop weapons of mass destruction, order indiscriminate killings, and engage in deceitful practices even against their own agents and other loyalists in order to win the Cold War by any means possible—justifying all of this through the jingoistic assertion of American moral certitude. This is a world of every man for himself, and the cunning Hemlock understands this clearly. Eastwood clearly relishes playing the intelligent, confident raconteur as a discerning art collector who is above the brutal, gut-slitting knife work of his fellow assassins. Hemlock views this type of animal violence disdainfully. Throughout the film, the international "sanctioner" eschews killing his rivals with his bare hands, preferring to shoot them in classic gunfighter scenarios in which the fastest draw and sharpest shooter wins, or abandoning them to the indifference of nature, whether it be the oppressive heat of the Arizona desert or the relentless Morderwand (death wall) of the Eiger itself. Hemlock's moral take on violence is a winking exaggeration of the code of retribution and moral superiority that would be familiar to earlier Eastwood characters, including Harry Callahan. Callahan would relate to the practice of meting out justified violence, though Hemlock has a much stronger aversion to killing those who have not personally wronged him, or those few to whom he feels a personal loyalty (McGilligan 241).

While Callahan acts violently as a means of retribution toward criminals that would otherwise go unpunished because of liberal policies that protect the rights of criminals even when they have committed egregious acts against humanity, *The Eiger Sanction* examines an imperial moral justification in which any violence perpetrated by Hemlock or his CII colleagues is justifiable because it is committed in the interests of America. Hemlock himself begins to see the irony of this morality. The film (as well as the novel it is based on) makes it clear that the premeditated sanctions are intended to protect the interests of the American government and by extension its people. Hemlock is told that his unknown target must be killed in order to keep a biological weapon from getting into the hands of the agents from the other side (a clear reference to the Cold War Communists); this sets up a clearly defined moral dichotomy of good and bad, and seemingly clears the ethical slate for any of the killings in which Hemlock may be involved, either directly or indirectly. But Eastwood's Hemlock questions the motivations and actions of his government. When discussing the principles of sanctions with Jemima Brown (Vonetta McGee), a CII agent sent to seduce him into completing his mission, Hemlock invokes the Geneva Convention, pointing out the immorality of the Americans having a biological weapon in the first place. "What the hell are we doing with it?" Hemlock asks. "We're not supposed to have one either." Hemlock also claims that the sanctions he's paid to perform are ultimately meaningless and are simply ordered as "retaliation." While the dubious moral justifications of CII's sanctions are not fully realized themes and often function more as throwaway plot devices, the idea of justifying the killing of others in the name of nationalism comes more obviously into play in Eastwood's later directorial work, including *Flags of Our Fathers* (2006), *Letters from Iwo Jima* (2006), and especially *American Sniper* (2014), which also deals with an American assassin killing enemies on a global battlefield in order to keep Americans safe at home. Furthermore, the issues of the value and the effects of revenge are more seriously considered in Eastwood's *Unforgiven* (1992). In *The Eiger Sanction*, Eastwood develops a more mature world view and a critique of the motivations behind many of his previously played characters. This shift would become more nuanced and central to his subsequent work as both an actor and a director.

The introduction to the protagonist in *The Eiger Sanction* reveals a shift to a more intellectual persona than those familiar with Eastwood's early body of work would recognize. Jonathan Hemlock first appears in the film as a dapper, sophisticated art history professor at an unnamed college. An establishing shot of the campus, with its manicured lawns and boxy buildings, illustrates that that lawlessness and freedom of the frontier have been usurped by intellect and order. As a retired assassin, Hemlock has tried to put his killing ways behind him. He is now a collector of precious art and spends his days lecturing unappreciative students that "art belongs to the cultured who can appreciate it. The majority of the great unwashed does not fit into this category. And neither, I'm sorry to say, do most of you." This arrogant, elitist character is worlds away from the Man with No Name, yet his sense of detachment and self-confidence—traits of the classic Eastwood persona on- and off-screen—are still portrayed as a sort of aphrodisiac for his beautiful female students, one of whom, during his self-righteous lecture on the nature of art, scrawls across a magazine article profiling Dr. Hemlock the international mountain climber: "He could climb all over me!" In a subsequent scene, when one of his young female students makes a suggestive pass at him in order to improve her grade, he paternally admonishes her to study and then smacks her on the buttocks. A CII henchman, Pope, has been eavesdropping on this conversation and inquires of Hemlock, "Why didn't you boff the little quiff?" Hemlock replies, "I don't pick on the students, or drunks." Hemlock clearly establishes a moral code early in the film—the professor doesn't need to take advantage of women because he can acquire them fairly, without needing to rely on their naïveté or chemically induced lack of inhibition. This illustrates a maturing Eastwood persona and sets the example of Hemlock maintaining a dignified set of standards for an aging man in regard to his own sexual needs.[4]

Hemlock misses his younger days as an international agent and world-class mountain climber, but the middle-aged professor seems content to live the civilized life, retiring to his comfortable estate where he sips wine, plays jazz records, and admires his collection of priceless black-market art. The desire to conquer the frontier as a hired killer has been superseded by the materialistic pursuit of the finer things in life.

What could possibly draw the now-content former assassin back to his violent past? The film posits two possible enticements for Hemlock to come out of retirement for one more job: money and vengeful justice.

It is the prospect of financial security that first draws Hemlock out of his comfortable intellectual life. Summoned to the hermetically sealed lair of his CII chief, Dragon, Hemlock is offered cash and a guarantee that the Internal Revenue Service will not inquire as to how a middle-class college professor was able financially to procure a world-class collection of paintings by the likes of Pissarro, Picasso, El Greco, and Matisse. At first Hemlock refuses the job, but Dragon finally agrees to Hemlock's terms for the assassination of Kruger, the enemy agent who killed Wormwood—the code name for one of CII's operatives in Zurich, Switzerland.

The scene of Hemlock's first on-screen sanction illustrates one of the film's key themes. Even as a professional assassin, Hemlock still employs a moral code borrowed from the white-hatted cowboys of the American frontier—he will not kill in cold blood, and he will only shoot a man that draws on him first. The young, callous killer of the Spaghetti Western is gone. Eastwood's Hemlock is a modern evolution of the gentleman gunfighter, the stock character of the Western, though Hemlock has much to live for and is not driven solely by principle. This code, in which the hero only kills when the death is morally justified, limits Hemlock's options and makes him less effective as an assassin. It is clear in this scene that it's time for him to get out of the game. When it comes to killing, Hemlock has lost his edge—he no longer maintains his cold, calculating killer instinct. His code has shifted, and the killing profession no longer suits him.

Having received his target and his payment in advance, Hemlock travels to Zurich in order to fulfill his last job. Dragon has also revealed to Hemlock that Wormwood was the code name for his old friend Henri Baq, and that their mutual former friend and colleague Miles Mellough was a double agent who set up the killing. Hemlock now has another reason for taking the sanction—revenge. Once in Zurich, he disguises himself as a deliveryman, and, in an effort to make his character appear nonthreatening, Eastwood speaks in an affected, effeminate voice when Kruger, the target of his sanction, answers the door. This is an early example in the film of Eastwood's rather narrow view of idealistic masculinity—Hemlock wants to appear nonthreatening to his target and feminizes his voice in order to do so. Rather than shoot Kruger in cold blood at the door, Hemlock instead opts to retreat from the building back down to street level. Prefiguring the film's climactic climbing scenes—and emphasizing both the actor and the character's physical agility despite his age—Hemlock then scales a four-story drainpipe to sneak into Kruger's office.

As Hemlock silently enters through a side door, one of Kruger's associates, warned by Kruger, turns toward Hemlock with a gun drawn and squeezes off the first shot, missing. Hemlock returns fire and kills the man with one shot. Kruger takes advantage of this distraction and kicks Hemlock's gun out of his hand while pulling out the same switchblade with which he brutally slit agent Wormwood's throat in the prologue. Hemlock and Kruger struggle in close combat, and the latter is flung through the fourth story window to his death on the cobblestones below. These scenes draw a comparison between Hemlock and the other international agents: Eastwood's character kills with honor and grace, often allowing nature and circumstance to eliminate his targets, while the other assassins stab, slit, and otherwise barbarically kill one another with brute force and a total lack of moral compunction.[5]

As is often the case with the "one more job" trope, Hemlock is drawn back into the world of international intrigue by the Zurich sanction. Through a series of plot points, including Hemlock's seduction by Jemima Brown and blackmail by Dragon, Hemlock is recruited for yet one more sanction—this time to kill an unknown adversary who has signed on to a small climbing party on the North Face of the Switzerland's Eiger mountain, a climb Hemlock has coincidentally attempted—and failed—twice before. The Eiger is another precious and rare trophy that Hemlock longs to add to his personal collection. He will take the job and this time make it his last.

To train properly for the physically demanding and highly dangerous climb, Hemlock embarks for the ranch owned by his old friend Ben Bowman (George Kennedy) in iconic Monument Valley, made internationally famous by John Ford in his classic Westerns. The frontier motif is further underscored when Bowman picks Hemlock up at the dirt airstrip in a Ford Bronco (standing in for the wild mustang of the traditional Western) and the two of them race off in the open-top 4×4 toward the distant rock spires trailing a plume of sunlit dust. To this point in the film, the viewer has seen Hemlock as a refined college professor, and the transition to this Western landscape (and Hemlock's apparent comfort in it) is somewhat incongruous for the film. It is, however, a familiar experience for the viewer to see Eastwood the actor returning to his Western roots, and the script intimates that Hemlock has spent time on Bowman's ranch years before.

Hemlock is expecting to see the rustic accommodations he remembers from previous climbing trips and is shocked to see what has become of Bowman's "ranch." The undeveloped frontier is gone, replaced by the civilized pursuit of material comforts and swaths of tanned human flesh. Bowman's place is now a luxury resort complete with an enormous swimming pool populated by young, bikini-clad women who spend their days tanning and sipping drinks from the outdoor bar. White-jacketed waiters serve seafood and steak to privileged guests who have parked luxury cars in the large paved lot. Hemlock realizes that Bowman, too, has succumbed to the self-indulgent materialism that has replaced the collective geographic conquest of the American frontier. Bowman laments that he can't stand to associate with the "phony bastards" who populate his guest list, but he, too, was unable to resist the material temptations of civilization.

Once he sees what has become of the former Wild West way of life, Hemlock can only set out into the last unclaimed virgin land before him: the vertical frontier of the rock spires and mountain faces as yet unclimbed by other men. Thus begins the film's transition to this subsequent frontier as he heads off into the wilderness to begin his training.

Eastwood continues to play with Western tropes as Hemlock begins his arduous days of physically preparing for the challenges of the Eiger. His physical and spiritual trainer, George (Brenda Venus), is presented to him by Ben, and, in a titillating twist on the Native guide archetype, George is a voluptuous, silent Native American woman who favors tiny denim shorts and loosely knotted half shirts. The montage sequence of Hemlock's training by George is composed of long shots of the two of them, the nubile

Native woman in the lead, as they traipse through an idyllic Western landscape—climbing red stone bluffs, fording rivers, and running through sylvan glades. In this sequence, Eastwood's character utters several irreverent one-liners that invoke numerous Native American stereotypes, telling George (who remains mute through most of the film) that she could refuse Bowman's mandate to get him into shape as a "chance to strike back at the white man," and telling her later that he wished "Custer would've won." This reiterates the similar anti–political correctness world view of Harry Callahan from *Dirty Harry* and *Magnum Force*.

While Eastwood is comfortable parodying the established tropes of earlier Westerns, the film's focus on a middle-aged man defining and retaining his sense of masculinity is the central motivation of the film's protagonist. Throughout the film, deviant masculinity is tied to moral depravity. Many of these parameters echo the rules laid out in Eastwood's overall body of work, which, Paul Smith argues, depends on conscious reiterations of this masculine code from film to film (134).

The most notable interpretation of deviant masculinity is seen in a pattern of gay villains in the Eastwood films of the early 1970s, and this is reinforced in *The Eiger Sanction*. The character of Miles Mellough is explicitly gay in both the novel and in Eastwood's film, though in the book Trevanian says Mellough "pulled off his epic homosexuality with such style that plebian men did not recognize it and worldly men did not mind it" (127). Actor Jack Cassidy portrays the cinematic Mellough as foppish and effeminate, opting for dazzling embroidered suits and speaking in an affected voice.[6] As Paul Smith points out in his criticism of the portrayal of gay characters in the Eastwood oeuvre, "Homosexuality in these films is merely, as I have suggested, a matter of fake or dishonest sexuality and constitutes—as in the ending of *Enforcer*— precisely that which needs to be blown away in order to keep the logic of the 'amongst men' free of any perverse taint" (143).

In *The Eiger Sanction*, characters that don't fit within a narrow delineation of acceptable masculinity are also portrayed as somehow morally corrupt, and the implication is that the perversion of masculinity and the lack of moral righteousness are implicitly connected. It was Mellough, after all, who betrayed Henri Baq in Zurich, and he admits as much to Hemlock, though he makes clear that Henri did not die by his hand. "I didn't actually kill him you know," claims Mellough, to which Hemlock replies, "Well I probably won't actually kill you." Hemlock makes his disdain for Mellough clear as he growls, "You have an incurable disease and lack the guts to kill yourself."

Mellough's deceitfulness (he also claims to know the identity of Hemlock's Eiger-sanction target and wants to trade the information in exchange for Hemlock sparing his life) is egregious enough to justify his own sanction according to Hemlock's moral code. Rather than shooting Mellough in cold blood, Hemlock creates an opportunity for him and his henchman Dewayne to follow him out into the desert. As Dewayne drives Mellough's white Ford Thunderbird through desert washes, trying in vain to run down Hemlock—who is in Bowman's Ford Bronco—Mellough (with his small dog in his lap) encourages Dewayne to corner and kill Hemlock. Eastwood expertly filmed and edited this scene to evoke a classic horseback chase drawn from the Western.[7] The close-ups of the drivers are intercut with beautifully framed panoramas of the cars speeding across a backdrop of the iconic mesas of Monument Valley. The men chase Hemlock into a box canyon where he is apparently trapped. Dewayne pulls a pistol as Hemlock turns the Bronco back toward them with a shotgun held out the driver's-side window in his left hand, steering the speeding car with his right. Keeping with the old gunfighter's code that Hemlock follows throughout the movie, Hemlock returns fire only after Dewayne has shot and missed.[8] Hemlock has once again committed a justifiable homicide: Dewayne shot first, and Hemlock only shot and killed him in self-defense. Hemlock forces Mellough into the Bronco with him at gunpoint and drives him further out into the desert (Eastwood includes a shot of the odometer rolling off forty miles to emphasize how far he is taking Mellough into the wild), finally forcing him out of the car and abandoning him to the elements. Hemlock, true to his moral code to not take a life without justification—and reinforcing Eastwood's love of animals as innocent beings—takes the dog back to civilization with him (McGilligan 181). Mellough is last seen in a long helicopter shot, hopelessly yelling after Hemlock's departing car as it disappears toward the horizon of the vast desert. While the film portrays the death of Miles Mellough as justified, even appealing, *New Yorker* film critic and frequent Eastwood antagonist Pauline Kael reproached him for the mortal violence meted out to characters such as Mellough in his films. "It's not that the villains are kidnappers and murderers—their real crime is that they're homosexual," said Kael in her 1977 review of *The Enforcer*. She mentions the Mellough character in *The Eiger Sanction*, as well as villainous gay characters in both *Magnum Force* and *The Enforcer*, before positing the question, "Is this the last outpost for the Western hero—killing homosexuals to purify the cities?" (88).

Other male characters in the film are similarly portrayed as deviants from the ideal form of masculinity embodied by the Eastwood character. Dragon is not only an albino with extreme light sensitivity, but he has an unnamed condition that makes him susceptible to fluctuations in temperature and has a severely compromised immune system, necessitating a complete blood transfusion annually. His physical corruption echoes his own moral corruption. He remains in the dim red light of his sealed lair, ordering men around the world to kill without remorse.

Hemlock's friend Bowman is also deficient—physically unable to climb the Eiger due to a limp caused by frostbite on a previous expedition. Because of this ailment, Hemlock must pull Bowman along behind him on their training climb. The limp is key to the film's plot as Dragon reveals to Hemlock early on in the film that his Eiger-sanction target also limps. At the end of the film, it is revealed that Bowman had been Hemlock's target all along. His deceitfulness is excused by Hemlock at the denouement, however, because he had noble and masculine motives for his treachery. Bowman reveals that George (Hemlock's Native American guide and sex partner) is his daughter and that she was addicted to drugs. Bowman made a deal with Miles Mellough to betray Wormwood in exchange for Mellough helping cure George's addiction. Bowman's masculinity is thus restored through a patriarchal loyalty. It is not his actions but his underlying motivations that redeem him according to Hemlock's personal moral code.

Perhaps the most interesting examination of masculinity is in the character of Montaigne, the French climber attached to Hemlock's Eiger team. Montaigne is, much like Hemlock, struggling with the effects of middle age on his body and on his identity. Montaigne claims that the Eiger will be his "last mountain" since he is forty-two years old.[9] Hemlock rebuffs Montaigne's wife's advances as the team is planning their climb and tells her that Montaigne is climbing only to keep her interested in him. Madame Montaigne later ends up in the bed of Freytag, the young German climber on the expedition, and the film implies that the distractions of cuckoldry, another form of deviant masculinity, lead to Montaigne's death, by freezing, after suffering a concussion caused by a rockfall. When Meyer, the Austrian member of the team, says of Montaigne's death, "The man inside couldn't keep the man outside from dying," it is clear that the Frenchman is intended to be a pitiful character who ultimately failed to maintain his masculinity, which contributed directly to his death. Montaigne serves as a doppelgänger of sorts for the Hemlock character. A clear comparison is made between the two men. Both are aging and lack the physical edge of younger climbers.

However, Hemlock's aloof romantic entanglements with Jemima Brown and George don't throw him off his game—whereas the emotionally vulnerable Montaigne allows a controlling woman to cloud his goals and actions; thus he lacks the masculine constitution necessary to overcome the physical deficiencies of his age.

In the final act of *The Eiger Sanction*, Eastwood transposes the extinct frontier of the American West onto the vertical face of an untamed mountain in the Swiss Alps. The final shot of the Monument Valley sequence—a long overhead wide shot of Hemlock's Bronco moving off into the fading sun—dissolves into a helicopter shot that rises over an Alpine ridge to reveal the awesome North Face of the Eiger, which appears accompanied by a dramatic flourish in John Williams's score. The two frontiers, the vanishing West of America and the vertical wilds of the Eiger, are now joined as Hemlock heads into the film's final daunting physical and psychological ordeal. The next shot shows the edge of civilization—the railway cars and station of the Jungfrau Railway that runs straight through the heart of the Eiger's North Face in a series of tunnels; and the charmingly rustic Hotel Bellevue des Alpes, built in 1840.

Eastwood examines the shift from the conventional conflicts and values of the Western frontier to the more personal and inwardly focused conquests of the modern American man. Without the possibility of geographic conquest, and in the slow physical decline of middle age, men like Hemlock turn to sport and other physical pursuits in order to stave off physical and spiritual decrepitude. In Joseph E. Taylor III's in-depth examination of Yosemite rock climbers, *Pilgrims of the Vertical*, he talks about the masculine needs fulfilled by climbing as modernization and civilization closed the frontier and agrarian American society gave way to the clock-punching workweek of factories and offices: "Very simply, the old ways of measuring success were losing meaning, the old paths to manhood fading" (17). Taylor states that this was the environment that led to the American investment in sports (climbing among them) as a new pathway to masculinity. Climbers in particular saw vertical walls as virgin frontiers on which to lay claim, and Taylor illustrates the sexual language with which climbers referred to lines and unclimbed walls, often describing them with violent misogynistic language. Taylor quotes noted Yosemite climber Royal Robbins proclaiming his "'lust to tattoo [his] name in indelible ink' in its 'flesh'"—referring to a wall that Robbins had lovingly named "Aphrodite's thigh" (144). Hemlock and his mentor, Bowman, share this passion for climbing. During Hemlock's period of training in Monument Valley for the Eiger, he leads Bowman on a climb up a narrow spire called Totem Pole. Bowman claims to have climbed it before, but as Hemlock summits and turns to help him surmount the final ledge, Bowman admits that Hemlock has just achieved a climber's one true objective—he's made a successful first ascent of the spire. Bowman's language echoes that of Robbins and his contemporaries who spent years seeking to claim first ascents and new lines up Yosemite's famous granite walls. "Congratulations, old buddy. You got her cherry!" Bowman reveals to Hemlock. "You're the first one ever to climb up here." The two men share a moment (and beer that Bowman has surreptitiously slipped into Hemlock's pack), and the camera spirals up and away as the music soars to a majestic crescendo, revealing a stunning southwestern sunset panorama that would have made an apt final shot to a Western.

A climber's first ascent is an evolution of manifest destiny: from divinely inspired geographic conquest in the name of a young nation-state, to an internally driven accomplishment marking the climber himself as exceptional. As the physical frontier has become civilized (and effectively closed off in the Turner view of the West), the rugged individual must find new places to claim.[10] The self-fulfilling, ego-driven nature of a first ascent is in line with Hemlock's sophisticated materialism. The new acquisition—in this case an unclimbed route up the face of a Swiss mountain—is no longer claimed by divine providence, nor for the benefit of a growing, exceptional nation. Instead, a first ascent is something to be bagged: a trophy for a collector whose collection exists only to validate himself. It is clear that reaching the summit of the Eiger, a peak on par with K2 and Mount Everest in terms of difficulty and risk to climbers, is something for Hemlock to acquire along with his Pissarros and Picassos (Schickel 313). As Hemlock finds himself disenfranchised with the idea of American exceptionalism in the muddied moral ambiguity of post-Vietnam geopolitics, he doubts the implied moral superiority inherent in the "we must keep the formula from the other side" mentality, and he decides to pursue individual exceptionalism instead. "You know I want another shot at this hill," Hemlock tells Bowman when they arrive in Switzerland. And so begins the film's third act, a chance for Hemlock to assert his masculinity and acquire something as rare and valuable as a Pissarro on his wall—the North Face of the Eiger. The German climber, Freytag, suggests that the men attempt the summit by a new route, and the chance to blaze a new trail on the vertical map offers a perfect frontier for Hemlock to attempt, once again, to conquer.

Hemlock meets his team—knowing that one of them is an assassin for the other side and bent on killing him before he can sanction his target—and all seem suspect. Freytag is headstrong and challenges Hemlock immediately for the leadership of the team. Meyer, the Austrian, is the most dedicated climber of the group and is known among the climbing community for having stabbed and killed a native porter for taking food on a previous climb. The Frenchman, Montaigne, rounds out the group. Like pioneers plotting an arduous journey, the men discuss Freytag's route, in this case by consulting a large map superimposed directly on a large photograph of the Eiger's North Face. Despite Freytag's obvious desire to lead the expedition, it is conceded that Hemlock will take charge of the group so that they can benefit from the experience of his previous climbs (though Freytag is quick to point out that both of Hemlock's previous attempts at the Eiger resulted in shameful retreats down the mountain without having reached the summit). By the end of the film, Hemlock is the sole survivor of the expedition. He has, without trying, successfully completed his mission: all three of his potential targets are dead, each the victim of a climbing accident not precipitated by Hemlock nor any of their fellow climbers. It is appropriate that, in failing once again to fulfill his personal manifest destiny and conquer the North Face of the Eiger, Hemlock rides back to civilization on the railroad that literally cuts through the frontier by means of open gallery windows in the rail tunnel running through the mountain's face. Ultimately, Hemlock has failed in his personal quest to conquer the Eiger, yet he has asserted his moral superiority to CII and its hired actors, and he has maintained his masculinity by aging gracefully and avoiding weakness of either mind or body. Hemlock will live to see another day: he can retire quietly to his mansion and enjoy his world-class art collection, a bottle of fine wine, and his jazz—a cultured man who appreciates the finer things and thus deserves to have them, away from the "great unwashed" he arrogantly despises.

Eastwood was successful in *The Eiger Sanction* at parodying elements of his earlier films around which he'd built a cinematic identity. He manages to direct a film that, intended as an action vehicle with elements of a spy parody, becomes a more thoughtful exploration of aging, masculinity, and the tropes of the Western—an art form he greatly admires, and to which he owes his storied career. *The Eiger Sanction* marks a turning point in his career that led to the refining of his on-screen persona in a more thoughtful and in-depth way.

Notes

1. Trevanian was the nom de plume of writer and film/television critic Rodney Whitaker. *The Eiger Sanction* was written as a broad satire of Ian Fleming's James Bond novels and was later followed by a second Jonathan Hemlock novel *The Loo Sanction* (1973).

2. In the book, Dragon is given the first name Yurasis, which is just one of the many characterizing puns meant to evoke the names of Bond villains such as Auric Goldfinger and Bond girls such as Pussy Galore, Solitaire, and Octopussy.

3. Director Sergio Leone wanted James Coburn to play the Man with No Name in the Spaghetti Western trilogy, and Dirty Harry was originally a vehicle for a middle-aged Frank Sinatra. See *Clint Eastwood: Out of the Shadows*, directed by Bruce Riker.

4. All three of the main female characters in the film are portrayed as deceitful. George, Hemlock's Native American personal trainer later revealed to be his friend Ben Bowman's daughter, pursues a sexual relationship with Hemlock, and after letting herself into his hotel room for sex one night, she drugs him with a sedative at the behest of Miles Mellough. Mrs. Montaigne, the wife of the French climber, tries to seduce Hemlock and, when that fails, sleeps with Freytag, another of Montaigne's fellow climbers. Jemima Brown, a black CII courier, is sent by Dragon to pose as a stewardess and seduce Hemlock. She succeeds and steals the sanction money out of his safe the next morning. While George and Mrs. Montaigne are never redeemed for their deceit in the film, Jemima Brown joins Jonathan in Switzerland prior to the Eiger climb, seeking his forgiveness. Hemlock knows that Jemima had a strong patriotic sense of duty to keep the biological agent out of Russian hands, and the two are together in the final shot of the film.

5. This is an evolution of Paul Smith's "Amongst Men" theory, a common film trope in which men tacitly agree to one-on-one combat to the death. In *The Eiger Sanction*, Hemlock realizes that his opponents practice deceit and cannot be trusted to enter into such a pact honorably. Hemlock's code of honor is internal, and he applies its expectations only to himself. See Smith, *Clint Eastwood: A Cultural Production*, 132–33.

6. The film also adapts from the novel Mellough's small dog named "Faggot," and the animal is used in the movie to further the homosexual stereotype of the Mellough character.

7. In an interview for *Clint Eastwood: Out of the Shadows*, Eastwood said, "I've always felt there are only two really authentic American art forms, jazz, and the Western movie." See *Clint Eastwood: Out of the Shadows*.

8. The scene of Hemlock, one hand on the steering wheel of the Bronco, the other clutching an Ithaca shotgun, is an obvious homage to John Wayne's suicidal cavalry charge, shotgun in one hand, pistol in the other, from *True Grit*.

9. It is intimated in the film that Montaigne is slightly older than Hemlock though in reality Eastwood was forty-four during filming.

10. Frederick Jackson Turner asserted, in his famous address to the American Historical Association in July, 1893, that the frontier led to several unique characteristics

that compose the American individual, including "that masterful grasp of material things," "that restless, nervous energy," and "that dominant individualism." He goes on to say that even with the geographic frontier conquered, "the American energy will continually demand a wider field for its exercise." See Turner, "The Significance of the Frontier in American History 1893."

Works Cited

Clint Eastwood: Out of the Shadows. Directed by Bruce Riker, Warner Home Video, 2000.

The Eiger Sanction. Directed by Clint Eastwood, performance by Eastwood, Universal, 1975.

Kael, Pauline. "Harlan County," The Current Cinema, *New Yorker,* 24 Jan. 1977, 84–89.

McGilligan, Patrick. *Clint: The Life and Legend.* St. Martin's Press, 1999.

Schickel, Richard. *Clint Eastwood: A Biography.* Alfred A. Knopf, 1996.

Smith, Paul. *Clint Eastwood: A Cultural Production.* U of Minnesota P, 1993.

Taylor, Joseph E. III. *Pilgrims of the Vertical: Yosemite Rock Climbers and Nature at Risk.* Harvard UP, 2010.

Trevanian. *The Eiger Sanction.* Three Rivers Press, 2000.

Turner, Frederick Jackson. "The Significance of the Frontier in American History 1893." *National Humanities Center,* Dec. 2005, www.national humanitiescenter.org/pds/gilded/empire/text1/turner.pdf. Accessed 17 Jan. 2016.

2

Forced Into Heroism

Clint Eastwood's Reluctant Protagonists in
The Eiger Sanction, The Gauntlet, and *Firefox*

Edward Lamberti

helicopter is flying over trees and snowcapped peaks. The sound of the rotating blades is very loud. Then the film cuts to the opposite: ground level, near silence, and Mitchell Gant (Clint Eastwood) running along a path through the trees. We can hear his breathing. Gant is bearded, and sweat has blotted the front of his gray sweat shirt. He is clearly out for some exercise, but when he first hears and then sees the helicopter, which he realizes has come looking for him, he panics, runs to his house—a lone shack in a clearing—and grabs a rifle, ready to defend himself. What is he afraid of? Why does he live in such a remote place? And why does he look both fit and ravaged? Gant, a former US Air Force pilot who served in the Vietnam War, has evidently sequestered himself away from civilization, and he is panicking because civilization has found him and is coming to reclaim him. This is the opening of *Firefox* (1982), and if I start with it, it is because it is illustrative of what I am going to explore in this chapter with regard to three Eastwood films: *Firefox, The Eiger Sanction* (1975), and *The Gauntlet* (1977).

These are films that Eastwood both starred in and directed, so they embody what we may consider an "Eastwood movie." Yet, despite all three films being made in the years when Eastwood was regularly a top box office draw,[1] they tend to be sidelined, not just by scholars but also by Eastwood fans, in favor of his more famous films of the period, such as the classic Western *The Outlaw Josey Wales* (1976), the Dirty Harry movies *The Enforcer* (1976) and *Sudden Impact* (1983), and the hugely successful comedies *Every Which Way but Loose* (1978) and *Any Which Way You Can* (1980). In this chapter, I wish to consider *The Eiger Sanction*, *The Gauntlet*, and *Firefox* both as Eastwood star vehicles and as fascinating examples of his work as a director and storyteller.

My contention is that, despite their diverse settings and subject matter, the films share two main qualities that produce a productive tension. The first quality is the figure of the Eastwood character as a loner who is reluctant to participate in the wider world and who is forced, coerced, into a heroism he must enact for other people. The second main quality the films share is found in the handling of their somewhat improbable yet engrossing stories. Each film has a plot based around a mission, and delivers on the visual spectacle of that mission being brought to the boil. The result, in each of the three films, is a tension between the solitary nature of Eastwood's performance and the crowd-pleasing professionalism of the storytelling. This tension paints the films as more complex than they at first appear, and it is this tension and complexity that my chapter will address.

Introducing the Eastwood Protagonists

Like *Firefox*, *The Eiger Sanction* begins with the Eastwood character being brought out of retirement. Jonathan Hemlock in *The Eiger Sanction* is an art professor who receives a visit at his university on the last day of the semester from an old acquaintance, Pope (Gregory Walcott). Pope has been sent to bring Hemlock back into the fold, to recruit him for a mission. Hemlock sees Pope off in inimitable Eastwood style, but he cannot ignore the request, and soon he has to go to meet with Dragon (Thayer David), the boss of a secret, though government-endorsed, intelligence unit called CII. The backstory is that Hemlock has worked for many years as a paid assassin for CII, using his fees to purchase priceless paintings by the likes of El Greco, Matisse, Picasso, Klee, and Pissarro, among others. Indeed, it is the lure of a Pissarro that has newly come onto the market that CII uses to bait Hemlock into coming out of retirement and accepting a new mission.

Although when we first meet Hemlock, he is not as obviously ravaged by experience as Gant is in *Firefox*, he is living an existence that, in its own way, marks him out as an equally isolated Eastwood protagonist. For it seems incongruous not just that Hemlock could be an ex-assassin turned art professor, but that Eastwood could play him. The brief glimpses we get of Hemlock at his college—dressed in scholarly jacket and professorial glasses, saying the final words in his last lecture of the semester, and then seeing off the advances of a student who is intimating that she would be willing to sleep with him to better her grades—make it very hard to imagine how Hemlock, as played by Eastwood, could possibly be sustained as a plausible character if CII had not come calling. Can we really imagine Hemlock as embodied by Eastwood existing in that world in 1975, the stage of Eastwood's career that had just seen him play a bank robber in *Thunderbolt and Lightfoot* (1974) and which would shortly see him reprise the role of Dirty Harry Callahan in *The Enforcer*? Those few brief scenes on the college campus near the start of *The Eiger Sanction* seem to be aware of their own incongruity—the odd, discouraging speech Hemlock gives to his students and the subsequent dismissive pat he gives to his female student's derriere counting as barely plausible sketches of the life of a professor. By the time Hemlock is disdainfully accepting the mission from Dragon, the film feels as though it is on firmer territory. If the US military's visit to Gant's hideout in *Firefox* initiates his reluctant reengagement with society, Pope's visit to Hemlock in *The Eiger Sanction* rescues him from an equally precarious existence: having to carry on as a decidedly un-Eastwood-like figure.

The opening to *The Gauntlet* is different in one crucial sense: Eastwood's character, Ben Shockley, a cop with the Phoenix Police Department, knows he has a meeting to attend. It is therefore not as though he has been expecting to be able to hide away from life (or from a story). Rather, Shockley is introduced to us as too disheveled and, indeed, too much of a mess generally to have prepared adequately for a meeting that is, as we find out, part of his job. Accordingly, no character comes to search out Shockley; it is the film itself that searches him out. The film begins, like *Firefox*, with a shot moving across territory—in this case, the city of Phoenix. It is a style of opening that a number of Eastwood movies of this era use, whether directed by him or by someone else—*The Enforcer*, *Every Which Way but Loose*, *Any Which Way You Can*, *Sudden Impact*, and *Tightrope* (1984) all begin like this, with a high, wide shot of a locale as the opening credits are shown, the camera then angling down so that the film can cut to action. In *The Gauntlet*, the film first presents Eastwood as Shockley in a long shot, walking unsteadily out of a bar at dawn after what appears to have been an all-night drinking session. He gets to his car and drives across town to the police station as the credits run. It is redolent of a moment a little way into *The French Connection* (1971) when the central cop, Jimmy "Popeye" Doyle (Gene Hackman), comes out of a bar after having been up all night drinking. It is never a good look for a cop, but at least by this point in *The French Connection* we know something about Popeye: he is devoted to his job. In *The Gauntlet*, since it is just the start of the movie and the long shots are continuing under the credits, almost two more minutes will pass before we get a good look at Shockley. When the first close-up on him comes, it confirms our worst fears: having brought his car to a lurching stop in front of the police station and opened the driver's door, Shockley is looking down in tiredness and disgust at the bottle of Jack Daniel's that has just slipped from the vehicle and smashed on the asphalt.

At this point, however, we still do not know who Shockley is. We do not know that he is a cop. What we do know is that he is played by Eastwood, directing himself, and that this is a startlingly unprepossessing way to introduce oneself on-screen. Paul Smith notes the contrast between the role of Shockley and Eastwood's most famous movie cop, Dirty Harry Callahan:

> Shockley is a down-at-the-heels version of Callahan, a drinker and a depressive, and someone who is chosen to do the movie's central task not because he gets a job done, but because his boss sees him as expendable. It seems clear that part of the movie's deliberate effort is thus to offer a kind of obverse of Harry, a Harry manqué. (128)

Of course, there is perhaps a seedy glamour in introducing oneself as a drunk and a mess—it offers ample room for improvement over the course of the story. And that is what will happen in *The Gauntlet*; indeed, the film finds a lot of humor in this presentation of its star. But my point here is that the *extent* of Shockley's dishevelment, and the way in which the film's narrative feeds off it by seeing him as a victim waiting to happen, positions him very much as a prime example of how Eastwood has enhanced his career through images of compromised masculinity. This means that, although *The Gauntlet* is a rather neglected film in Eastwood's filmography, we can see it as paradigmatic of how his star persona works. The beginning establishes not just ample room for Shockley to improve but also ample room for Eastwood to display his talents as an actor, as he sets about playing a character whom we can slowly come to root for.

These three character introductions, then, are similar in the way in which they home in on a person who is somehow living a life that is unsustainable. Gant, Hemlock, and Shockley have all chosen an existence that will permit them to nurture their solitary preoccupations—Gant's evasion of his post-traumatic stress disorder, Hemlock's love affair with his art collection, and Shockley's affiliation to the bottle. As such, the missions they are called up for are at once unwelcome disruptions of their private equilibriums and opportunities for them to confront the world. All three men are recruited into situations in which, to succeed, they will need to find it in themselves to become heroic. This is why I am calling these solitary men reluctant protagonists. And as these characters are all played and directed by Eastwood, we can read these instances of reluctance as tests for Eastwood the star and Eastwood the filmmaker.

His Missions, and Why He Chooses to Accept Them

It is, of course, in the nature of story that a character's peaceful existence is shattered by an event that initiates the drama. And this type of incident has proved the springboard for many an Eastwood film. My point in this regard in relation to these three films, however, is that in each case the character is quickly dramatized by the film as *weak* in the face of the mission being presented and the organization presenting it. And this weakness may account in part for the degree to which these three films have been somewhat overlooked over the years. By the time of *The Eiger Sanction* in 1975, Eastwood *had* played weak before: his disc jockey, Dave Garver, in *Play Misty for Me* (1971) is stalked by a one-night stand, Evelyn Draper (Jessica Walter), who comes close to overpowering him, and in *The Beguiled* (1971) he is a Union soldier at the time of the American Civil War who, due to injury, is taken in by the women of a girls' school but then held captive by them. And in *Thunderbolt and Lightfoot*, when his character, Thunderbolt, succeeds in his aim of recovering some long-buried loot, it comes at quite a price: the breakdown of his relationship with his bitter former associates (George Kennedy and Geoffrey Lewis) and the loss of his upbeat friend, Lightfoot (Jeff Bridges). In each case, however, Eastwood is playing an individual untied or cut adrift from authority and contending with life on his own terms. By contrast, *The Eiger Sanction*, *The Gauntlet*, and *Firefox* are three instances of Eastwood's playing a character beholden to authority—and in each case, the authority is controlling, compromised, or corrupt. The weakness of the Eastwood protagonists in the face of these unavoidable missions is, therefore, made even more pointed by the missions not even being something he can unequivocally support, and it is this control, compromise, and corruption that I now wish to scrutinize.

The Eiger Sanction and *The Gauntlet* both feature very obvious, self-contained mission scenes. They take place in offices and feature the Eastwood character's boss explaining the mission and why the character has been chosen for it. Dragon in *The Eiger Sanction* is a cartoon-like figure—and this is the first indication that the film is a hybrid, a work of indeterminate genre, and thus of variable tone. The film has begun as a standard espionage thriller, with credits over shots of a man walking through central Zurich while John Williams's spy-theme music plays on the soundtrack. The man we have been observing is then attacked in his apartment by an assailant who murders him and then flees with an accomplice. These opening scenes establish a mood of intrigue but also one of secure genre, the European-set espionage thriller in step with other similar films such as Alfred Hitchcock's *Topaz* (1969) and Fred Zinnemann's *The Day of the Jackal* (1973). When *The Eiger Sanction* cuts to Eastwood as Hemlock in his art lecture, however, the tone is lightened by comedy; even Hemlock's confrontation in his office with Pope is shot through with the kind of tight-lipped, grimly delivered, tough put downs for which Eastwood is justly enjoyed. Hemlock's first meeting with Dragon, however, shifts the tone yet again (all this in the film's first fifteen minutes): Dragon is an albino, and, as the dialogue rather ploddingly explains, this particular albino has to exist in near darkness because even the softest direct light hurts his skin. Thus, Hemlock's meeting with Dragon takes place in a space lit like a photographer's darkroom, red-lit and hushed. Furthermore, Dragon is made up and played very much as a movie villain, heavyset, with white hair, pale eyeballs, and a high, rasping voice. The film has therefore lurched from serious espionage to campus comedy to an almost science-fiction environment, and it is here that Dragon explains the situation: CII requires that the murdered man in Zurich be avenged, and Hemlock is the man to do it. When Hemlock protests, Dragon threatens to inform the Internal Revenue Service of Hemlock's precious collection of art masterpieces, for which Hemlock has not paid tax. Hemlock counters this with some fierce negotiation over his demands for carrying out the retaliatory killing (or "sanction," as Dragon calls it), but his weakness for his artworks ensures that he is caught in a trap: the art is clearly all he enjoys in his life, and he cannot comprehend losing it. The mission, then, is presented with a mixture of flattery (that Hemlock is the man for the job) and menace (if he does not accept, consequences will follow). It is Hemlock's *acceptance* of the mission that reveals his weakness: he is powerless to refuse. And this is somehow emphasized in Eastwood's playing of the scene: Hemlock's grudging acceptance conveys the need for the film to capitulate to genre requirements. The story will come to require that he join a climbing expedition to the Eiger to assassinate the remaining target. The film will, therefore, take him to Monument Valley to train and from there to the Swiss Alps. With Hemlock's acceptance of the mission, the story proper can begin.

The mission in *The Gauntlet* is presented in a tidier way and without a break in tone, simply because it comes about as part of the Eastwood character's daily work. This mission, on the surface, is routine. Shockley is late for his meeting with the new police commissioner, Blakelock (William Prince), who—according to Shockley's friend and colleague Josephson (Pat Hingle)—is apparently "very spit-and-polish." When Shockley meets with Blakelock, the film's presentation of the moment supports Josephson's claim. The scene is Blakelock's office, and Shockley stands subserviently in front of Blakelock's desk throughout the meeting while Blakelock sits behind it. Eastwood as director shoots the conversation very similarly to that between Hemlock and Dragon—as a succession of medium shots and close-ups, here conveying Blakelock's granite-like intransigence and Shockley's bafflement as to why he has been chosen; Blakelock tells him, "Your division commander says you're a man who gets a job done." Their meeting ends with Blakelock reminding Shockley, "You represent the Phoenix PD. Get a shave," and Shockley's quiet, rather sheepish agreement to do so. Shockley, then, is thoroughly beholden to carrying out this mission—it is his job to accept it; plus he may feel as though he should make something of an impression with the new commissioner. And so he sets about his task with weary efficiency. The mission, after all, appears simple enough: Shockley is to take a round trip to Las Vegas to extradite a prisoner back to Phoenix for a trial. What Shockley does not yet know is that he is being set up. The prisoner he has been sent to collect, a prostitute named Gus Mally (Sondra Locke), is a vital witness in an upcoming trial. Furthermore, as we will come to discover, she has been raped by Blakelock, and he is desperate to silence her. Blakelock's plan is for Shockley and Mally to be killed on the return journey from Vegas to Phoenix. *The Gauntlet*, therefore, is a story about corruption, and Edward Gallafent notes the difference between this film and previous Eastwood work:

Part of the film's premise, and the way that it differs from a vigilante movie like *Magnum Force*, is its cognisance—expressible after Watergate and Richard Nixon's resignation—that the system in which the hero is situated is corrupt not just in details or in particular places, but specifically at the point of high command. (171–72)

Gallafent's observation thus identifies in *The Gauntlet* a signal anxiety of post-Nixonian America, namely, a growing realization that the powers that be cannot be trusted, that they are out for themselves, and that they do not have the people's best interests at heart. Much of the tension in the first half of *The Gauntlet* concerns the contrast between this rapidly growing sense of dread and the slowness with which Shockley himself wakes up to it. Indeed, one senses that if the smart captive Mally were not to raise her concerns— first tentatively, then insistently—it is likely that the two of them would be dead shortly after leaving the police cells in Vegas. Eastwood the actor, therefore, is playing the part of a slow-witted, institutionalized man, and Eastwood the director presents him so unflinchingly to serve the larger thrust of the narrative: good cops must stay alert to the possibility of corruption not just within the expected places but also within the force that should be fighting it.

Mitchell Gant in *Firefox* is, like Hemlock, coerced into his mission. The military has come to his remote house, and the sight of the helicopter has caused him to lapse into a traumatic memory, which the film will present a number of times: Gant, captured by enemy forces, witnesses the death of a Vietnamese girl in a US napalm attack. Gant, hunched and in torment, is brought round from the memory by Buckholz (David Huffman), who calls him "Major" and treats him with respect. But, as they begin to discuss the reasons for the visit, Buckholz mentions that Gant's house is on government land and that it could be reclaimed if he does not cooperate. US Intelligence needs Gant to go to the USSR to steal a supersonic MiG-31 jet, nicknamed "Firefox," which the Soviets have developed. Gant is called on not only because he is an excellent pilot but also because he speaks Russian. To be sent to the USSR on such a mission—when one is clearly unfit for active duty and has been unaccustomed to pressure since Vietnam—would be something that surely no one would accept without hesitation, and the government's coercion of Gant is their tacit admission that anyone could see the foolishness of what they are attempting. But attempt it they will, and Gant is soon in a flight simulator getting refresher training and being briefed in

London by Buckholz and the British mastermind involved in the plan, Kenneth Aubrey (Freddie Jones).

Part of the thrill of these three films is that Eastwood's reluctant protagonists have all been placed in situations that will afford opportunities for them to sharpen their wits and to show what they are capable of. Any wrong move they make could mean death. But while Hemlock, Shockley, and Gant are all on paper eminently actable parts, Eastwood's performances warrant attention for the ways in which they manage to sustain interest in these characters that remain, in many senses, unappealing, even charmless. The tension in these films between crowd-pleasing storytelling and a borderline moroseness is incarnated in their central figures, and it is this tension to which I shall now turn.

Charmless but Compelling Figures

Eastwood's screen persona is so established and so recognized that it is very easy to forget that, before his movie career took off with *A Fistful of Dollars* (1964), his most famous role was as the genial cowboy Rowdy Yates in TV's *Rawhide* (1959–1966). As François Guérif puts it, "the European foray [to star in the Sergio Leone films] would sweep away, in one fell swoop, the image he had worked so long and hard to create. Enter the macho cynic, lawless and without faith to boot—an image which would not be nearly so easy to shake" (31). Eastwood's popularity in the immediate post-*Rawhide* years was founded on just this sort of character, beginning with the Man with No Name in the Leone trilogy. After *A Fistful of Dollars*, *For a Few Dollars More* (1965), and *The Good, the Bad and the Ugly* (1966), Eastwood proved himself a hardheaded central figure in films as diverse as the cop movie *Coogan's Bluff* (1968), the war films *Where Eagles Dare* (1968) and *Kelly's Heroes* (1970), and the Westerns *Hang 'Em High* (1968), *Two Mules for Sister Sara* (1970), and *Joe Kidd* (1972). He showed his softer side with his role in the big-screen version of the musical *Paint Your Wagon* (1969) and his direction of the drama *Breezy* (1973), in which he did not appear. But those two films flopped, as did the downbeat film *The Beguiled*; audiences were clear as to how they liked their Eastwood.

But that more popular side to early Eastwood was in itself a curious phenomenon. There was, in those first years of superstardom, an impassivity and an impregnability to Eastwood on-screen that enabled him to create compelling centers of attention, but which also raised the question as to what audiences were actually being invited to enjoy—and why they might be enjoying it. Writing about the Westerns that Eastwood made with Leone and Eastwood's own films of the 1970s, Dennis Bingham says, "The feeling persists that for a major star, Eastwood in these films is a schematic and insubstantial figure. He would seem to possess little of the individuality and distinction of a studio-era star" (174). My sense here is that what Eastwood as a screen persona has often lacked is charm; charm is a rare quality, of course, but surely one that, if it is to be found on-screen, is to be found in the star. Eastwood in more recent years—whether falling off his horse as the out-of-shape cowboy in *Unforgiven* (1992), romancing fellow secret service agent Rene Russo in *In the Line of Fire* (1993), or being a trainer-cum-father figure to Hilary Swank's boxer in *Million Dollar Baby* (2004)—has displayed great charm, warmth, and likability. But in so many of his leading-man roles in the first two decades of his career, he appears as a rather non-ingratiating screen presence.

I believe this accounts in part for the quality of depressiveness that emanates from his characters in *The Eiger Sanction*, *The Gauntlet*, and *Firefox*. In one sense, this is simply Eastwood's familiar "cool" image on display: the characters he plays live their lives so much on their own terms—or like to think they do—that they cannot muster up much enthusiasm for the parts they play in the lives of others. In each of the scenes in which the Eastwood character receives his mission, he does so with an element of disdain for his superior—much as he does in the Dirty Harry films. But in *The Eiger Sanction*, *The Gauntlet*, and *Firefox*, this disdain more obviously masks a sense of disappointment, even resignation.

And yet Eastwood is compelling on-screen. It is not just his look—the tall head, the abundant hair—but also his walk—purposeful yet rangy, strong yet refreshingly unselfconscious. David Thomson says that "it is often preferable to have a movie actor who moves well than one who 'understands' the part" (43), and he says of Humphrey Bogart in *The Big Sleep* (1946) that the shots of him walking "draw us to the resilient alertness of his screen personality. . . . Bogart's lounging freedom captures our hopes" (43). I do not mean to suggest that Eastwood does not understand the parts he plays, but I do mean to draw attention to his nonverbal—and even nonfacial—qualities. Our "hopes" reside in how Eastwood "moves," at least as much as in what he says and the facial expressions he makes. Bingham suggests that something similar occurs in *High Plains Drifter* (1973):

The film needs spectators to complete the scene; they supply the desire and passion missing from Eastwood. This is because Eastwood in his persona and his presence is oddly incomplete; the cause of his phenomenal success might lie partly in the fact that he is only a schematic figure whose desires and motivations the spectator willingly fills in. (168)

In *The Gauntlet*, however, Shockley's dishevelment and incompetence make him more relatable, more human. Josephson says to him, "You should've put on a tie. You should've shined your shoes. You should've made some kind of an effort to spruce up a little bit." Shockley, as we have seen, starts off as a portrait in weakened masculinity. Guérif observes that "Ben, like Harry [Callahan], is an inspector, solitary, obstinate, and incorruptible" (125). And he notes how the film quickly shows these traits in an ambivalent light: "Within the first twenty minutes, Eastwood puts all of Ben's sterling 'qualities' in question: 'obstinate' might also mean narrow-minded, 'solitary' could mean vulnerable, and 'incorruptible' doesn't mean a whole hell of a lot when your higher-ups have become the symbol of corruption itself" (125). When Mally asks Shockley why he thinks he was chosen for the mission and he tells her that he gets the job done, she replies: "They don't want the job done. They picked you because you're a drunken bum [. . .]. You're a nothing, Shockley—a nobody. You're a faded number on a rusty badge, and you've been set up by your own people to take the fall with me. Wake up, for Christ's sake!" This exasperated scrutiny does wake him up. It is worth noting that the film's poster, by famed graphic artist Frank Frazetta, shows Shockley as a kind of He-Man, bulging muscles bursting out of his vest, handgun held aloft, Sondra Locke as Mally chained to his free arm and wrapped around his leg. The image is a cheerful exaggeration since in the film no equivalent image of Shockley exists: even as he begins to understand the drastic situation in which he and Mally find themselves, Shockley remains relatively unremarkable as a physical specimen—in good shape but not excessively eye-catching. The Shockley of the film seems older than the Shockley of the poster too. But his unremarkableness—and the modesty that comes with it—is perhaps his most attractive quality. And this attractiveness is indistinguishable from that of Eastwood in this film. In his cop's white shirt and holster, dark trousers, and shoes impractical for a night clambering about in the desert—and with a five o'clock shadow on his jaw and shades he dons at judicious moments—Shockley has a haphazard sort of nobility that is enormously appealing precisely by dint of its being incarnated in Eastwood as movie star, actor, and highly capable storyteller behind the camera.

Giving the Films Their Best Chances

Eastwood's talent as a storyteller is especially evident when one considers the question of genre in relation to *The Eiger Sanction*, *The Gauntlet*, and *Firefox*. Something that marks all three films is the difficulty of defining them in relation to any particular genre. *The Eiger Sanction* is, variously, an espionage tale, a whodunit, a travelogue, and a mountaineering story. *The Gauntlet* is a cop thriller, a road movie, and a screwball comedy; Smith calls it "a rather strange and almost unclassifiable film" (127). *Firefox* has been characterized by a number of critics as a war film (Cornell 147; Smith 198),[2] but it is also, more specifically, a Cold War story, and Eastwood himself has said it "started out like a classic spy film" (qtd. in Henry 106). All three films, however, wear their generic variables lightly. *The Eiger Sanction* is Eastwood's fourth film as a director, *The Gauntlet* his sixth, and *Firefox* his eighth, and each of them showcases an abiding sense of what Eastwood's film direction is generally like in the years before his acclaimed, Oscar-winning 1992 Western *Unforgiven*. Up to that point, Eastwood as a director generally appears content to deliver stories in an unforced, logical way, covering action in a no-nonsense fashion and exhibiting little artistic will that would seek to push the material beyond the comfort zone of broad-brush popular entertainment. There are exceptions to this: *High Plains Drifter* is a radically austere Western that manages to transcend Leone's influence to achieve a mercilessness of its own, *The Outlaw Josey Wales* is a richly staged and surprisingly sensitive look at race relations in the post–Civil War South, and *Bird* (1988)—Eastwood's biopic of jazz saxophonist Charlie Parker—is an ambitiously constructed, hard-hitting look at a tortured legend. If *Unforgiven* is an artistic breakthrough in Eastwood's career, it is not so much for its semi-revisionist look at the West as for its quality of predetermination, the sense that Eastwood has chosen everything that has gone into the film very carefully and judiciously. Since then, films such as *Mystic River* (2003), *Million Dollar Baby*, the Iwo Jima movies—*Flags of Our Fathers* and *Letters from Iwo Jima* (both 2006)—and *American Sniper* (2014) have shown us sides to Eastwood's filmmaking we haven't seen from him before. But this is not to denigrate early Eastwood: starting with his directorial debut, *Play Misty for Me*, and with very few exceptions, he has given his films their best chance at succeeding.

His comments on *The Eiger Sanction*, for example, display his awareness of its place within popular trends as well as his true interest in the tale, and the need to meld the two:

It was the kind of thing a lot of people were doing, these tongue-in-cheek spy drama things, but there was an element of it that was more interesting because the mountain-climbing stuff seemed like it actually could be suspenseful. The whole thing on height. I got wrapped up with the challenge of trying to make the picture all in the mountains, which I did. (qtd. in Avery 98–99)

As such, the film affords numerous opportunities for Eastwood to display his physical prowess. The most obvious example of this is the dizzying sequence in which Hemlock climbs the Totem Pole in Monument Valley, the bird's-eye view making sure we cannot fail to notice that it is actually Eastwood (and George Kennedy) sitting at the top. The "tongue-in-cheek spy drama things" to which Eastwood refers are, of course, James Bond and its parodies, and he clarifies this elsewhere, acknowledging the film's proximity to the Bond saga (McGilligan 39; Henry 102). *The Eiger Sanction* is based on a novel by Trevanian that takes a satirical look at the world of a spy; the comparison with Bond helps explain not just Hemlock's mission but also the film's globe-trotting spectacle, from Zurich to the US desert to the Alps. The attractive shooting of these locales by cinematographer Frank Stanley, showing off their physical properties, aids the film by diverting attention away from some of its more dubious narrative elements, such as Hemlock's cold-blooded abandonment of his old friend-turned-nemesis Miles Mellough (Jack Cassidy) in Monument Valley. The wide-screen imagery and Williams's sweeping score draw out Hemlock's solitariness by placing him squarely in an imposing physical world that dwarfs him and which he is required to master. The training sequences in the United States are superseded in spectacle by the sequences on the Eiger itself, shot on location in difficult conditions and providing a thrilling setting for the culmination of Hemlock's mission, wherein he must try to identify and then assassinate his target. Pascal Mérigeau has noted of *The Eiger Sanction* that "Eastwood's major merit here, yet again, is to not be contemptuous of the script he has agreed to make, but to do his very best to deliver quality entertainment" (qtd. in Guérif 112). Eastwood's own assessment of the film sums up his unpretentiousness: "*The Eiger Sanction* was a modest story with good physical productions" (qtd. in Avery 99).

With regard to *The Gauntlet*, too, Eastwood displays a pragmatic awareness of its potential and its areas of interest. Eastwood told his director friend and mentor Don Siegel: "I wanted a certain believability about the story, but at the same time there had to be an entertainment quality" (qtd. in Avery 117), and the film very effectively uses a succession of increasingly outlandish action set pieces to put across its themes in as entertaining a way as possible. Yet Eastwood explains:

> What attracted me to the story was that it was a good relationship story. It's an action picture with a ton of action, but at the same time, great relationships. The girl's part is a terrific role, not just token window-dressing like in so many action films. Her part is equal to the male part, if not even more so. It's in *The African Queen* tradition: a love-hate thing that turns out to be a love story. It's a bawdy adventure, too. (qtd. in Thompson and Hunter 59)

As in *The Eiger Sanction*, the expressive location filming of *The Gauntlet*—here by cinematographer Rexford Metz—and the way in which the film's pacing allows it to avoid falling into its plot holes give Shockley's mission a propulsion. As the film moves forward, its protagonist has to sharpen himself up and help Mally so that they might save themselves from dying on the journey back to Phoenix. A key sequence in this regard comes when they commandeer a car driven by a cop (Bill McKinney) nearing the end of his day's shift. The sequence begins in Vegas, Shockley and Mally forcing their driver at gunpoint to take them to the Nevada-Arizona border, where, Shockley believes, they will be met by colleagues from the Phoenix PD. Given that Shockley has arranged this through the same channels—that is, a call to Blakelock—that previously resulted in his and Mally's ambush by cops at her house, Mally believes something is wrong, and slowly she starts to probe Shockley as to whether there isn't a chance he is being betrayed by his own people. The cop driving them, having taken the opportunity to quiz Mally about her work as a prostitute—and having received both a humiliating verbal takedown from Mally and a beating from Shockley for his efforts—now asks Shockley whether he will stand for Mally's implying that his people are betraying him. But Mally's reasoning is sound, something Shockley eventually has to admit, and Eastwood as director uses a wonderful series of close-ups to depict Eastwood the actor's performance of Shockley's growing realization that there is more to the situation than he at first believed. "Pull over," he says to the cop, and with that utterance Shockley admits the possibility that Mally may be right. It is a marvelous sequence, brilliantly written and beautifully performed by the three actors—a sequence in which Shockley has been scrutinized by Mally, by the cop, and by the movie.

Something that *The Eiger Sanction*, *The Gauntlet*, and *Firefox* share is this sense of propulsion, in taking a rather solitary figure, a loner, and placing him at the center of a narrative with a momentum that will carry him far beyond the confines of the life he has created for himself. This is evident in the titles of the films: the Eiger sanction being the mission Hemlock must work toward and carry out, the gauntlet being the test that Shockley and Mally must face in their climactic return to Phoenix, and the Firefox being the prize that awaits Gant—and the United States—if he successfully infiltrates Russian Intelligence. In each case, the titular element is treated almost as a star of the movie in its own right; as with classic star introductions, the Eiger, the gauntlet, and the plane are talked about, anticipated, and finally revealed. In particular, the sequence in *Firefox* in which Gant finally enters the hangar housing the plane and sees it for the first time with his own eyes is a thrilling payoff not just for him but also for viewers after so much plotting, speculating, and waiting by Gant and his partisan helpers. The sequences that follow—wherein Gant must steal the Firefox and then try to fend off the Russian pilot in hot pursuit in a second, similar plane—are especially welcome in what is a long film and one in which the protagonist has for so much of the running time been tense and unwell through the stress of what he has to do. In contrast to *The Eiger Sanction* and *The Gauntlet*, there is no humor or romance in *Firefox* to offset the reluctant protagonist's tension or ours. Indeed, the film gains immensely from Eastwood's convincing performance of Gant's physical and psychological weaknesses. In the Moscow scenes especially, and those set in the hangar where Gant is preparing to steal the Firefox, there is genuine suspense created through the possibility that his weakness and illness will give him away, will somehow expose him as a fallen hero, as *Eastwood* out of shape. Eastwood has since shown himself elsewhere to be good at playing the ailing, for example in *Honkytonk Man* (1982), *Unforgiven*, and *Blood Work* (2002). Because of the thinness of his voice, it can easily be made to sound afflicted by the common cold or worse. In *Firefox*, this weakness in itself creates a life-or-death situation: if Gant cannot find the strength to steal the plane, he will have no way out of Russia.

Thus in each of these films there is a tension between the protagonist's solitude and the drive of the narrative, which requires that the protagonist cast off that solitude in order to win through. I have argued that there is a depressive quality to the Eastwood characters, and in the final section I shall consider ways in which that depressiveness can be read productively within the contexts of the films.

Stories of Corruption and Liberation

The violence in *The Gauntlet* is worth noting. At the time, the film was Eastwood's most expensive, costing in the region of $5.5 million ("Box Office / Business for *The Gauntlet* [1977]"), a million of which was spent on special effects (Hirschhorn 430). But there is not much in the way of physical, one-on-one action or combat. As Gallafent notes, Shockley only fires his gun twice in the whole movie—once at a locked door and once at the fuel tank on a motorbike (170). Instead, most of the violence is directed at objects—Mally's house, shot to pieces by the cops who surround it; the hijacked cop's car as it arrives at the Nevada-Arizona border and is attacked by Blakelock's squad (Shockley and Mally having bailed out in time); a helicopter pursuing the fugitive couple across the desert until it hits power lines and explodes; and, most memorably, the bus in which Shockley and Mally enter Phoenix to run the gauntlet of armed cops at the film's climax. Eastwood has stated that these scenes were designed to express the pent-up frustration of cops trained for such a rare moment: "Imagine what it's like for a cop to be out there training all the time. The big *if*: what's going to happen if I have to pull the gun? . . . All of a sudden it comes over the radio that there's a house with, say, some known criminal, armed and dangerous, shooting. Something wild's going to come down" (qtd. in Avery 116). The actions of the police are therefore seen as unrestrained, in excess of require-ments—clearly there is no need for Shockley and Mally to be met with such a show of force. And this show of force only demonstrates in practice what the film has been saying all along, and what Shockley has reluctantly come to realize; the film has, in Gallafent's words, "the uneasy knowledge that the actual practice of this law enforcement has somehow gone horribly wrong, with the figures of command corrupt and the men in the field impotent as a result" (173). Shockley's heroism is borne of a dissociation from the institution to which he has pledged his devotion for his profes-sional life. Being the hero of his tale has brought him a profound disquiet; if it is liberation, it is only liberation from his own ignorance.

As is the case with Shockley, the fulfilment of the missions that Hemlock and Gant carry out brings the realization that their missions are based on profoundly ambivalent premises: Hemlock despairs that his retaliatory sanction serves no purpose while Gant is presumably healed in some senses by stealing the Firefox but remains a rootless figure, barely more resolved by the film's end than he was at its start. Smith reads the opening of *Firefox* as an illustration of a broader tendency of reemerging and newly active US foreign policy:

> [T]he helicopter has come searching for him to bring him out of retirement—in other words, to make the serviceman serve again. The premises of this opening sequence are, thus, almost stunningly allegorical in the sense that the 1980s became precisely the time, after more than a decade, that the symbolically traumatized and debilitated American forces were called from their post-Vietnam seclusion and began to serve again. (199)

If servicemen began to be called on to serve again in the US armed forces, then Hollywood, too, was beginning to play its part in addressing the trauma of Vietnam by putting it front and center in movies. Thus 1978 had seen two big, Oscar-winning films, *Coming Home* and *The Deer Hunter*, that depicted veterans back home, and 1982, the year of *Firefox*'s release, also saw the release of *First Blood*, another film about a Vietnam vet, played by another established star, Sylvester Stallone. Smith has noted how the release of *Firefox* played into narratives around the reemergence of US military might (the film premiered as a benefit for the United Service Organizations, with inflated ticket prices and attendance by prominent political figures):

> Both Eastwood and the movie, then, function in this situation as points around which the then prevailing right-wing understanding of America's military destiny and its enemies can be articulated. The individual hero is released from the "exile" of his post-Vietnam trauma, and returns to outwit the cold war enemy. (201)

But the portrayal of Gant in the film is not in step with a rosily patriotic reception. As we have seen, Gant is a troubled man, physically and psychologically weakened by his trauma. For Drucilla Cornell,

> [t]he film's purported optimism is belied throughout by the weakness and demeanor of Eastwood's hero. . . . Though he is obviously a skilled pilot, his technical prowess and daring never fully overcome his

personal struggle with his past or with what he needs to do to complete the mission. In this sense, the film sends a much more mixed message about war (even cold war) than the Reagan administration was prepared to see. (148)

And the film affords him no comforting way out. As Gallafent notes, "At its close Gant says, conventionally enough, 'Let's go home.' But the film is substantially silent on the subject of home. Given the absence of the usual ways in which such a subject might be presented . . . we cannot know very clearly what this line is to be taken to mean" (150). Gant, then, is stranded—or at least the film does not give us an opportunity to see where he might go from here. Hemlock, too, is left in a state of suspension: there is the suggestion of a tentative romance with Jemima (Vonetta McGee), with whom he has become allied during the course of his mission, and his days as an assassin appear to be over, but can we really see him returning to his job as art professor? And if not, what sort of job does Jonathan Hemlock do next? As for Shockley, the gauntlet he runs gives him a chance at a future with Mally. We know they have fallen in love and discussed a possible life together. But that romance does not seem large enough to assuage the disquiet over the film's portrayal of the police. Larger questions about society remain in the air, and Shockley may not be the person to address them.

Nevertheless, if Shockley, Hemlock, and Gant are all trapped by the missions they find themselves on, they are at least, in some senses, liberated by them. And their actor and director may have been liberated by them too. Guérif believes *The Gauntlet* represents "a sort of exorcism for Eastwood. The heightened violence, cranked up to fever pitch, frees him for a while from the noise and fury of his preceding characterizations. After the gauntlet has been run we are left, if only for an instant, with a character at peace with himself" (127). And this is the point I want to end on: that *The Eiger Sanction*, *The Gauntlet*, and *Firefox*—all generally considered to be relatively minor films in Eastwood's career—are liberating in their conclusions: we can enjoy the fun and the heroics of these stories, but it is also invigorating to recognize their disconcerting undertows. In their portrayals of their reluctant protagonists, the films deepen the achievements of Eastwood's body of work. In all three films, Eastwood shows he is strong enough to present himself as weakened—so as to pose important questions about our institutions.

Notes

1. Eastwood topped the Quigley's "Top Ten Money Making Stars Poll" of film actors in 1972, 1973, 1983, and 1984, and was in the top three on five occasions in the intervening years.

2. Also, Gallafent includes *Firefox* in his chapter entitled "The War Movies."

Works Cited

Avery, Kevin, editor. *Conversations with Clint: Paul Nelson's Lost Interviews with Clint Eastwood 1979–1983*. Continuum, 2011.

Bingham, Dennis. *Acting Male: Masculinities in the Films of James Stewart, Jack Nicholson, and Clint Eastwood*. Rutgers UP, 1994.

"Box Office / Business for *The Gauntlet* (1977)." *IMDb*, www.imdb.com/title/tt0076070/business?ref_=tt_dt_bus. Accessed 10 Jan. 2017.

Cornell, Drucilla. *Clint Eastwood and Issues of American Masculinity*. Fordham UP, 2009.

Gallafent, Edward. *Clint Eastwood: Filmmaker and Star*. Continuum, 1994.

Guérif, François. *Clint Eastwood*. 1984. Translated by Lisa Nesselson, Roger Houghton, 1986.

Henry, Michael. "Interview with Clint Eastwood." 1985. Translated by Kathie Coblentz, Kapsis and Coblentz, pp. 96–116.

Hirschhorn, Clive. *The Warner Bros. Story*. 1979. Octopus Books, 1986.

Kapsis, Robert E., and Kathie Coblentz, editors. *Clint Eastwood: Interviews*. UP of Mississippi, 1999.

McGilligan, Patrick. "Clint Eastwood." 1976. Kapsis and Coblentz, pp. 21–41.

Smith, Paul. *Clint Eastwood: A Cultural Production*. UP of Minnesota, 1993.

Thompson, Richard, and Tim Hunter. "Eastwood Direction." 1978. Kapsis and Coblentz, pp. 42–61.

Thomson, David. *The New Biographical Dictionary of Film—Sixth Edition*. Alfred A. Knopf, 2014.

"Top Ten Money Making Stars Poll." *Wikipedia*, en.wikipedia.org/wiki/Top_Ten_Money_Making_Stars_Poll. Accessed 10 Jan. 2017.

3

Why Are We Stuck in Low-Earth Orbit?

Sexagenarian *Space Cowboys* and the Failing Body of
Their American Dream

W. D. Phillips

"Send my team up. We'll fix your broken satellite for you."
—Frank Corbin (Clint Eastwood) in *Space Cowboys* (2000)

"I fix things."
—Walt Kowalski (Clint Eastwood) in *Gran Torino* (2008)

Clint Eastwood fixes things. At least that is what his cinematic oeuvre, in its many phases and stages, seems to reveal. Walt Kowalski, *Gran Torino*'s (2008) crotchety protagonist, directly claims as much, though, when pushed, elaborates that he simply fixes things like dryers and sinks. False modesty and narrative misdirection notwithstanding, Eastwood's various characters have "fixed"—across fifty years—everything from broken satellites to Old West towns, San Francisco crooks, assassination attempts, false imprisonments, America's 0–1–1 post-WWII military record, the at-risk future of his Hmong neighbors, and Meryl Streep's aching heart.

Eastwood's capacity to overcome, as a protagonist in American narrative cinema, the obstacles placed in front of him by the end of the film is, of course, hardly remarkable. More remarkable, though, is his ability to do so persistently from his thirties up through his eighties in such a manner that it continues to have meaning for contemporary audiences. Still, as Bob Batchelor and Norma Jones note in the introduction to their recent collection of essays, *Aging Heroes: Growing Old in Popular Culture*, actors such as Robert De Niro, Kevin Costner, Sylvester Stallone, Michael Douglas, and

Jeff Bridges have all continued to engage American audiences even as they have aged into their sixties and beyond. As an aging performer playing aging characters, Eastwood's choices nonetheless seem to exhibit greater consistency of conceit, and this goes beyond simply the performance mode of "stubbornness and eccentricity" (Gates 176) that runs across his many elderly characters. We can, to a degree, assign that type of consistency to the fact that, since 1990 and the age sixty, he has performed what I refer to as the "old-man Eastwood" character thirteen times, all but two of which were under his own direction. Moreover, of those thirteen films, only *In the Line of Fire* (1993), directed by Wolfgang Petersen for Columbia Pictures, was made outside of Eastwood's own Malpaso Productions.[1] Eastwood's control over his own characters and performances has therefore been extremely superintended, even in relation to the degrees typically exhibited by A-list stars with familiar screen personas. That his "senior persona," as Craig Rinne calls it, is generally incapable of repairing broken relations with his immediate family or constructively addressing the flaws in his characters has been noted by numerous critics.[2] Nonetheless, his characters do, with significant consistency, fix all other diegetic problems assigned to the story's protagonist.

William Beard, in his essay "Lies of Our Fathers: Mythology and Artifice in Eastwood's Cinema," analyzes the nature of the diegetic solutions and effectively argues for a recognizable pattern of artificial mythologies in the films both starring and directed by Eastwood. What this means for Beard is that Eastwood "almost always accompanies his representations of heroic or super-heroic character and action with indications of their impossibility and/or their artifice" (224). In performing his role as "fixer," Eastwood, according to Beard, repeats throughout many of his films a particular form of narrative closure that is "reassuring and redemptive, on the one hand, and highly visible in its portrayal of artifice and fakery that enables that reassurance and redemption," on the other ("Lies" 230). The character of old-man Eastwood may save the day, but Eastwood the director makes sure to show, at some level, just how constructed and hence ersatz such narrative closure is for both the diegetic world of the character and especially the extradiegetic world of the viewer. In Eastwood's precise manipulation of what Beard elsewhere calls the "trope of the flag" (*Persistence* 143), the filmmaker reveals the protagonist's diegetic successes to be at best a weak suture for the larger societal issues for which they stand: a tent made up of American flags woven together by inmates of the local asylum allows the Wild West show (and the frontier myth it perpetuates) to go on in *Bronco Billy* (1980); Eastwood's ex-wife welcomes him home from "victory" in Granada with the tiniest of toy flags in *Heartbreak Ridge* (1986); and a media circus surrounds "the photograph," the results of which were "the crassest hucksterism" and "a sickening series of boosterish pageants" (237), in *Flags of Our Fathers* (2006).

Though Beard stops short of calling these films allegorical, Craig Rinne, looking at Eastwood's performances of the early 1990s, does not, and he goes beyond Beard's claims to argue that Eastwood's characters, in looking to redeem themselves, are "explicitly tied to historical American events or period settings, suggesting that the film narratives with these characters serve as allegories for . . . America" (131). Rinne focuses his study on *Unforgiven* (1992) and *In the Line of Fire*, both released shortly after the end of the Cold War, and argues that "variations on the senior persona persist in Eastwood's later films," such as *Space Cowboys* (2000), but "those films lack the intertwined allusions to specific, grandiose historical events and frontier mythology that enabled an obvious, allegorical connection to post–Cold War America" (146).

This paper will perform an extended analysis of *Space Cowboys* and the "grandiose historical events and frontier mythology" with which the film and its protagonists are engaged. In doing so, I will expand Beard's reading of artificial mythologies in this film and several others made in the same period. I will also, as a result, extend and correct Rinne's claims in regard to this work. What will result is an argument for the *inability* of Eastwood's aging characters to single-handedly fix the ills of contemporary America, but also an argument for Eastwood's *ability*—as representative of a certain American generation whose own bodies have begun to falter—to diagnose these ills as symptoms of a failing American body. Through his narrative agency in response to these symptoms of American decline, Eastwood's characters and the generational wisdom and experience they embody also work to indicate how such collapse might be slowed, altered, or—ideally—reversed.

Recognizing the Severity of the Problem; or, "Old Enough to Know Your Ass Is in a Sling"

In her December 2008 *New York Times* review of *Gran Torino*, Manohla Dargis made claims that far exceeded her response to that film alone, calling forth the films of Clint Eastwood, and American cinema more generally, from the previous two decades: "Few Americans make movies about this country anymore, other than Mr. Eastwood" and "even the misfires show an urgent engagement with the tougher, messier, bigger questions of American life." Such a statement may not immediately appear to apply to *Space Cowboys* and its geriatric wish fulfillment of outer space adventures. Closer analysis, however, clearly reveals the significance of Dargis's claim to an understanding of this film as well.

On the surface, *Space Cowboys* engages Eastwood's interest in the efficaciousness of older male screen bodies/heroes, a theme running through nearly all of his films since at least *Heartbreak Ridge*, including *Unforgiven*, *Absolute Power* (1997), *True Crime* (1999), *Blood Work* (2002), and *Gran Torino*. In these films, Eastwood as a filmmaker brings this forward in multiple cinematic registers: through the dialogue (drawing attention, often through self-deprecating humor, to his character's age); in relation to his protagonist's actions and physical condition (careers requiring high-level physical performance, heart transplants, cancer); and via the on-screen image (his shirtless body is regularly displayed, and in *Space Cowboys* he literally shows his ass—and those of his similarly aged colleagues[3]).

Space Cowboys starts in the monochromatic historical past of 1958, just before the beginning of the space race, when Air Force test pilots flew new, experimental aircraft, pushing the envelope of both the human body and the developing technology. It opens on the Bell X-2 aircraft, navigated by Frank Corvin (Clint Eastwood) and piloted by Hawk Hawkins (Tommy Lee Jones). Airmen Jerry O'Neill (Donald Sutherland) and Tank Sullivan (James Garner) round out the elite team as ground and air support.[4] After Hawk pushes the envelope too far, breaking height and speed records but also destroying the expensive plane itself, their commanding officer, Bob Gerson, is only too happy to inform them that while they may be the "best of the best" as test pilots, they are no longer among America's chosen ones for the impending race to the moon. When Eastwood's elite (but fictional) Team Daedalus is supplanted by a chimpanzee, Eastwood as a filmmaker—with screenwriters Ken Kaufman and Howard Klausner—marries two historical displacements to undermine the heroic nature of the characters, raising the bar for their eventual modern-day redemption. It is a deft narrative conflation, referencing two historical decisions in setting up the dramatic situation that the second act of the film will work to redress. The first decision referenced here is the National Aeronautics and Space Administration's (NASA) determination to require Mercury astronauts to have a college education. Though many military test pilots were chosen to compete for the seven

Mercury spots, many others (some argue the best) were passed over for that reason alone. Chuck Yeager—lionized in 1979 by Tom Wolfe in *The Right Stuff*, a narrativized history of the early space program—is simply the best known. Sam Shepard's iconic performance of Yeager in Philip Kaufman's 1983 film adaptation reinforces this characterization of the test pilots as uniquely in possession of "the right stuff." Moreover, Kaufman's use of the film Western's iconography in his representation of Yeager frames these men as the last of a certain breed of western hero (Charity). This characterization is important, if less explicitly so, in *Space Cowboys* and is recognizable in the choice of the film's title. The second historical choice of consequence here is NASA's decision to have the first American "pilot" in space be a chimpanzee.[5] Again, Wolfe and especially Kaufman make much of the challenge to the pride and swagger of the Mercury astronauts whom this choice affects; *Space Cowboys* follows this as well. Eastwood thus multiplies the perceived injustices to his Daedalus team before bringing them, and us, up to the present.

The present we find in *Space Cowboys* is one fully colored by the post–Cold War politics of internationalized space flight. As the film enters the fictional present of 2000, the Russians have an oversized communications satellite in a quickly degrading orbit that will fall to earth, if uncorrected, in just over a month. Its destruction will result, supposedly, in a communications blackout and widespread turmoil in Russia unless the Americans can send the space shuttle to tow it back into a stable orbit and have an astronaut repair its antiquated and unresponsive control system. Frank Corvin, as Eastwood's senior persona, turns out to be the design engineer for the original system, which somehow made its way from *Skylab* in the 1970s to a Cold War Russian satellite.[6] As it happens, he is now also the only one with the specialized knowledge and skills to repair it and bring the dead satellite back online. Recognizing the predicament that Gerson, now a NASA administrator, is in (see old-man Eastwood's quote that serves as the subtitle for this section), Corvin negotiates/blackmails him into bringing on his original team, though Gerson adds the condition that they must all meet the same physical requirements as any regular astronaut. Despite the odds against them, and assisted by John Glenn–like media coverage and public interest (for his 1998 return to space), Corvin, Hawk, Jerry, and Tank crew the space shuttle mission, accompanied by two young, "hotshot" astronauts.[7]

The communications satellite is ultimately revealed to be a cover for a Cold War era nuclear platform with missiles that are programmed to launch at the United States should the satellite itself ever be in peril. When one of the young astronauts errantly activates the launch codes and damages the space shuttle in the process, it is up to the four members of Team Daedalus to save the day—and the world. Hawk, whose NASA physical revealed previously undetected (and inoperable) pancreatic cancer, uses the missile's boosters to heroically pilot the loaded satellite out into deep space, flying himself—literally—to the moon. Corvin is then tasked with piloting the damaged shuttle and its remaining crew members safely home without the benefit of computer assistance, something that the younger generation considers impossible but that old-man Eastwood as a member of the earlier test-pilot generation and possessor of their "right stuff" is able to execute successfully.[8] The film's final shot pans across the lunar landscape to reveal Hawk's body resting against a boulder as he faces out toward the once-promised, now-realized surface of the moon. Like the ironic, commentative "trope of the flag" that Beard finds in *Bronco Billy*, *Heartbreak Ridge*, *Unforgiven*, and *Flags of Our Fathers*, the tiny American flag on the arm-patch of Hawk's moon-shot body amounts to a similar destabilization of the heroic gesture of this final scene, if to a significantly lesser degree. However, in this last shot of *Space Cowboys*, the use of nondiegetic music in the form of Frank Sinatra's "Fly Me to the Moon" more effectively undercuts any note of serious accomplishment on the part of Hawk—the most self-sacrificing and, by that measure, most heroic of the four. In relation to the narrative structure of the film, this musical selection bookends the story, as Hawk had sung bars from the song in the prologue. Thematically, though, the choice had the potential to elicit nostalgia from a certain audience for whom that ballad—written and released originally in 1954 but made famous by Sinatra's 1964 recording—had actual ties to the Apollo missions: it was famously played both on Apollo 10 as it circled the moon and again on the moon's surface by Apollo 11 astronaut Buzz Aldrin from a portable cassette player.[9]

The stakes here seem to be those typically associated with the "dream factory" notion of Hollywood, according to which the film's protagonists are forced to save the world, in this case from the threat of a Russian-motivated nuclear annihilation carried over from the Cold War. This is true despite the advanced age of the protagonists, who are clearly written and cast to appeal to older viewers.[10] I want, however, to read the film in terms of the meaning of the space race and the American space program for Eastwood and his generation, the dovetailing of the diegetic story world and the extradiegetic world of the audience here purposefully emphasized. As A. Bowdoin Van

Riper reminds us in his study of "Hollywood and Aging Astronauts," "the quartet's experience with the space program is older than Apollo, Gemini, or Mercury—older than even NASA itself" (58). And this generationally ascribed experience and the memories associated with it thus recall the greatness and elite status of the American space program—its early failures but especially its ultimate triumphs. The Apollo missions to the moon in the late 1960s and early 1970s offered Americans a glimmer of hope when nearly every other political and military operation was under intense scrutiny for its accretion of failures. In fact, the space race narrative of setbacks and failures giving way—through strength of will and intellect (collective and individual)—to victory in the form of the successes of Apollo 11 and the other lunar landings was one of the few aspects of American society in that period that continued to match the established narrative of what Tom Engelhardt calls America's "victory culture," its centuries-old legacy of overcoming all adversity and adversaries. For Engelhardt, this perspective on America's greatness was predicated on a time before nuclear weapons (pre-1945) when America was assured through its historical trajectory to come out as the winner of any conflict, no matter how overmatched the country appeared at the start. Engelhardt further recognizes the threat of imminent *mutual* destruction that the atomic age and the Cold War jointly precipitated as the mortar and pestle that ground down the myth of that victory culture; the Korean and Vietnam Wars only helped to sever what was therefore already withering. The global preeminence of the American space program then was one of the last bastions where such a narrative of victory could find a place to survive among the new, more corrosive myths of the Cold War era. However, after the glories of lunar exploration ended—and with it the superiority of American technology and the ethos that the Apollo program signified for that generation—America's space program turned to more reusable technologies such as the space shuttle. The shuttle, however, never assumed the same symbolic stature as the lunar missions because the goals associated with it seemed less challenging (despite the advanced science actually in play). The *Challenger* disaster in January 1986, and the thirty-two-month moratorium on shuttle flights that followed, took even more polish off its shine.

In the course of those thirty-two months, three separate government reports were published, each suggesting new directions and bold initiatives for the American space program—*Pioneering the Space Frontier: The Report of the National Commission on Space*, subtitled "An Exciting Vision of Our Next Fifty Years in Space," published just one month after the tragic explosion (though begun in 1984); *Leadership and America's Future in Space* (the so-called "Ride Report" after its author Dr. Sally Ride), published in August 1987; and *The NASA Program in the 1990s and Beyond* by the Congressional Budget Office, published in May 1988. Where the first two made clear arguments for expanding the space program for reasons of science and human advancement, they also made clear the underlying motivation of national pride that such adventurous and high-risk/high-reward missions would produce. Looking at the third report, the most balanced of the three, we still find a rhetoric highly aware of the nation-building stakes:

> The core program lies between two extremes that clearly illustrate the difficult choices involved in setting future U. S. space policy. At one end of the spectrum, new and ambitious initiatives beyond the core program, such as a lunar outpost or a manned expedition to Mars at the turn of the century, could more than triple NASA's current real budget by 2000. At the other end of the spectrum, if NASA were to limit its future spending to its current real level, it would be forced either to stretch out into the next century its planned space station and the other projects in the core program, or to adopt a less ambitious set of goals that de-emphasize manned space flight activities in favor of unmanned missions. Holding the NASA budget to its current real level would therefore limit the international leadership of the United States in space activities. This, in fact, is the difficult choice facing the Congress: whether to increase dramatically the commitment of the United States to preeminence in space exploration or to adapt the U. S. space program to a limited budget. (ix)

Two years later, in another report, this one titled *Report of the Advisory Committee on the Future of the U. S. Space Program*, the conclusion was seemingly reached. "That group's most important finding," according to NASA historian Thor Hogan, "was that the space program needed to shift its fundamental rationale from one dominated by national prestige, national security, and foreign policy . . . to one predicated on global economic competitiveness and environmental protection" (126).

The end of the Cold War at the end of 1989, just one year after America's return to space, seemingly gave Congress a way out of this quandary by opening up new possibilities of *internationalized* space exploration. In making recommendations for America's future in space, the "Augustine Report," as the 1990 *Report of the Advisory Committee* was known, openly recognized that "the jewel represented by the vision of a seemingly unattainable goal" provided critical motivation "to our nation's scientists and engineers, its laboratories and industries, its students and its citizens" (Advisory Committee 28). Nevertheless, they also noted that the "long term objective of human exploration of Mars . . . is a challenge that could be constructively shared among a number of nations" (9). Through similar logic, *Freedom*, the proposed American space station, was at first delayed and ultimately replaced with a new international space station while, in the meantime, *Mir*, Russia's already functioning space station, was employed to serve the broader needs of science and technology. For a time, in fact, the adjustment to international collaboration and the modification and development of new hardware and technology to physically dock the shuttle with *Mir* determined the course of America's space program (Evans 10). For those whose pride and prejudice were bound up in the earlier nation-building glories of Apollo, the American space program was no longer attempting to fulfill its own unique destiny but, for the first time, appeared to be serving another master (and, as with the *Mir* docking technologies, sometimes an old—but not so old— nemesis at that). Whatever symbolic hope for America that the space program had seemed to carry on its broad shoulders in the late 1950s and '60s now seemed lost in a new era of international cooperation, the greatest immediate hope of which was the establishment of a shared space station. Though manned extraplanetary exploration was regularly promised as an eventual by-product of a permanent orbiting structure, budget cuts or at least stasis throughout the 1990s made such prognostications increasingly less likely in the short term. Rather than shooting for the moon and stars, the new generation of astronauts, and the American public that observed them from afar, had to be contented with space stations placed in what is called low-earth orbit, only 250 miles above the earth. The moon, to which the previous generation of American "star voyagers" had dared to travel, is 240 thousand miles away and thus a goal (via the most simplistic comparative schema) nearly one thousand times greater.

This is, as they say, where *Space Cowboys* comes in. The story has clear echoes of the role adjustment described above, for America is forced, in the film, to play janitor to Russia's past sins rather than forging ahead with its own goals; the opening of the film, in fact, makes clear that the original shuttle mission has been scrapped in favor of this rescue mission. In the end, though Eastwood and his senior citizen cohort may have saved the world, they have not returned America's space program to its previous position of international preeminence but simply preserved the new status quo. Such a reading of *Space Cowboys* lines up neatly with similarly available readings of Eastwood's other films from this period. For example, at the end of *True Crime*, Eastwood's Steve Everett has saved an innocent man, literally at the last minute, from being executed for a crime he did not commit, but the inadequacies of America's judicial system and the racial biases that continue to inform and influence those shortcomings are not any closer to being resolved. And again, the corrupt politician uncovered by Eastwood's cat burglar in *Absolute Power* gets his comeuppance at the end, but the political corruption—which here specifically runs all the way up to (or down from) the president—remains wholly uncorrected. In both of these cases, the severity of American society's problem is much too great for one protagonist to correct alone. Eastwood's aging characters can see the larger problems, and help these films' viewers see them as well, but as agents of change they can only, at best, address the symptom and not the more pervasive disease. Nevertheless, taken together, the films articulate—from the perspective of Eastwood's characters, Eastwood the director, and the generation they both represent—the scope of America's problems as well as their unresolved nature.

Unforgiven presents a similar, if somewhat more aggressive, critique. In order for Eastwood's William Munny to achieve personal redemption for unintentionally leading his only friend to his death, he must actively participate in the code of violence that the rest of the film had worked to deconstruct. Eastwood's angel of vengeance does again what his characters have done so many times before, wiping the slate clean as a (temporary) corrective for the flawed direction society had taken. The ending, where the flag clearly flies behind Munny's drunken threats, affirms that our civilization is built on fears of violent retribution more than ideological dreams of a better tomorrow. Like *Space Cowboys* then, this film is also heavily steeped in the aura of the Cold War, its symbolic position anchored in fears of imminent destruction. We can read *Unforgiven*—as many have already done—as the deconstruction of the values of regenerative violence, yet Eastwood's grand finale there ultimately provides us with no alternative mythology to replace our understanding of America's Western history. Beard, in fact, indicates that Eastwood's use of the Stars and Stripes in that penultimate scene literally and figuratively flags for the audience such a gap between textual and extratextual meaning ("Lies" 234). The Western, an integral part of the

American myth that Eastwood's generation affirmed to make sense of its own culture and history, is shown to be hollow. More importantly perhaps, no effort is made to refill it.

In *Gran Torino*, as a final example, Eastwood saves his young neighbors from the gang that is terrorizing them and holding their bright futures hostage. Still, his "victory" does nothing to return Detroit, or the American industrial might it so clearly stands in for, to its previous position of repute. In the face of the racialized fragmentation of America we find in *Gran Torino*, Kowalski's Polish surname (as well as his now-deceased neighbor's) highlights the capability—now also passed—of Ford, Detroit, and America to create the cultural "melting pot" that they long touted.[11] Though old-man Eastwood and his Hmong neighbors ultimately bridge their own culture gap, the film's resolution (a victory in defeat, as it were, for Eastwood's protagonist) offers no solution to the larger economic and societal problems that motivate the film's dramatic tension.

Uniquely among these films, *Space Cowboys* is the only one in which Eastwood's character is not simultaneously struggling with family redemption, though the interpersonal dynamics are nominally displaced onto the "family" of Team Daedalus and particularly Hawk (played by Jones, significantly the youngest in the bunch). The question of restitution here is not nearly as significant as in the majority of those other films, especially *Absolute Power* and *True Crime*, the two films that immediately preceded *Space Cowboys*. This is largely a function of the genre conventions of the buddy movie supplanting those of the family drama in the film's B story; the multi-character focus of the film also plays a role here, as it takes narrative precedence in the film's second act, story time normally devoted to the Eastwood protagonist's own backstory. This extraction of the otherwise recurring failed father / family man as the principal subplot/subtext allows us, in *Space Cowboys*, to more easily recognize another of Eastwood's recurring themes across these films: the diminution of the American dream and the manifestations (and sometimes mechanisms) of its decline.

On the surface of the narrative, all these films borrow the structure of classic Hollywood cinema's hero story and apply it to an *aging* hero who is similarly able to overcome the obstacles and adversaries placed immediately in front of him. But they also, like the American films of the late 1950s and the '70s (of which Eastwood was a key contributor), shine a light on the failures of key American institutions: the judicial system in *True Crime*; political corruption in *Absolute Power*; the inability of the Western, as a genre, to offer sufficient myths for new generations in *Unforgiven*; the failure of America's industrial cities in *Gran Torino*; and, in *Space Cowboys*, the insufficiency of NASA to continue to embody the American dream and along with it the "immensely consoling" "dream of a golden past where Americans . . . gave the world a living example of the superiority of their ideology and unique national gifts" (Beard, "Lies" 239). The expansive reach of these national issues behind Eastwood's dramatic situations is arguably what Dargis notes in her review. The (anti)heroes of those '60s/'70s films are unable, unwilling, or unconcerned with correcting the deep-seated social ills their adventures reveal. The "victories" these characters experience (when they do) are dramatized as personal victories but of a scale that attempts in no way to repair the vast breach the film's narrative has exposed at the social level. Throughout his "old-man" period, Eastwood—more frequently and with more regularity than arguably any other mainstream American film-maker—has crafted cinematic narratives that do not attempt to erase, or fully integrate with the hero's personal victory, the larger social issues the stories implicitly activate in establishing the protagonist's dramatic situation. So beyond Dargis's claim that Eastwood's films engage the "tougher, mess-ier, bigger questions of American life," they also leave the social and political-economic wounds they expose open at the end of the film—wounds generally erased in Hollywood via the dramatic displacement of social prob-lems onto the protagonist's journey and the reverse transferal of the hero's resolution back onto society. Eastwood's senior persona achieves the protag-onist's principal goal at the end of his films, but that resolution in no way resolves the larger societal issues that originally motivated the narrative action. This is a key element of what Beard recognizes as the slippage between Eastwood's transcendent heroes and the artificiality or impossibil-ity of the resolutions that they enact on the diegetic and extradiegetic worlds. To this we can now also add the impossibility, identifiable by a specific generation of Americans represented in the Eastwood characters, of fully achieving the older generation's American dreams or—more accurately—the dream(s) for America they once, long ago, shared.

Passing the Reins in Eastwood's Cinema;
or, He Who Has Eyes, Let Him See

Reading *Gran Torino* as he might a Western, Art Redding argues for a gen-erationally defined "hand-off" from the figure of past authority to a new carrier of the torch:

this story is told across generations: the winning of the west will mean that the "violent" older generation must hang up their guns, retire, and cede power to a new generation (the "kid") who stands for and inherits the new "civilized" social order. . . . We witness more or less the same plot line being developed in *Gran Torino*, as the violence of the contemporary urban frontier gives way, through the heroic actions of Kowalski, to a new, peaceable order to be inherited by 21st century immigrants. (13)

This torch passing is part of the final act of redemption and thus must occur at the end of the story, after the heavy lifting has been done to clear the field for the next generation's success. The hero, here as in the Western, must die or ride away in order for civilization to grow out of his or her sacrifice; *My Darling Clementine* (1946), *Shane* (1953), *The Searchers* (1956), and many, many more Westerns repeat this trope. It should be noted, however, that the questions in those films, as in Eastwood's old-man films, often revolve less around whom the reins should be passed to than who has the capacity to see the problem, assess the best solution, and alter the course in order to put America's extradiegetic future back on the "right" track. By regularly choosing stories that he can both star in and direct, Eastwood makes it clear that the capacity to make the necessary changes, even at the most surface of levels, must come from the wisdom and experience of old age.[12] Even more specifically, this is wisdom gained and experience assembled during America's "golden past," whether defined by Engelhardt's "victory culture" or—as I have argued in relation to *Space Cowboys*—the space race of the 1950s and '60s.

Eastwood's protagonists and the generation that produced them had different dreams for America. According to these films, only those with firsthand knowledge of those dreams are qualified to implement them for the next generation. Later generations of Americans dreamed different dreams, and these were—as *Space Cowboys* makes clear—made up of less rarified stuff. Eastwood regularly grants his characters the agency needed within the narrative space to effect change; this simultaneously takes such agency out of the hands of those younger protagonists to whom American cinema most often grants it—characters that for him have neither the experience nor the perspective to address the "tougher, messier, bigger problems of American life."

Frank Corvin and his Team Daedalus cohorts came of age dreaming of the moon and stars. As Hawk's final mission demonstrates, low-earth orbit would never satisfy them. If NASA and, by extension, America are to be redeemed, then from the viewpoint of the heroes in *Space Cowboys* and other Eastwood films from the same period, only those who know what that view looked like through the lens of "victory culture" are capable of providing redemption. As I have argued, Eastwood's aging heroes never fully resolve the larger social problem their dramatic situations reveal. Their personal, protagonist-level victories, however, do serve to restore some of the aura of America's past glories. Like Hawk, perhaps these characters realize that though they cannot save their own failing bodies, they can still attempt to save the failing body of America or, at least, their generation's dream of America—one which later generations cannot fully share. Possessing more than just "stubbornness and eccentricity" then, Eastwood's old-man characters overcome later generations because they have both the experience and the perspective to see what later generations cannot and hence the capacity and desire to act more effectively. If Clint Eastwood is the fixer mentioned at the beginning of this essay, then in his films of the last two and a half decades, he is a fixer—partially, if ultimately insufficiently—of the broken body of his generation's once vital and virile American dream.

Notes

1. This number does not include Eastwood's appearance in *Casper* (1995). The other film that Eastwood starred in but did not direct, besides *In the Line of Fire*, is *Trouble with the Curve* (2012), a Malpaso production directed by Robert Lorenz, Eastwood's assistant director or producer on sixteen films.

2. Craig Rinne defines this "senior persona" as "an aging, single, flawed, heroic character grappling with the sins of his youth and hoping to redeem them through a second opportunity" (131). I will utilize his descriptor somewhat interchangeably with my own, though I have avoided using it solely because one aspect of Rinne's definition does not apply to *Space Cowboys*. As I will discuss briefly later in this essay, Eastwood's character in *Space Cowboys* is not single. My periodization here closely resembles that suggested by Philippa Gates, who argues: "Although [Chris] Holmlund suggests that Eastwood's last (as of yet) phase of films—those that present him as 'visibly old'—began in 1985, I would argue that it was not until *Unforgiven* that Eastwood's films offered narratives and themes related to advancing age or that Eastwood highlighted his aging body" (172).

3. When filmed in late summer / early fall of 1999, the actors' ages were as follows: Eastwood, 69; James Garner, 71; Donald Sutherland, 64; and Tommy Lee Jones, 53.

4. During this historical prologue, each character is physically performed by an actor that is age appropriate and thus apparently in their mid-to-late twenties, yet through the manipulation of postsynchronous sound each character's voice is

provided by the older actor who will portray him through the rest of the film. Bob Gerson, their commanding officer, is given a similar treatment and played by James Cromwell.

5. The chimpanzee's name in the script is Sam, a variation on Ham—the chimpanzee that, in January 1961, was the first "American" in space. In the film it is changed to Mary Ann. Eastwood, as some have noted, also hints toward his own cinematic history here in both *Firefox* (1982) and *Every Which Way but Loose* (1978).

6. The film ultimately assigns this "mystery" to a Cold War KGB theft, implicating Gerson in the act of 1970s-era espionage. It is worth noting that after *Skylab*, America and the Soviet Union did engage in a brief international collaboration of their space programs—the 1975 Apollo-Soyuz Test Project docking mission— which makes Soviet access to such a system more plausible, though the film never mentions this. As an interesting sidenote, according to Roald Sagdeev, a Russian space scientist during the Cold War, the John Sturges space film *Marooned* (1969) was used to help facilitate this collaboration.

7. John Glenn, the Mercury astronaut that flew America's third mission, and the first man to perform a full orbit of the planet, returned to space aboard the space shuttle in October 1998 (STS-95) at the age of seventy-seven. Eastwood's dialogue references this at one point in the first act, but otherwise neither the film nor the final, May 1999 revision of the script directly address this resonance or influence. The fact that Team Daedalus goes on *The Tonight Show* with Jay Leno as part of their premission goodwill building, however, replicates Senator Glenn's appearance there in November 1998, by which point Eastwood was attached and the script was in rewrites. As ridiculous as the physical-condition rider on Team Daedalus's contract with NASA/Gerson may seem to the film's viewers, according to Glenn's memoir, he was held to this same qualification for his return to space. Though the script would appear to be an attempt to capitalize on the attention paid to Glenn and his space shuttle adventure, the spec script was sold to Warner Brothers in September 1997, and Glenn's return was not announced by NASA until the following January (Glenn 364, 369; Chetwynd; Galloway; Getty; Madigan). Audience response was unusually high for both: Glenn notes that more press requested credentials for the launch than at any time since the end of the Apollo lunar missions (364); *Space Cowboys*, according to Box Office Mojo, ranked twenty-fifth for the year in terms of domestic gross, with box office receipts in excess of ninety million dollars.

8. Van Riper makes this argument with respect to the older astronauts in all three films he studies closely—*Space Cowboys*, *Red Planet* (2000), and *Deep Impact* (1998)—arguing that younger astronauts (at least in their cinematic representations) are less able to troubleshoot on the fly due to an increased reliance on both computers and Houston's committee of engineers who are present to solve any unexpected problems.

9. However, no review that I found referred to that level of connectivity; additionally, the ironic or even satiric note that the disjuncture between sound and image creates frustrated as many reviewers as it appealed to.

10. The early August release date follows late-summer counterprogramming trends that attempt to activate alternative audiences. *Blood Work*, Eastwood's next film (also distributed by Warner Brothers) was released in the same early-August slot two years later.

11. For a discussion of the actual mechanisms of cultural assimilation employed by the Ford Company in the name of American industrial might, see Grieveson. Of course many groups were marginalized by the melting-pot assimilation paradigm and the mythology that grew up around it.

12. One interpretation of Eastwood's delay between acquiring the rights to *Unforgiven* (originally written during the height of revisionist Westerns in the 1970s) and bringing it to the screen is that he wanted to wait until he was sixty years old (Buscombe).

Works Cited

Advisory Committee on the Future of the U. S. Space Program. *Report of the Advisory Committee on the Future of the U. S. Space Program* ("Augustine Report"). National Aeronautics and Space Administration, 1990.

Alaniz, José. *Death, Disability, and the Superhero: The Silver Age and Beyond*. UP of Mississippi, 2014.

Batchelor, Bob, and Norma Jones. "Introduction—Bad Abides: Jeff Bridges, Ideal Aging Hero." *Aging Heroes: Growing Old in Popular Culture*, edited by Norma Jones and Bob Batchelor, Rowman & Littlefield, 2015, pp. xi–xx.

Beard, William. "Lies of Our Fathers: Mythology and Artifice in Eastwood's Cinema." *New Essays on Clint Eastwood*, edited by Leonard Engel, U of Utah P, 2012, pp. 224–48.

———. *Persistence of Double Vision: Essays on Clint Eastwood*. U of Alberta P, 2000.

Blackburn, Al. *Aces Wild: The Race for Mach 1*. SR Books, 1999.

Buscombe, Edward. *Unforgiven*. BFI Publishing, 2004.

Charity, Tom. *The Right Stuff*. BFI Publishing, 1997.

Chetwynd, Josh. "Warners Mad about *Cowboys*." *Hollywood Reporter*, 23 Sept. 1997. *LexisNexis*, www.lexisnexis.com.lib-e2.1ib.ttu.edu/hottopics/lnacademic/?verb=sr&csi=12015.

Chivers, Sally. *The Silvering Screen: Old Age and Disability in Cinema*. U of Toronto P, 2011.

Dargis, Manohla. "Hope for a Racist, and Maybe a Country." Review of *Gran Torino*. *New York Times*, 11 Dec. 2008, p. C1. *LexisNexis*, www.lexisnexis.com.lib-e2.1ib.ttu.edu/hottopics/lnacademic/?verb=sr&csi=6742.

Engelhardt, Tom. *The End of Victory Culture: Cold War America and the Disillusioning of a Generation*. Revised edition, U of Massachusetts P, 2007.

Evans, Ben. *The Twenty-First Century in Space*. Springer, 2015.

Galloway, Stephen. "'Cowboys' Film on Eastwood's Launching Pad." *The Hollywood Reporter*, 31 Aug. 1998. *LexisNexis*, www.lexisnexis.com.libe2.1ib.ttu.edu/hottopics/lnacademic/?verb=sr&csi=12015.

Gates, Philippa. "A Good Vintage or Damaged Goods? Clint Eastwood and Aging in Hollywood Film." *New Essays on Clint Eastwood*, edited by Leonard Engel, U of Utah P, 2012, pp. 168–89.

Getty Images (NBC). "Astronaut John Glenn during an Interview with Host Jay Leno on November 20, 1998." www.gettyimages.com/detail/news-photo/episode-1493-pictured-astronaut-john-glenn-during-an-news-photo/138394846.

Glenn, John, with Nick Taylor. *John Glenn: A Memoir*. Bantam Books, 1999.

Gourlie, John M., and Leonard Engel. "*Gran Torino*: Showdown in Detroit, Shrimp Cowboys, and a New Mythology." *New Essays on Clint Eastwood*, edited by Leonard Engel, U of Utah P, 2012, pp. 266–76.

Grieveson, Lee. "The Work of Film in the Age of Fordist Mechanization." *Cinema Journal*, vol. 51, no. 3, Spring 2012, pp. 25–51.

Hogan, Thor. *Mars Wars: The Rise and Fall of the Space Exploration Initiative*. National Aeronautics and Space Administration, 2007.

Kaufman, Ken, and Howard Klausner. *Space Cowboys*. Screenplay. May 1999 Draft. *Daily Script*, www.dailyscript.com/scripts/Space_Cowboys.pdf.

Madigan, Nick. "Feature Flight on Sudden Climb." *Daily Variety*, 7 Apr. 1999. *LexisNexis*, www.lexisnexis.com.lib2.1ib.ttu.edu/hottopics/lnacademic/?verb=sr&csi=140595.

McDougall, Walter A. *The Heavens and the Earth: A Political History of the Space Age*. Basic Books, 1985.

Metz, Walter. "The Old Man and the C: Masculinity and Age in the Films of Clint Eastwood." *Clint Eastwood, Actor and Director: New Perspectives*, edited by Leonard Engel, U of Utah P, 2007, pp. 204–17.

The NASA Program in the 1990s and Beyond. A Special Study. Congressional Budget Office, 1988.

National Commission on Space. *Pioneering the Space Frontier: An Exciting Vision of Our Next Fifty Years in Space—The Report of the National Commission on Space*. Bantam Books, 1986.

Redding, Art. "A Finish Worthy of the Start: The Poetics of Age and Masculinity in Clint Eastwood's *Gran Torino*." *Film Criticism*, vol. 38, no. 3, Spring 2014, pp. 2–23.

Ride, Sally K. *Leadership and America's Future in Space: A Report to the Administrator* ("The Ride Report"). National Aeronautics and Space Administration, 1987.

Rinne, Craig. "The End of History and America First: How the 1990s Revitalized Clint Eastwood." *New Essays on Clint Eastwood*, edited by Leonard Engel, U of Utah P, 2012, pp. 130–47.

Sagdeev, Roald, and Susan Eisenhower. "United States-Soviet Space Cooperation during the Cold War." *NASA—50th Magazine*, www.nasa.gov/50th/50th_magazine/coldWarCoOp.html.

Simmons, David. *The Anti-Hero in the American Novel: From Joseph Heller to Kurt Vonnegut*. Palgrave Macmillan, 2008.

Van Riper, A. Bowdoin. "Under a Wide and Starry Sky: Hollywood and Aging Astronauts, 1996–2000." *Aging Heroes: Growing Old in Popular Culture*, edited by Norma Jones and Bob Batchelor, Rowman & Littlefield, 2015, pp. 49–61.

Wolfe, Tom. *The Right Stuff*. Farrar, Straus and Giroux, 1979.

Filmography

Absolute Power. Directed by Clint Eastwood, performances by Eastwood, Gene Hackman, and Ed Harris, Castle Rock Entertainment / Malpaso Productions / Columbia, 1997.

Blood Work. Directed by Clint Eastwood, performances by Eastwood and Jeff Daniels, Malpaso Productions / Warner Bros., 2002.

Bronco Billy. Directed by Clint Eastwood, performances by Eastwood, Sandra Locke, and Geoffrey Lewis, Second Street Films / Warner Bros., 1980.

Casper. Directed by Brad Silberling, performances by Christina Ricci and Bill Pullman, Amblin Entertainment / Universal, 1995.

Deep Impact. Directed by Mimi Leder, performances by Robert Duvall and Téa Leoni, Dreamworks SKG / Paramount, 1998.

Every Which Way but Loose. Directed by James Fargo, performances by Clint Eastwood, Sandra Locke, and Geoffrey Lewis, The Malpaso Company / Warner Bros., 1978.

Firefox. Directed by Clint Eastwood, performances by Eastwood and Freddie Jones, The Malpaso Company / Warner Bros., 1982.

Flags of Our Fathers. Directed by Clint Eastwood, performances by Ryan Phillipe, Adam Beach, and Jesse Bradford, Dreamworks SKG / Malpaso Productions / Warner Bros., 2006.

Gran Torino. Directed by Clint Eastwood, performances by Eastwood and Bee Vang, Malpaso Productions / Warner Bros., 2008.

Heartbreak Ridge. Directed by Clint Eastwood, performances by Eastwood, Marsha Mason, and Mario Van Peebles, Jay Weston Productions / The Malpaso Company / Warner Bros., 1986.

In the Line of Fire. Directed by Wolfgang Petersen, performances by Clint Eastwood, John Malkovich, and Rene Russo, Castle Rock Entertainment / Columbia, 1993.

Marooned. Directed by John Sturges, performances by Gregory Peck and Gene Hackman, Frankovich Productions / Columbia, 1969.

My Darling Clementine. Directed by John Ford, performances by Henry Fonda and Victor Mature, Twentieth Century Fox, 1946.

Red Planet. Directed by Antony Hoffman, performances by Terrence Stamp, Val Kilmer, and Carrie-Anne Moss, Village Roadshow / Warner Bros., 2000.

The Right Stuff. Directed by Philip Kaufman, performances by Sam Shepard, Ed Harris, and Scott Glenn, The Ladd Company / Warner Bros., 1983.

The Searchers. Directed by John Ford, performances by John Wayne and Jeffrey Hunter, C. V. Whitney / Warner Bros., 1956.

Shane. Directed by George Stevens, performances by Alan Ladd, Jean Arthur, and Van Heflin, Paramount, 1953.

Space Cowboys. Directed by Clint Eastwood, performances by Eastwood, Tommy Lee Jones, Donald Sutherland, and James Garner, Malpaso Productions / Warner Bros., 2000.

Trouble with the Curve. Directed by Robert Lorenz, performances by Clint Eastwood and Amy Adams, Malpaso Productions / Warner Bros., 2012.

True Crime. Directed by Clint Eastwood, performances by Eastwood and Isaiah Washington, Zanuck Co. / Malpaso Productions / Warner Bros., 1999.

Unforgiven. Directed by Clint Eastwood, performances by Eastwood, Morgan Freeman, and Gene Hackman, Malpaso Productions / Warner Bros., 1992.

4

Empowering the Victim
Eastwood as a Director of Women

Raymond Foery

I f ever there were to be an acting award given for the archetypal "man's man" in Hollywood, Clint Eastwood would easily win it. As an actor, he almost never betrays the softer side that might occasionally characterize a Humphrey Bogart—or even a John Wayne—performance. Even the titles of Eastwood's films suggest the powerful masculinity of the world his characters inhabit: *White Hunter Black Heart*, *Unforgiven*, *Absolute Power*, *True Crime*, *Blood Work*. And while Leonard Engel and John M. Gourlie, in Engel's previous collection of essays on Eastwood's work, have suggested that his later films reveal not just a "tough guy" but "a tough guy with a heart of gold," the heart therein is not worn on the sleeve of the characters that the veteran actor so often portrays (10).

As a director, on the other hand, Eastwood has developed a reputation for being able to probe the inner angst of the male hero; he is often complimented for the subtlety of the performances he is able to draw out of his actors. The great populist critic Roger Ebert, for example, pointed to this achievement in his online review of *Mystic River*: "He [Eastwood] shows here a deep rapport with the characters and the actors, who are allowed lancing moments of truth. Always an understated actor himself, he finds in his three actors pools of privacy and reserve."

Often overlooked, at least until recently, has been Eastwood's remarkably sensitive direction of women. Indeed, the first scholar to pay considerable attention to this aspect of his work was Drucilla Cornell, whose 2009 *Clint Eastwood and Issues of American Masculinity* broke new ground in a field that had lain fallow for decades. Her examination of gender designation is poignantly articulated in her claim that Eastwood's films "show us what it means to be a good man . . . but what a struggle it is to even make an attempt" (186). I would argue here that in a select body of his work, Eastwood endeavors to show us what it means to be a woman, and not merely a victim.

I have written on his splendid direction of Meryl Streep and his sensitivity to her character in one of the few films from his first quarter century as a director that is not focused on male prerogatives, the underrated *The Bridges of Madison County* (1995). What I attempted to point out in that essay was how Eastwood shaped his directorial approach—articulated by his choice of camera angles and camera movement—to foreground the "other" in that film, in this case the wife left in an empty farmhouse at the outset of the plot. Eastwood's orchestration of the narrative—what I called a "cinematic waltz"—displayed his intention to make clear, as I put it then, that this film is her story and that it is being told from her point of view (Foery 196). The result was a narrative that was directed by Eastwood while the story was told by Streep's character. She became, then, not only a narrator by virtue of the film's narrative framing device but also a privileged teller, sharing with the director in the film's story-telling devices. I attempted to demonstrate that Eastwood's directorial choices made this clearer as the film progressed.

In the two decades since the release of *Bridges*, Eastwood has directed several projects that foreground female characters, and in those that do not, he has managed to render the portraits of his female characters in brushstrokes that suggest courage and dignity. To be examined here as examples of his prowess are five films made during the past twenty years that are quite individually distinct but whose central coherence can be gleaned from the approach Eastwood takes to one or another female character. In each one, I would suggest, Eastwood manages—using devices occasionally obvious but more often subtle—to empower the female character, whose individual travails have often characterized her as a victim not only of circumstances but also of an overbearing patriarchy.

Midnight in the Garden of Good and Evil, completed in 1997, just two years after *The Bridges of Madison County*, provides a fine example of Eastwood's subtle redirection, if you will, of the narrative from the one he inherited from the novel itself to one that offers the viewer (as opposed to the reader) a wider and deeper feminine presence. With the very first shot of the film, Eastwood redirects our attention—that is, if we have been readers of the novel—or directs our attention—if we have not read the novel. (The best adaptations, it could be argued, occur when the director assumes that the viewer has not read the source material.) The novel itself opens by introducing the reader immediately to the male protagonist, Jim Williams. In fact, the novel begins with the male pronoun: "He was tall, about fifty, with darkly handsome, almost sinister features" (3). Eastwood, on the other hand, structures his film around three strong women, each of whom serves at one point or another to motivate the plot.

His first strong woman is Minerva (played by Irma P. Hall). The film opens by introducing us to her sitting serenely on a bench overlooking one of the town squares. It is a grand, sweeping introduction, employing the sort of moving camera shot that Eastwood likes to use for emphasis. After the title sequence (which concludes on the iconic "Bird Girl" statue that was the cover illustration of the book), we see a mounted police officer from a low camera angle. The camera pans left to right to follow the horse and rider until they pass in front of a park bench. The camera then tilts up and introduces us to Minerva, a black woman dressed like a homeless person. She is feeding a squirrel and cackling. The camera movement, though, indicates to us that she is important: the grand gesture of the movement bringing us toward the grandeur of the individual. Minerva, indeed, is important to this story, and Eastwood acknowledges this at the outset of the plot. This introductory scene concludes with a high camera angle looking down on Minerva as she looks up, seemingly at us. She is, in fact, looking up at a descending jetliner that is bringing a New York journalist to Savannah. The plot has now been put in motion. Minerva will be an important presence throughout the plot, but we will not see her again until the middle of the film. By then the plot will have become as cloying as the moss dripping from the live oaks surrounding Savannah's famous Forsyth Square.

The second strong woman we meet is Mandy (played by Alison Eastwood, the director's daughter). "Y'all got some ice?" she asks as she barges into the journalist's apartment. She is single, independent, and somewhat free-spirited, although the role she plays here is that of the "ordinary" girl, at least by comparison to the other two women. Later in the development of the story line we shall see her as a foil to the other female characters, and as a fulcrum for the kind of normal and "ordinary" existence that our visiting journalist eventually seeks.

The third strong woman is perhaps not biologically female: "I've got a man's toolbox," announces "The Lady Chablis" from the witness chair at the murder trial that completes the story arc. But Lady Chablis (played by Savannah's the Lady Chablis herself, or Chablis Deveau) is, in every other way, "a lady." Eastwood's camera makes that clear to us. In virtually every scene, she is shot from slightly below, always suggesting a towering presence. (Yes, she is a tall person, statuesque, and Eastwood continuously reminds us of this.) In many ways, Chablis is as much a driver of the plot as Minerva. Eastwood films her as if she, indeed, were the diva she wants to be. On the street, as the journalist follows her in his car, the camera glides along, giving her some space. At the club where she performs her transgender numbers, the camera treats her as if she were the marquee attraction she would so like to be. And, finally, when she crashes the cotillion, Eastwood covers her wild and impetuous dancing with due respect and restraint. In short, for Eastwood, she is a lady—the Lady Chablis, as she calls herself—and not once does his camera diminish her stature.

Eastwood's approach to all three women is similar: he gives them their dignity. While they each might find themselves to have been victims of life's slings and arrows, he never diminishes them or pities them. His manner of filming them elevates each one in such a way that each shares a role as a catalyst in the unraveling of the gothic tale. And in a lovely final gesture, the three women are brought together at the end of the film, though they never share a scene before this one. The scene serves then as a kind of celebration of survival, but it also amounts to a declaration by Eastwood that these three women have brought us the story, that they, indeed, have been the tellers of the tale. It is an apt conclusion, which serves well not only the characters but Eastwood, for it centers the narrative while concluding the story. Minerva, of course, has the last word—or rather, the last image. The film ends with her back at her park bench, cackling at us once again.

Hereafter, released in 2010, concerns itself with a different kind of dignity, the dignity of the spiritual life, the dignity accorded to suppositions about an afterlife. It is not an easy film, and it was not one of Eastwood's commercial successes. (It actually lost money for Warner Brothers, something an Eastwood film rarely does.)[1] But it reveals a strong feminist presence, and one that is again embraced by the directions Eastwood gives to his camera operator. Once again, the Eastwood camera embraces the characters and places each on a sort of podium where we can observe them. While Eastwood uses this approach toward each of the characters in the film, it is clear from the opening sequence that we are going to be led through this particular narrative by a woman, in this case a journalist. Marie (played by the marvelously named Cécile de France) is the first person we see when the film opens. More importantly, she immediately takes charge of the situation: finding gifts for her lover's children, securing the hotel bill from the front desk, having breakfast sent up to the room. She leaves the hotel and walks to the shopping district, the camera following her and merely observing. It is, we are to discover in a moment, December 26, 2004. Marie is almost immediately swept away by the enormous wall of water triggered by the Indonesian tsunami, washed away several hundred yards, and then miraculously saved by a couple of good Samaritans. Eastwood shows us her battered face. She has survived.

But while under water and close to death, Marie experiences a vision. Out of focus and unclear, the image she sees causes her to come to feel that she has sensed the "hereafter" of the film's title. It is at this point that Eastwood's direction begins to color in the outline of the character of Marie. He never diminishes her or belittles the notion she has that she has come across something that is truly beyond the explicable. She is always shot from a slightly low angle and almost always given full frames in conversation with other characters. In convincing a group of publishing executives that they should support her book proposal, for example, she is framed in such a way that there is never a doubt as to who commands the space of the room. Basically, Eastwood's framing and subtly moving camera tell us that Marie is to be respected, that she is the agent of change, that she is the heroine of this section of the film. (There are three separate "sections" to *Hereafter*, three separate story lines, the strands of which are tied together during the last movement of the film.)

It is important for Eastwood to establish this sense of respect because the subject matter of the film is one that can be so easily dismissed—and usually is—by those who live in the "normal" world. (The word "normal" is significant here because in one of the other strands of the film, Matt Damon plays a character, George, who continually claims that all he wants is a "normal" life.) By giving such credence to the character, Eastwood gives credence to her concerns. This then legitimizes these concerns in the eyes of the viewer.

The "normal" world, of course, rejects them. Her publisher refuses to publish the book she presents (he thought they had agreed on another topic), and her boss at the TV station where she works—and was once the "star" news anchor—feels that she needs "more time" to get over the trauma of the near-death experience she suffered when the tsunami struck.

Once again, Eastwood's careful composition and rock-steady framing of her render Marie not only believable but also courageous. "I am never a victim," she declares to her boss (who had also coincidentally been her lover), describing herself as one who is "never vulnerable, never complains." She is indeed the furthest thing from a victim. She refuses to give in, she refuses to compromise, she refuses to return to her previous existence. The tsunami experience has changed her life, and she has accepted the change and even relishes it.

At the end of the film, Marie takes the hand of George. Once again, she is framed as the protagonist that she is, this time taking the lead with a new soul, just as she had with the previous lover. The film then concludes with one of Eastwood's trademark overhead crane shots. A bird's eye view, one might call it, or in this case perhaps a view from the hereafter.

One of the points I would like to make about Eastwood the director has to do with his astute choices of female performers for the various films under examination here. Cécile de France, as an example, is hardly known in this country, although she is credited with over two dozen films in France. Her performance for Eastwood in *Hereafter* is, as I have tried to point out, virtually flawless and a model of the kind of restraint that so often characterizes an acting performance on an Eastwood project (including, of course, virtually all his own). Eastwood tends to find actors who are philosophically suited to the role in question, and he then directs them with a sure hand that allows them to become perfectly credible before our eyes. And they are often actresses who have been virtually unknown to us. Cécile de France is a paradigm of this approach.

Take, as another example, Sienna Miller. While it is true that she had appeared in over a dozen films before Eastwood cast her in the role of Chris Kyle's wife in *American Sniper*, it can be fairly stated that she was at that time virtually unknown to the general movie-viewing public. Eastwood's direction of her is another example of his respect for characterization and his refusal to allow the trite attitudes associated with "victimhood" to sully the performance of this brave woman. Like Cécile de France at the opening of

Hereafter, Sienna Miller makes clear from the moment we see her that her character, Taya, is independent, strong, and even tart of tongue. We first see Taya in a bar. A guy sidles up to her and asks if she would like him to buy her a drink. "Will a drink make you six inches taller and charming?" she responds quickly and evenly. The camera frames her in perfect light. She will very soon be Kyle's equal, then his wife, and finally his soul mate. Later in the film, Eastwood makes this clearer. The two of them are in bed. (Kyle is home from one of his four missions to Iraq.) Contemporary films contain dozens of shots of couples in bed, of course. This one is a bit different from most. It is shot from directly overhead. The two are side by side, lit precisely the same way, occupying precisely the same amount of space in the frame: yet another example of Eastwood's way of exalting the female performer, making her easily and gracefully the equal to the male. There is no tussling between the couple, no "she-above-him" or "he-above-her"—the commonly used parlance for questions of "equality" in so many contemporary films. Rather, Eastwood gives us a zen-like, almost classically oriental composition: the yin and the yang of this couple made so strikingly obvious.

In some ways, it is more of a challenge to direct a "known" actress than an unknown one. It has often been observed that well-known actors and actresses come to a new project with a persona and often an acting style that has been etched into their very psyches over the years. To break that mold can be challenging. With both *Million Dollar Baby* and *Changeling*, Eastwood faced that very task.

Million Dollar Baby (2004) has become one of Eastwood's most successful films over the past two decades. In addition to its financial return of more than $100 million on an estimated budget of $30 million, the film won numerous accolades, including four of the most prestigious Academy Awards for that year. Best Actor in a Supporting Role went to Morgan Freeman and Best Actress in a Leading Role went to Hilary Swank; the film was named Best Picture, and Eastwood himself was named Best Director of the year. (Perhaps more satisfying to Eastwood was that he was also named best director for that year by the Directors Guild of America, an enviable recognition of his work by his peers.)[2]

The approach that Eastwood undertook in directing Hilary Swank was a complex and subtle one. In terms of overall composition, he made a conscious effort to alternate light and dark as motifs whenever he framed her. My colleague John M. Gourlie, in a fine chapter on this film for a previous collection of Eastwood essays, identified Eastwood's approach in the first paragraph of his article: "In the cinematic images Eastwood gives us, dark shadows consistently fall across patches of light" (242). Indeed they do, but it is more than a few dark patches, I would argue. It is really a programmatic approach to the eternal battle between light and dark (good and evil) that Eastwood uses as his modus operandi for this film.

Million Dollar Baby is in fact a tale told through alternating images of light and dark. Figures are always stepping in and out of shadows. Characters are seen as having one shadow or another hovering over them. Even the settings of the film fluctuate between light-and-open and dark-and-closed. Take, for example, the first time we see the "million dollar baby" herself. Emerging out of the shadows from a stairwell of a dreary boxing gym while a fight is in progress is Maggie Fitzgerald (played by Hilary Swank). Perhaps unnoticed on first viewing is that the shot just before we see Maggie is actually a point of view (POV) shot from her perspective as she enters the arena. It is only later that we realize this is Eastwood's way of announcing—clearly yet subtly—that this is to be her story, and that, as with some of the other tales from his oeuvre, the leading lady is going to tell it her way. The camera moves in to her as she looks down at the fighter's corner. There she sees Frankie Dunn (played by Eastwood), and the telling of the tale begins. This is an especially interesting opening because we have already seen a few shots of the film—a boxing match in progress—and, more importantly, we have heard the strongly modulated tones of a male narrator. So, from the opening moments of the film, we have the juxtaposition of a story told through the eyes of a male, in this case Dunn's assistant and general go-between (Morgan Freeman), and a tale that is focused on a female, in this case an independent young woman who wishes to excel at the customarily male sport of boxing.

When we next see Maggie, she is standing in a hallway that appears to be located just outside the locker room of the fight arena. Dunn emerges and they walk down this hallway together. As they pass under the individual overhead lamps, she (occupying the center of the frame) moves in and out of shadow. While under one of the lamps, we see her face; while not under a lamp, she is in complete darkness. The metaphor that will characterize Eastwood's entire approach to this film has therefore been articulated within the very first few minutes. Over seven minutes of screen time pass before we see Maggie again. In any film, this is a considerable amount of time. In an Eastwood film, characterized as most of them are by his meticulous pacing, this can seem like an entire chapter. When we see Maggie this time, it is from Frankie's POV. There she is, in a far corner of his gym, punching a large bag, her back to him—and to us. She is not in shadow this time, but she is lit by the dreary lights of the industrial space that defines the gym. Frankie approaches her—camera taking us forward to where she is standing by the bag—and their first conversation within that space establishes the nature of their relationship. She wants his help as her trainer; he "doesn't train girls."

The pattern of light and dark continues as we learn more about Maggie. The next scene shows her in the brightly lit, little restaurant where she works. Just after that, we see her in an extremely dark room, no doubt within her tiny apartment, counting the coins she has earned as tips from her restaurant work and munching on a cold piece of meat that she scavenged from the table of one of her customers. It is a grim existence, made more visually poignant by the juxtaposition of her light and dark surroundings.

Back at the gym, Maggie is discovered by Freeman's character, Eddie (also called "Scrap" in the film), as she continues to work the large bag. Eddie is turning out the lights to conclude the day. In one of the strongest images of the film, we see him look over at her and we see her through his eyes: outlined against the gym wall in total silhouette. The only sound we hear is the thudding of her glove against the bag. It is a powerful image, and a moment of pure cinema.

The story line of the film progresses along a predictable fashion for a good while. Dunn eventually agrees to train Maggie, and their partnership proves successful—for a while. In another of the film's beautiful moments, they seal their deal with a handshake in front of us; they are in semisilhouette against the gym wall. The shot echoes the previous one where she was in total silhouette, but now, of course, there is some light on the scene, some hope for Maggie.

Most of the rest of the film shows us her progression as a fighter and their progression as friends and, eventually, "relatives": he, the father figure; she, the daughter who has come to replace his real daughter who is mysteriously estranged from him. (And that is precisely the shadow that hangs over him throughout his life; during the film, we learn no details and can only imagine the reasons.)

We see Maggie through five fights, rendered through a classic montage sequence. In the sixth, she has her nose broken but manages to win the fight anyway. She and Frankie embrace. They are in full light. The background around them is dim. The juxtaposition of light and dark has reached its apogee. It plays itself out in the road-trip scenes that have nothing to do with the world of boxing. Maggie has used her earnings to buy a house for her mother. In the most brightly lit scene in the film, the mother demonstrates what a lowlife human being she is as she rejects the gift and in so doing reminds Maggie of why she is on her own. It is painful to watch—in broad daylight. The next scene shows Maggie and Dunn in the car. It is dark; he is driving. We see each of them in precisely equal close-ups, dim shadows of dusk around them. "I got nobody but you, Frankie," Maggie says to Dunn. "Well, you've got me," he replies. The irony is clear: the brightly lit scene is full of sadness; the scene that takes place in the dark of dusk is full of joy. And what is also made clear is that Maggie—the strong, independent woman, the focus of the light within the dark world of prize fighting—has asserted her dominance over her male mentor. When the character that Eastwood plays says "you've got me," we know what the director Eastwood means: Maggie has become empowered. She is now the dominant character within the world of the film.

The last thirty minutes of the film are excruciating as Maggie drifts into her final darkness. Most of the scenes before the end, however, take place in brightly lit spaces. Even the hospital corridor is full of light. The darkness returns when Frankie prepares to assist in Maggie's suicide. He enters the now darkened hospital corridor and as he proceeds toward her room he is in total silhouette. As he leaves, Eastwood gives us the exact reverse of the entry shot: Frankie in full silhouette walking down the corridor and out of the hospital. The darkness has fully descended.

Eastwood's approach to this film results in yet another demonstration of his ability to ennoble a character, and he elicits a performance from Hilary Swank that may indeed be the best of her career. Once again, his direction elevates the character, removes her from any self-pitying sense of victimhood, and empowers her as she makes her journey.

With *Changeling* (2008), Eastwood was again directing a seasoned performer. Like Hilary Swank, Angelina Jolie had already won an Academy Award before she came to work on an Eastwood project (for the 1999 *Girl, Interrupted*). She was also possessed with what Eastwood called "the most beautiful face on the planet," which, Eastwood went on to say, often prevented audiences and critics from appreciating her actual talent ("Beautiful Face," *Sidney Morning Herald*). Eastwood's direction of her in this largely underappreciated film strongly revealed that talent.[3] In fact, Jolie's portrayal of Christine Collins may, in time, come to be seen as one of her defining roles. If it is, it is in large part because of Eastwood's careful, restrained direction, never allowing her to appear stereotyped, always giving her the kind of attention that allows her to develop the richly nuanced performance of a complex and yet charismatic character.

What makes this performance so powerful—and at the same time so persuasive—is that Jolie's character is perhaps the most oppressed and maltreated of all of the women we have been examining. She is truly victimized, a consequence of her having to live under the most egregious aspects of a patriarchal society. She lives in a world where virtually every male individual—including a young boy—tries to take advantage of her. And yet, as with so many of Eastwood's female characters, she manages not only to survive but to flourish, to fully overcome the fierce resistance she faces in this male-dominated world.

Indeed, Angelina Jolie is perfect in this part, as Eastwood's camera often reminds us. All the techniques and approaches that have been examined in this essay come into play in this film, from the careful delineation of spaces of light from spaces of darkness—evident in the very first interior shot of the little house where Christine lives with her young son, Walter—to the steadfast caressing of the character by the gentle camera movement. Of particular note is a short but perfectly executed movement that takes place at the very beginning of the film. Christine is on a streetcar with her young son, accompanying him to school. Sitting beside the window, costumed in the simple yet elegant garments of the day, the two of them suggest nothing less than a Norman Rockwell moment. They arrive at his school; she gets up to lead him off the streetcar. The camera executes a very elementary shot: a slight tilt down followed by a simple right-to-left pan. But in this moment, what we see is the grasping of his little hand by hers; the camera focuses entirely, in medium close-up, on this precise moment and pans to accompany it. Without a cut, the shot continues as Christine reenters the trolley and takes her seat, Walter visible through the window in the background as he approaches the entrance steps of the school. Christine is thus seen as the maternal force that she is, and in the very next scene, we will discover that she is also a very capable professional with leadership qualities, a 1920s example of the single mother trying to do it all.

After a two-shot transition (the second ending with a medium close-up of that iconic face), Eastwood cuts to a spectacular tracking shot of a woman on roller skates. It is Christine doing her job as a supervisor of telephone operators, getting to each one as fast as she can (hence the skates). It is an unusual way to introduce a character in her work environment, but Eastwood, of course, is fully aware of the classical grammar of cinema and of the meaning of angularity in a chosen shot. The traditional view of the low angle shot is that it tends to elevate its subject, putting that subject above us, if you will.

Here Eastwood simply chooses to exaggerate the grammatical rubric, elevating his subject to a height so far above the rest of us that she is bound to suffer from the fall. And in this film, suffer she does.

The profound suffering begins the next day. In one of the most cinematically eloquent passages of the entire film, Eastwood balances Christine's departure from her house in the morning—with Walter looking out at her from the living room window—with her return several hours later, both moments orchestrated through camera movement. It takes one long, languid tracking shot (interrupted only once by a medium shot of her) to have her leave the house; her return is another tracking shot, this time interrupted by four medium shots of her as she makes her way back to the house. This juxtaposition of the two tracking shots serves to increase our level of tension as we begin to wonder what might be amiss at the house. It is the kind of cinematic resolution Eastwood so often exhibits. Here it marks a perfectly symmetrical movement. Once within the house, Christine will discover that her life has unraveled.

Changeling tells such a powerful story that it might have been successful in the hands of any number of directors. What Eastwood brings to it is his characteristic poise, and his particular refusal to let the negative elements overwhelm and subjugate his heroic character, in this case a single mom who has every male authority figure coming down hard on her. She survives. Her son does not. That is the plot (based upon a true story). But like the other Eastwood heroines under examination here, Christine Collins is treated with dignity, with respect, in fact with honor, by her director.

And yet in this case she remains a victim, and Eastwood is aware of this. He summarizes her situation near the very end of the film. The man suspected of killing her little boy has been apprehended. He is scheduled to be executed by hanging. She manages to convince the authorities to let her see the condemned killer. At the prison, she continually asks him: "Did you kill my son?" "Did you kill my son?" He will not give her the satisfaction of an answer. It is one of the most emotionally searing scenes in the film. Eastwood chooses to let it play out, one actor looking into the eyes of the other, demanding an answer, demanding justice. The condemned man, now intimidated but still refusing to answer, calls for the guards to take him back to his cell. The concluding image of the scene shows us Christine, alone and behind the bars of the door that has just been closed; as the camera pulls away, she crumbles to the floor. And there she is as the scene ends, behind bars, down on the floor, alone. Yet, she has done more than survive. She has confronted the killer of her son. She now knows the truth. She can watch impassively as he goes to the gallows. She is a victim no more.

I have argued that Alfred Hitchcock's reputation as a director uninterested in his actors is a largely undeserved one. It is really an aspect of the Hitchcock persona, created by studio public relations executives, not a personification embodied by Hitchcock the artist. The evidence I have cited in these discussions has been simply the performances given in Hitchcock films. Was Cary Grant, to offer one example, ever better than when he was working for Hitchcock, whether it be in *Notorious* (1946) or in *North by Northwest* (1959)? Was Jimmy Stewart ever better than when he appeared in *Vertigo* (1958)? Did Doris Day ever give a performance that came anywhere near her characterization of the worried and anxious mother in *The Man Who Knew Too Much* (1956)? Something similar can be said about Clint Eastwood: he elicits remarkable performances from a range of actors, many of whom can be said to have done their very best work for him. I would conclude here by asserting that Angelina Jolie has never given as nuanced, as complex, as finely tuned a performance as she does in *Changeling*. It might very well come be seen as her signature role. But she is merely one of the many female performers who have responded to the brilliance of her director. Clint Eastwood—man's man, action-film icon, master of the male-oriented universe—is, as it turns out, a masterly director of women. He achieves this distinction by his ability to empower them, and he seems to do this effortlessly.

Notes

1. According to the Internet Movie Database (IMDb), the film's budget was $50 million and it made a little more than $32 million. See www.imdb.com/title/tt1212419/business?ref_=tt_dt_bus.

2. See the official website of the Academy of Motion Picture Arts and Sciences, www.oscars.org/oscars/ceremonies/2005, and that of the Directors Guild of America, www.dga.org/Awards/History/2000s/2004.aspx.

3. This film also lost money. On an estimated budget of $55 million, it returned about $36 million. See www.imdb.com/title/tt0824747/business?ref_=ttspec_ql_4.

Works Cited

"Beautiful Face Hampers Jolie: Eastwood." *Sydney Morning Herald*, 6 Oct. 2008, www.smh.com.au/news/entertainment/film/beautiful-face-hampers-jolie-eastwood/2008/10/06/1223145233452.html. Accessed 8 May 2017.

Berendt, John. *Midnight in the Garden of Good and Evil: A Savannah Story*. Random House, 1994.

Cornell, Drucilla. *Clint Eastwood and Issues of American Masculinity*. Fordham UP, 2009.

Ebert, Roger. "*Mystic River*." Review. *RogerEbert.com*. Oct. 8, 2003, www.rogerebert.com/reviews/mystic-river-2003. Accessed 8 May 2017.

Engel, Leonard, and John M. Gourlie. Introduction. *New Essays on Clint Eastwood*, edited by Leonard Engel, U of Utah P, 2012, pp. 1–17.

Foery, Raymond. "Narrative Pacing and the Eye of the Other in *The Bridges of Madison County*." *Clint Eastwood, Actor and Director: New Perspectives*, edited by Leonard Engel, U of Utah P, 2007, pp. 195–203.

Gourlie, John M. "*Million Dollar Baby*: The Deep Heart's Core." *Clint Eastwood, Actor and Director: New Perspectives*, edited by Leonard Engel, U of Utah P, 2007, pp. 242–50.

5

Manufactured in America

Clint Eastwood, Chrysler's *Halftime in America*, and the Republican National Convention

Craig Rinne

This article closely analyzes the formal elements and ideological implications of *Halftime in America*, a two-minute Chrysler commercial
that aired during Super Bowl XLVI on February 5, 2012. Written by
American poet Matthew Dickman and directed by David Gordon Green,
the short film stars Clint Eastwood, mainly with voice-over narration but
also with shots of Eastwood intercut with a montage of Americana images
and scenes. In this collection dedicated to Eastwood's filmography, one of
the richest and most enduring of any American filmmaker, why study a
seemingly minor commercial work? I do so for three reasons.

The first is the widespread viewing of *Halftime in America*, which may
dwarf that of any of Eastwood's feature films, and its accompanying discussion. The Super Bowl has over one hundred million viewers in the United
States alone, with millions more abroad, and within thirty-six hours of its
airing at the close of halftime, Eastwood's *Halftime in America* was viewed
over four million times online (Corliss, par. 1). The commercial quickly
became a national talking point, perhaps most famously by Karl Rove

attacking it as propaganda for President Obama and the automotive industry bailouts.

The second reason is its airing during the Super Bowl—which has become an unofficial national holiday—and the commercial's use of professional football tropes alongside the frontier myth elements with which Eastwood is so closely associated. Will Wright, in *Sixguns and Society: A Structural Study of the Western*, argues that the individual focus of Westerns shifted to a more team-oriented "professional Western" in the 1960s, reflecting the rise of corporate culture and dependence on technology in American society. The first Super Bowl was in 1967, marking the beginning of professional football's rise as an American cultural force. Richard Slotkin, in *Gunfighter Nation: The Myth of the Frontier in Twentieth-Century America*, details how the decline of the Western film in the 1960s and '70s was accompanied by a dispersal of frontier narratives into other genres; the territorial battles of football and the narratives around it (e.g., the gunslinger quarterback) also mark an affinity between football and the Western. The intersection of the Super Bowl, the frontier Western, and Eastwood makes for an intriguing study.

The final reason is my reading of this short film as the climax of Eastwood's move towards allegorical monumentality—as a voice of America. In a previous work, I argue that Eastwood's success in the early 1990s was due to a meshing of his frontier, Westerner persona with the opening of new possibilities in post–Cold War America; Eastwood's films of that period contain references to actual historical incidents that suggest he was speaking and acting for America (Rinne). In conjunction with one of the most popular of his recent films, *Gran Torino* in 2008—which expanded Eastwood's representative American persona to Detroit and the automotive industry— *Halftime in America* becomes perhaps Eastwood's sharpest, most explicit narrative of monumentality.

Additionally, examining such a brief text enables a comprehensive, intense formal analysis that reveals the short film's intertextual and ideological elements. I have divided *Halftime in America* into nine segments, each containing a thematic and/or formal point, and I will closely analyze each segment in turn. The commercial has forty-five individual shots; I have provided the numbers of the shots and their time locations within the commercial, and lines from Eastwood's voice-over are within quotation marks. In my conclusion, I will provide an overarching analysis of the commercial and also connect it to Eastwood's performance at the Republican National

Convention later that year (August 30, 2012) to further examine its socio-political impact.

Eastwood and America's Shadow

2 shots (1–2, 0:00–0:11), shots joined by a fade to black

These first two shots introduce but disguise Eastwood visually, although his voice-over narration could identify him to those listening closely. However, the visual style also identifies "Clint"; the shots employ chiaroscuro, film noir–style lighting, one of the markers of Eastwood's directorial visual style, with Eastwood's figure in silhouette (his face is not visible at all), walking generally toward the camera, while his elongated shadow is projected on the tunnel wall to the left—for a similar Eastwood image, think of the shots at the amusement park leading to the climactic shootout in *Sudden Impact* (1983). Obviously, Eastwood is not directing this piece, but Gordon Green clearly knows the power of Eastwood's iconic images.

The tunnel leads off the field in a football stadium; on the right side of the frame, the field, a goal post, and some people are framed by the tunnel entrance in the background. The leaving-the-field motif, as Eastwood states "It's halftime," begins the metaphorical link between the game and the theme—the "Super Bowl" and "America," of course—but for the Eastwood aficionado, the noirish shot of Eastwood and shadow in a tunnel at a football / track stadium references very similar shots in the original *Dirty Harry* (1971). Those previous *Dirty Harry* shots reside in a sequence that is perhaps the nadir of Harry Callahan's violent conservatism—the scene where Callahan, in Kezar Stadium, previous home of professional football teams the San Francisco 49ers and the Oakland Raiders, tortures Scorpio to reveal the whereabouts of the kidnapped girl. Post-Iraq/Afghanistan and waterbcarding, evoking this self-righteous torture underscores the shadowy dark side of contemporary American ideology and undercuts this commercial's superficial message of unity. Many of Eastwood's films are rife with internal contradictions, and *Halftime in America* is no exception.

Note also that Eastwood wears a suit but with hands in his pants' pockets—both formal and familiar, stern yet friendly, in his position as patriarchal spokesperson for America.

Halftime, or the Frontier?

2 shots (3–4, 0:12–0:16)

The two shots of this segment create a brilliant visual synecdoche that taps into Eastwood's Westerner, frontier persona. The first is a long shot along a railed porch with wooden furniture, including a rocking chair, and there is a sunrise/set behind the hills in the background—rural, nature, red states, conservative—buttressed by a visual echo of the porch and rocking chair in John Ford's classic Western *My Darling Clementine* (1946), where Henry Fonda / Wyatt Earp rocks and balances against the rail. The second is a helicopter shot of the New York City skyline at sunrise/set—urban, civilization, blue states, liberal—with echoes of Eastwood's Western sheriff flying into New York with his prisoner in *Coogan's Bluff* (1968). Matched by forward tracking/flying camera movement, the two shots supposedly represent all of America (conveniently eliding any other categories, particularly the independent or dissident) and begin the commercial's main social theme of moving forward together, unified, which is reinforced by the voice-over: "It's halftime in America, too." However, while halftime is the middle of a single, unified game, it also divides that supposed unity—a frontier division that will resurface in my reading.

Unspoken and unseen here, but always along the boundary line (or the halfway point) between rural/nature and urban/civilization, is the boundary-straddling frontier hero—which the commercial subtly began with by having Eastwood walking alone gradually toward the camera, the individual Westerner hero who moves across the frontier (or, in the police films, most obviously *Coogan's Bluff* and *Dirty Harry*, the transplanted Westerner, the lawman caught between poverty/crime and established authority / the law). The first sequence of Eastwood alone is followed by these two establishing shots, positing a combined, unified America; Eastwood has again become a monument, the individual "American spirit" who precedes and settles frontier America. But the segment ominously ends with "people are out of work . . ."

The Problem is Personal

4 shots (5–8, 0:17–0:25)

The voice-over "and they're hurting" accompanies a close-up of a woman sleeping—in the frontier myth stereotype, the woman needs protecting—but her male partner sits up and holds his head, seemingly unable to protect: "They're all wondering." Then another intimate shot, a medium shot of an African American man fixing his tie in front of a bathroom with pastoral scenes on the wallpaper. Race is not an issue; all Americans are *in the same boat*: "We're all scared." The *in the same boat* motif visualizes in the next shot, a long shot of several silhouettes (like Eastwood at the start) leaning on a harbor rail, watching sailboats in the background. One man appears to be facing the camera, watching a young girl walking a dog (in medium close-up in the foreground) as "because this isn't a game" is voiced. The silhouettes at the rail watching sailboats tie all Americans to Eastwood (*in the same boat*), and they are all focused on the future symbolized by the young girl. The woman sleeping, the young girl with an uncertain future— "this isn't a game": this is the gendered stereotype where weak women need masculine, heroic protection.

Motor City

8 shots (9–16, 0:26–0:38)

First, a close-up of the official Detroit flag, undulating—an immediate call to rally—and then an image of a ruin, an old brick façade without a building behind it, as Eastwood says, "The people of Detroit know a little something about this": the ruins of Detroit, decaying without the auto industry. Then a low-angle low shot of the American flag on top of a flagpole over and behind a chain link fence with cloudy skies behind, and the line "They almost lost everything." This one-second shot reinforces the "we're all scared" idea, cloudy skies over the flag because "people are out of work," an idea that the first two shots of the sequence visually implied with the Detroit flag followed by ruins. Eastwood's '90s films often used the Stars and Stripes to emphasize the American monumentality of his characters and narratives—perhaps most notably after the climax of *Unforgiven* (1993) as Will Munny / Eastwood warns the town that he'll come back and kill them all if they don't behave—and the Detroit and American flags here reinforce the narration that Detroit represents America, while post–*Gran Torino* Eastwood represents both. Also, the shots of both the ruin and the American flag/pole are fast-moving tracking shots, right to left, implying that the camera is in a moving automobile, beginning a recurring camera movement that suggests the audience—and the answers—are to be found in movement, in cars, in a modern form of frontier escape.

The next five shots show factories: first steel making (an industry that was lost) and then automobile making on an assembly line, as "we all pulled together" refers to the American and the assembly line teams, ending with "now Motor City is fighting again" over the assembly line shots. One shot shows robotic manufacturing, following the words "almost lost everything," an almost buried reference to the automation and offshoring that crippled the Detroit auto industry. The shots of the assembly line employ rack focus, both with the robotics and with an African American line worker, beginning partly blurry and then snapping into focus, suggesting that the previous cloudiness/haziness of the auto industry, and of the Great Recession, is now receding and the present/future is clear; Americans, workers, images have "all pulled together" and are "fighting again."

Clint the Patriarchal Historian

7 shots (17–23, 0:39–0:55)

The line "fighting again" overlaps the first shot of the next scene, a medium close-up of the silhouetted Eastwood, face still in shadow, walking towards the camera on the left side of the frame, out of focus lights on the right—the solution is still hidden, still cloudy, blurry, hazy, but closer, as Eastwood then narrates: "I've seen a lot of tough eras." The word "fighting" leads directly to the Eastwood shot since his core persona is the violent action hero, the Westerner, but not the youthful hero; rather, he is the patriarchal, experienced Westerner who has seen it all. Here Eastwood explicitly speaks for America, shifting from singular "I" to royal "we": "I've seen a lot of tough eras, a lot of downturns in my life, and times when we didn't understand each other. Seems that we've lost our heart at times, the fog of division, discord, and blame made it hard to see what lies ahead." Accompanying these lines are *moving* images— which again emphasize the *moving forward* motif—either on a boat (*all in the same boat*) or apparently from an auto: ship cranes passing in the distance at sunrise/set, a car driving down a residential street in the early morning (evoking *Gran Torino* neighborhoods as well as that film's explicit racism and themes of not "understanding each other"), and a silhouetted man with a cap at a boat prow moving toward the sunrise/set.

I write sunrise/set because whether an individual shot was actually filmed at sunrise or sunset (regardless of the fictional narrative context) is not usually apparent, but more importantly because of the ambiguous nature of the stereotypical *riding into the sunset* ending of Western films. The act of riding into the sunset laments an always already past way of life (the Western frontier is gone), but concurrently the Westerner hero has usually succeeded and helped establish lawful civilization—the sunset seems a sunrise for the future town, or at least the sunrise will follow. Consider Josey Wales riding into the (apparent) sunrise at the end of *The Outlaw Josey Wales* (1976). *Halftime in America*, poised at an imaginary midpoint, looks back at the setting and forward to the rising; thus the sunrise/set imagery—while apparently that of the sunrise and the new hope after halftime—always implies the setting of the past, Eastwood's walking in darkness in the Great Recession.

This darkness resurfaces with two key images, accompanying "the fog of division, discord, and blame." The first is a silent television clip of a commentator pointing angrily, with "fog of division"—the media is subtly blamed for keeping America divided. More disturbingly, a shot of protestors at a capitol building follows, with "discord and blame." The equation of rights to assemble and protest with discord and blame is disturbing enough, but the commercial proceeds to digitally alter the found footage of a pro-teacher union rally in Madison, Wisconsin, protesting Governor Scott Walker's attempts to limit collective bargaining by state employees. The commercial digitally erases pro-union messages from the protest signs and replaces them with generic statements. As Michael Shaw argues in his *Huffington Post* analysis of the changed footage, the effect is that the commercial seems more of "a pro-corporate, anti-union advertisement than any other kind of political statement" (par. 16). The commercial elides the reality of the pro-union protest, instead transforming the rally footage into a generic statement against divisive protest. The unity that the commercial strives for must delete the past—yet another manifestation of the frontier myth, further emphasized by this segment ending with another shot on a moving boat (*all in the same boat*), with multiple silhouettes in the sunrise/set, where the discord/division/blame "made it hard to see what lies ahead." Eastwood can name his version of history, but only to forget it.

Black-and-White Advertisements

9 shots (24–32, 0:56–1:13)

After a cut to black and a slow fade-in, this segment begins with a series of three black-and-white still photographs, the camera slowly tracking in on each (*moving forward*). These photos are posed family portraits, the viewer assumes—a brother and sister, a mother holding her daughter, a family of five (mother, father, two sons, daughter). Although the pairs in the first two shots appear racially diverse—and soon following these black-and-white photos is an African American father dropping his son at school—the core, the middle, the nuclear family of five, is white, not surprising considering that these *black-and-white* portraits suggest tradition, heritage, the American Way, with the narration "After those trials, we all rallied around what was right and acted as one": *e pluribus unum*, the one cannot be other than the dominant, the mainstream, of ideology.

The next shot underscores the mainstream ideology: a medium shot of two firefighters, also black and white, and at first glance another photograph; but the firefighters swaying slightly, one blinking, reveals the recorded video. In the context of "rallying" and "acting as one," this shot references the cult of heroism around firefighters post-9/11, arguably the last moment where America seemed unified, and the master justification for Eastwood using "we." The sentiment is not only about doing what is right, however—it includes violent, forced application of ideology, as in the invasion of Iraq or the manifest destiny of the frontier mythos. The final lines of the narration in this segment clarify: "Because that's what we do, we find a way through tough times, and if we can't find a way we'll make one." Although the original version of this line is attributed to another one-name icon, Hannibal, before he crossed the Alps, Clint's use could not better summarize the frontier myth in this commercial. And the double meaning of "one" is inescapable: not only to make "a way" but to force everyone to unite as "one."

Before the "we'll make one," though, comes an image of *what is made*, the inevitable explicit product placement—this film is a commercial, after all. The shots of the assembly line and the fast-moving tracking shots have anticipated the commodities, the automobiles, and they appear following the two firefighters. First, three shots show an African American father and son—there is a medium shot of the boy exiting a car, followed by a bit of a jump cut to a medium close-up of the father (the man fixing his tie in shot 7) carefully watching his son, and finally the camera crosses to the other side of the car (over the 180-degree line) to reveal not only the black (with glare, dark *blue*) Dodge Challenger but also the African American boy going to meet his white friends ("because that's what we do," suggesting America has accomplished upward mobility and racial unity, a needed point after *Gran Torino*'s racist depictions of African Americans). The next shot briefly shows a woman closing the back of a *white* Jeep Wrangler ("We find a way through tough times" linking to a potential off-road vehicle). Finally, for this segment, we see a man loading the side bin of a *red* Dodge Ram, the bed already filled with bricks, while men in hard hats walk by in the background (the bricks/construction reinforcing the "if we can't find a way, then . . ." narrated over this shot, and the " . . . we'll make one" over the next). By making patriotic red, white, and blue cars, Detroit and the automotive industry are *making a way*—a grasping twist on the frontier, holding on to the past to blaze a new path.

The Cowboy Way

8 shots (33–40, 1:14–1:28)

The next segment extends the frontier argument, beginning with a three-shot Western, all bathed in golden sunrise/set, all shots tracking quickly to convey auto movement:

Shot 33

An extreme close-up of a forearm and hand on a wheel in silhouette, the driver window behind, the arm pointing forward (to the right) as the auto moves to the right; "we'll make one" plays over this shot.

Shot 44

A slight low-angle close-up of a cowboy-hat wearing man driving in silhouette on the left of the frame, the sunrise/set looming large in the driver-window background on the right, only music audio.

Shot 45

An extreme long-shot of the sunrise/set (with the sun now higher in the sky, implying a sunrise), again with fast tracking implying auto movement, but the direction is reversed, moving to the left, only music audio.

The frontier cowboy driver is blazing a trail, moving forward as we read, left to right, beginning with an assumed new dawn behind his profile—so he's driving south? And left to right suggests west to east. But the third shot (shot 44) is moving right to left, backwards, yet suggesting east to west, the movement of American frontier history. Unless this is a minimovie and the third shot is a sunset and the cowboy driver is still heading south? With too many contradictions and negations, the frontier myth and imagery is folding in on itself; the frontier is closed, although the narration will not admit it.

The narration pushes forward: "All that matters now is what's ahead" over a long shot of an empty, curving road, the camera on the front of an auto moving right to left, and then a close-up of the woman driving the Wrangler (the viewer assumes), facing right/forward again (but not to the frontier) as the auto moves to the right. "How do we come from behind" follows, over a shot of the right Wrangler bumper (on the left of the screen) driving through a town intersection (the light is green, of course) into the sunrise/set on the right of the frame. The true "sunrise" is in the next shot, of a young girl, a daughter, looking to screen left (presumably toward the sunrise) as Eastwood narrates: "How do we come together…"—frontier, sunrise, and unity connect to the symbol of a hopeful future for America.

Cut to Eastwood stepping forward and stopping, in close-up, his face now finally revealed, the shot beginning blurry, then in focus, then a slight blur before the next shot—the camera can't quite believe it has captured Clint—along with the voice-over "and how do we win" (the narration is still voice-over, not yet synced with the image of Eastwood speaking). In this three-shot Western, the cowboy driver and the mother/daughter have both led to Clint—he is the future and the past, the present winner who contains multitudes, the monumental symbol of America. Now the confusion of the cowboy driver moving east or west or south is clear—while frontier progress is traditionally westward expansion, east to west and left to right on the map, *Halftime in America*'s progress is from left to right, to the east on the map, because *eastward* sounds like (leads to) *Eastwood*. Left to right also suggests political movement, liberal to conservative, which I will further explore in the conclusion.

Detroit is Savage War is America

3 shots (41–43, 1:29–1:36)

This segment, though short, has three of the most interesting shots in the commercial. The first is a long shot of a robotic assembly line (no employees), apparently of sport-utility vehicle (SUV) bodies, with a motionless, incomplete body (no engine) positioned head-on in the background while a side shot of a similar incomplete body passes from right to left in front of the still camera (between the camera and the head-on body), creating an illusion of camera movement to the right. The camera and viewer nearly become visual and mobile apparatus, located within the manufacture and movement of the automobile. The very viewing of the commercial is an interpellation, forcing the viewer into the industrial process; the mechanization and the lost jobs of Detroit and the auto industry are "true about all of us."

The second shot is a left to right tracking long shot of (presumably) three finished SUVs (Jeep Grand Cherokees) from the previous shot, lined up one behind the other in three colors: *white*, *red*, and dark *blue*. These "Cherokee" SUVs indirectly reference the Cherokee Nation and other Cherokee American Indians, suggesting *The Outlaw Josey Wales*'s Cherokee character Lone Watie (played by Chief Dan George) and reanimating the savage war history between American Indians and European settlers that is behind the frontier myth in this advertisement, the original conflict of *red* and *white* (and *blue*)

America, eventually leading to the SUV, the covered wagon of modern America, crucial to its lifestyle and economy.

The third shot, a low-angle, fast-tracking shot to the right, shows a high sun behind the treetops, and it eventually escapes the trees and shines high in the sky before fading to black. The trees tamely suggest the wilderness, the vestigial frontier, while the high sun suggests that the new dawn has already been reached. The assembly line and the SUVs lead to the brilliant sun, to a pagan god, to (in the next segment) Clint Eastwood (with only a brief fall to black beforehand; Eastwood always falls before he rises in his films). "This country can't be . . ." begins here as a bridge between segments.

Clint and Credits

2 shots (44–45, 1:37–2:00)

Narration: "This country can't be knocked out with one punch. We get right back up again and when we do the world's going to hear the roar of our engines. Yeah. It's halftime, America, and our second half's about to begin."

The climactic shot is one long take, a tight close-up of Eastwood speaking into the camera, the voice-over finally synced with his image, the right side of his face (screen left) still in slight shadow and the blurred overhead light in the background on the right. If the viewer hasn't yet realized, the omniscient narrator is revealed as the monumental Eastwood, here in an iconic, Clint-tough-guy close-up delivering his lines and explicitly speaking for America: "We get right back up again. . . . our second half's about to begin." In fact, with the shading on the right side of the face and the blurred background on the right, the shot composition is similar to Eastwood's infamous close-up delivering his most notorious line, "Go ahead, make my day" in *Sudden Impact* (1983)—minus the .44 Magnum, of course—a one-liner that former actor President Reagan appropriated for a speech against tax increases (note also that Eastwood closed his Republican National Convention speech in 2012 with this line). Eastwood's aspirations to American monument—present from his earliest Westerner roles in frontier-commentary narratives and accelerating to historical arrogance in and past the post–Cold War 1990s—has reached its apotheosis in this commercial where he explicitly adopts a presidential role (unfortunately, one assumes, as a counterpoint to President Obama's convention-defying election and presidency).

The metaphorical "world's going to hear the roar of our engines" line neatly ties Chrysler and the auto industry in to representing the supposed rebirth of America on the global stage in the imagined upcoming second half. As Eastwood finishes his narration, he walks off-screen, both forward and to screen left (but to his right)—always *moving forward*, but also moving into the American audience and with the dominant motion of the tracking shots.

The final shot is a black screen with white letters, with the slogan "IMPORTED FROM DETROIT" at the top as the Chrysler logos appear one by one below, left to right: Ram, Dodge, Jeep, Chrysler. Although the commercial was apparently a monumental Eastwood statement, the financial source of the commercial is finally made clear with "trademarks of Chrysler Group LLC" at the bottom—now, in 2016, ironically recalling that the world did "hear the roar" when Chrysler become a subsidiary of Italian automaker Fiat in 2014. Whatever Eastwood's intention at halftime in 2012, global capitalism found a way to win two years later.

Summary Analysis; Post-text:
The Republican National Convention

Halftime in America reads as a condensed Clint Eastwood frontier film that explicitly presents his aspirations to American monumentality. The commercial begins by establishing a frightening, despairing wilderness and a history of "downturns and tough eras"—like the frontier settlements in his Westerns, the shadowy streets of San Francisco in the Dirty Harry films, or the decaying metropolis of Detroit in *Gran Torino*. The lone hero, the Westerner Clint, enters the narrative, stoic and powerful among the frightened ordinary public who are struggling with "division, discord, and blame" in their wilderness ("fog of division" may even be a San Francisco reference). That hero is near invincible but often endures a vicious beating (from *A Fistful of Dollars* to *Unforgiven*) before rising again—"can't be knocked out with one punch." And while the public rarely unifies and "acts as one" in Eastwood films, Clint does act as the representative "one" who wins, who "makes" ("my day") or "finds a way," usually through violent retribution, when the villains hear the "roar" of his pistols. And in many of his post–Cold War films, that victory is a victory for some aspect of the American Way that supposedly enables an American future (or American present for those films set in the past—the Westerns, *A Perfect World*), and often a past wrong or trauma tied to an actual historical event is righted to enable a better future (the Kennedy assassination in *In the Line of Fire*, the Korean War in *Gran Torino*). These historical references combined with variations on the frontier myth provide Eastwood with a platform to speak as a grandfatherly, patriarchal voice of America, or at least the still-fighting, masculinist, Westerner aspect of it.

The rise and fall of the American automotive industry, centered around Detroit, roughly parallels that of the Western film (including television series)—beginning around the turn of the twentieth century, rapidly advancing in the first half of the century, peaking in the 1950s, and slowly declining in the 1970s, with a secondary though continuing status since then and occasional cycles of mainstream relevance. And both industry and genre appeal to stereotypical American values of hard work (the cowboy, the line), the open frontier (the car on the open highway), and even teamwork in the later, professional Westerns. Thus, the attempt by monumental Eastwood and *Halftime in America* to use Western, frontier tropes both to call for a rhetorical American unity and to reestablish the relevance of the auto industry, a Detroit-centric one, is not surprising—disingenuous as such a hopeful comeback win for us all may be in the global marketplace.

Clint Eastwood's effectiveness as a monumental spokesman, however, depends on cleverly crafted film imagery and narrative. Without that editing and production process, his iconicity wavers and monumentality crumbles, as shown by his rambling oratory at the 2012 Republican National Convention. Infamous for his staged device of addressing an empty chair representing President Obama—who, he implies, utters obscenities from the chair—his speech weakly attacks Obama on several minor points (Guantanamo Bay, a deadline for withdrawal of troops) while conveniently avoiding any discussion of the Great Recession corporate bailouts: bailouts that included Chrysler, Eastwood's recent employer, and that enabled the automotive industry to survive for his *Halftime in America*. Eastwood even undermines himself during the speech. He begins by criticizing Obama for being a lawyer—"Attorneys are so busy, you know they're always taught to argue everything, always weigh everything, weigh both sides." But then Eastwood ends his speech with a wavering appeal to all Americans—"Whether you are a Democrat or Republican or whether you're a libertarian or whatever, you are the best"—a waffling that seems inappropriate at the Republican convention.

To tie the convention speech further to *Halftime in America*, Eastwood also accuses Obama of being an ecological hypocrite with his "big gas guzzler" presidential plane, again ignoring his own recent campaigning for Chrysler and the American auto industry, the creators of the "gas guzzler."

Eastwood's attempt at speaking for America at the convention fails not only due to its rambling, unpolished nature but because it begins with a series of ineffectual attacks on Obama, and by implication his constituency, before ending with a watered-down, general appeal to America. These attacks on President Obama reveal what is missing from *Halftime in America* as a typical Eastwood film narrative—a villain, an antagonist; the savage war of the frontier always requires the Other. Could it be the Great Recession itself? On the surface, but a recession is a very abstract notion to match up against Clint. Or the rest of the world and their economies? Perhaps, but the global is a subject carefully avoided in the commercial, only obliquely referred to with the line "the world will hear the roar of our engines." Eastwood's convention attacks on Obama suggest that the implied villains of *Halftime in America* are the imagined liberal welfare state and its proponents on the left, those non-patriotic dissidents (the Wisconsin protestors) who do not truly believe in the American Way and traditional corporate culture (as opposed to current global conglomerations). This realization deconstructs Eastwood's apparent message on behalf of the automotive industry in *Halftime in America*, implicitly attacking the unions that formed the core of that industry. Perhaps that rabidly indiviudalistic sentiment is why the commercial shows robotics as often as line workers and focuses more on the consumers of the commodity. Eastwood's monumental American persona worked in the post–Cold War 1990s, despite any internal contradictions, but by 2012 the cracks and flaws had surfaced in that aging, manufactured product.

Afterword

I finished the initial version of this article in early 2016, when Donald Trump's presidency still seemed a very remote possibility. Now, making final revisions in early 2017 after President Trump's election, *Halftime in America* seems almost prophetic. The commercial (and Eastwood) tapped into working class fears and a nostalgic vein for mythical American greatness, represented by the relatively affluent, suburban lifestyle that the Detroit automotive industry once helped provide for both its workers and its consumers. Trump's campaign also clearly tapped into this fear (now anger) and nostalgia, resulting in shocking electoral victories in Michigan and Pennsylvania (once home of the steel industry)—Trump's post-halftime strategy outmaneuvered that of his opponent, Hillary Clinton. Viewing the Trump campaign and presidency through the lens of *Halftime in America*, the shift from Obama to Trump completed the work of the commercial that the

commercial could not do for Chrysler (as they were bought out by Fiat)—
Trump completed the left/liberal to right/conservative movement that the
commercial suggested, away from the imagined liberal welfare state toward
a conservative fantasy to "make America great again" (Trump's campaign
slogan). While the world heard the "roar" of Chrysler's "engines" only
through its merging with a global conglomerate, the world currently hears
President Trump's "roar" against globalization in his continued plans to
build a wall on the Mexican border and his executive order banning immigrants and refugees from reputed terrorist states. Ronald Reagan once
appropriated Eastwood's "make my day"; similarly, Trump capitalized on
the nostalgic themes of *Halftime in America* by promising to "make America
great again," a message that helped win him the presidency. One can imagine a sequel to both *Halftime in America* and *In the Line of Fire* starring
Eastwood as a former secret service agent, now a cabinet member, monu-
mentally assisting a President Trump figure and preventing a terrorist-cell
assassination attempt.

Works Cited

Corliss, Richard. "Clint's Halftime Ad: From the Director of *Pineapple Express*." *Time*, 7
Feb. 2012, entertainment.time.com/2012/02/07/clints-chrysler-ad-from-the-director-
of-pineapple-express/.

Eastwood, Clint. Speech at the 2012 Republican National Convention. 30 Aug. 2012,
Tampa Bay Times Forum, Tampa, Florida. "Watch Clint Eastwood Speak at Republican National Convention." *YouTube*, uploaded by PBS NewsHour, 30 Aug. 2012,
www.youtube.com/watch?v=3DGl-4gByV4.

Halftime in America. Directed by David Gordon Green, performance by Clint Eastwood, Wieden+Kennedy for Chrysler, 2012.

Rinne, Craig. "The End of History and America First: How the 1990s Revitalized Clint
Eastwood." *New Essays on Clint Eastwood*, edited by Leonard Engel, U of Utah P,
2012, pp. 130–47.

Shaw, Michael. "Reading the Pictures: The Clint Eastwood Chrysler *Halftime in America* Controversy, and the Doctored Wisconsin Footage." *Huffington Post*, 8 Apr.
2012, www.huffingtonpost.com/michael-shaw/chrysler-superbowl-ad_b_1260740.
html.

Slotkin, Richard. *Gunfighter Nation: The Myth of the Frontier in Twentieth-Century
America*. HarperPerennial, 1993.

Wright, Will. *Sixguns and Society: A Structural Study of the Western*. U of California P,
1975.

6

The Real War That Got into the Movies
Eastwood and Spielberg in the Pacific

John Streamas

One of the first functions of my field, ethnic studies, was to expose racial stereotypes in media: the "dragon lady" Asian woman, the spiritual but vanishing Indian, the hypersexual, athletic black man, the indolent Latino, and others. Students in our introductory courses enjoy this work partly because it is easy. The stereotypes have a long and flagrant history, and even conservative students recognize and readily condemn them. More recent stereotypes take a liberal turn, and, though as easy to identify, are more difficult to condemn. These include the noble but embattled woman of color rescued by an enlightened white man. Liberal stereotypes are found in such films as *To Kill a Mockingbird* (1962) and *Dances with Wolves* (1990) and, in my specialization of wartime Japanese American culture, *Come See the Paradise* (1990) and *Snow Falling on Cedars* (1999). This latter film, based on the 1994 novel by David Guterson, extends its liberal reach so far that the white protagonist denies himself the love of a Japanese American woman by producing evidence that exonerates her Japanese American husband from a wrongful murder charge. The newer, liberal stereotypes assign dignity to people of color but still turn them into victims needing the rescue of a white man. The people thus labeled by stereotypes are denied agency, a right to tell our stories in our own voices.[1]

This is not to say that whites must never tell our stories, or that white men can never be our allies, even our heroes. It is simply to say that stereotypes still rule mainstream American visual culture and that the newer, liberal stereotypes represent an improvement so scant that it insults the progress we claim to have made since the civil rights movement. Aside from documentaries and low-budget, marginalized works, where can we tell our own stories on film?

At first glance, Clint Eastwood's *Letters from Iwo Jima* (2007) would seem to be another disastrous example of a white man telling our stories, even if it is based on actual documents written by real Japanese soldiers. Who gave Eastwood the right to tell Asians' stories? That the film is part of what has been called a diptych, partnered with *Flags of Our Fathers* (2006), certainly grants an artistic claim, but this is still no moral or political claim. That a defining feature of many modern and postmodern narratives is the construction of multiple perspectives reinforces the artistic claim, but Eastwood is still a white man telling Asians' stories. Besides, in most stories with multiple perspectives, the characters are relatively homogeneous. *Rashomon* (1950) is the classic example in film, with the perspectives of only Japanese people. Films that risk cross racial perspectives may win the praises of liberal white media—the classic example here is *Crash* (2004), written by Paul Haggis, a cowriter of *Flags of Our Fathers*—but they are usually scorned by critics of color for posturing condescension. Thus, if Eastwood's Iwo Jima films form a diptych, then they, too, assume the risk of cross racial perspectives.

My aim here is to argue that the films of Asian wars that Eastwood made in the first decade of the new century, his Iwo Jima films and *Gran Torino* (2008), mostly rise above the most common stereotypes perpetuated by American films of those wars, and that even when he fails and succumbs to a liberal cliché—the white savior in *Gran Torino*—he recognizes a need to grant at least Asian visibility. Because many Asian American critics and scholars savaged *Gran Torino*, my point can best be served by comparing these films to another on Asian war made by a filmmaker of Eastwood's generation, Steven Spielberg, whose *Empire of the Sun* (1987) I will briefly examine.

Before discussing the films, cultural context is in order. Most critics agree that a few decades ago US culture took a conservative and libertarian turn; they disagree only over whether the turn began with the Nixon presidency in the 1970s or the Reagan presidency in the 1980s. The so-called culture wars of the 1980s represented a white male backlash against gains made by the civil rights and feminist movements, and they manifested themselves in rejections of affirmative action programs, the rise of a "prison industrial complex" that filled an emerging private prison industry with the bodies of young black men, and increasingly racialized immigration policies. Anti-Asian "yellow peril" discourse revived in the late 1980s, and when, a few years later, journalist Tom Brokaw published his best-selling *The Greatest Generation* (1998), the revisionist histories of World War II published in the second half of the twentieth century were tossed aside so that the "good war" narrative might be revived, and Japanese were cast once again not as an enemy but as a racialized enemy. This is not to suggest that the "good war" narrative went unchallenged, but the persistent revisionism of scholars such as John Dower, Lisa Yoneyama, and Yoshikuni Igarashi, and of activists such as Studs Terkel, were mere whispers beside the shouts of Brokaw and pop historian Steven Ambrose and politicians such as Ernest "Fritz" Hollings.[2] Nor is it to suggest that all of popular culture embraced the "good war." Shortly after Brokaw's book coined the adoring phrase "the greatest generation" to name Americans who fought in the war, two major films of that war appeared: Spielberg's *Saving Private Ryan* and Terrence Malick's *The Thin Red Line* (both 1998). Spielberg's film surely recalls mythmaking wartime Hollywood movies, but it is set in Europe and its combatants are white. Malick's film is set in the Pacific and it does show, briefly, the results of Japanese soldiers' atrocities, but it is mainly concerned with the fears and failings—including the violence—of American soldiers; and, in its exoticizing but largely sympathetic depiction of indigenous islanders, it can hardly be accused of stirring racial angers.[3] Finally, the 2000 publication of James Bradley's *Flags of Our Fathers*, on which Eastwood based his film, took up Brokaw's tribute to American soldiers even as it demythologized much of the "good war." Still, as the new century and millennium arrived, the "good war" narrative continued to define many Americans' understanding of the war, and few would have been surprised if Eastwood, in filming Bradley's book, had chosen to exalt soldiers while ignoring, or even bolstering, the myth.

To be sure, the racial narrative that mostly drives *Flags of Our Fathers* involves not a clash between whites and Asians but the role of Native American soldier Ira Hayes. The film is less the story of one of the fiercest battles

of the racialized Pacific War than it is the demythologizing of patriotic iconography; and a tragic irony abides in the fact that a principal agent of the
mythmaking campaign was a man whose racial community was the victim
of America's founding frontier myth. The focus of Bradley's book is understandably Bradley's own father, one of the six flag raisers immortalized in
the photograph on Mount Suribachi, but Eastwood devotes almost as much
attention to Hayes. Only twelve minutes into the film, Hayes is identified as
a Pima Indian; and then, twelve minutes later, he is provoked into showing
his fellow soldiers photographs of Japanese beheadings of prisoners when
they accuse him of leering at images of his "squaw" in their "wigwam." Less
than a quarter hour later he denies being a flag raiser, and Rene Gagnon, one
of the six, calls him a "dumb Redskin" for refusing credit. When he, Bradley, and Gagnon are sent home to be paraded across the nation by politicians, hailed as heroes selling Americans on the urgency of buying war
bonds, he occasionally plays the role of the patriotic hero, telling President
Truman that his people are "very proud" of him, even deferentially pretend-
ing to have lost some of his native language when a politician tries to greet
him in a garbled version of it—a politician who later confides to a friend that
the Pima language is "gibberish." But for each deference, Hayes suffers
revulsion, depression, and despair. He calls the fundraising campaign a
"farce." He drinks heavily, pukes out of trains, and calls out desperately to
fallen comrades.

Lest Hayes seem vulnerable to the stereotype of the "drunken Indian"—
and Gagnon does accuse him of having been too drunk in battle to fire his
weapon—Eastwood carefully plants corroborating views of the mythmaking. When, in Chicago, the three men are presented a large statue of the flag
raising made of ice cream, and when chocolate sauce is poured over it, the
perspective is not Hayes's but Bradley's. A senator, in a racist offering of
good-natured advice, urges Hayes to say that he had used a tomahawk in
battle since it would make a better story. And when Hayes, refusing to plant
a fake flag on a fake Mount Suribachi, goes on a rampage, Eastwood carefully turns sympathy toward him when a bartender says, "We don't serve
Indians!" and a commanding officer says, "Jesus Christ, he's drunk! Goddamned Indians." Finally, Eastwood shows glimpses of Hayes after the war,
a man broken by his experiences but made sympathetic, not pitiful. White
tourists, recognizing him as he labors in a field, stop and ask for photographs. He is photographed in jail. He walks to meet the father of Harlon
Block, an uncelebrated flag raiser, to tell him the truth about his son. And,

in a voice-over, an elderly Bradley recalls glimpsing Hayes a few years after the war, at the side of a desert road. In fact, Eastwood shows this glimpse twice in the film's final half hour.

In the single moment in which Hayes's characterization is at best ambiguous and at worst part of a white, liberal construction, Hayes addresses the Congress of American Indians, assuring them, "It's going to be a better world." While this view was apparently common in indigenous communities whose young men served in the two world wars—a view based on a belief that military service would prove the people's Americanness[4]—Eastwood refuses to explain whether Hayes's words are ironic or merely a desperate attempt at self-assurance. Regardless, the history of indigenous Americans in the past seven decades imposes its own irony on the words. Author James Bradley accepts the irony but focuses it too narrowly in his account of Hayes's death, at thirty-two, in January 1955, which he attributes neither to guilt nor to racist exploitation nor to a slight by his community, but rather to what would today be called post-traumatic stress (333).[5]

But irony is unwelcome in myth. The first raising of the US flag on Mount Suribachi was restaged for the benefit of a photograph, and that image, reproduced on front pages of newspapers all over America, came to stand "for everything good that Americans wanted it to stand for" (Bradley 282). One of the first images in Eastwood's film is of a nighttime fireworks display over Soldier Field in Chicago where the three fundraising flag raisers are to be celebrated; Eastwood lingers over the glare of the fireworks so that it might slowly melt into the glare of flares over the battlefield of Iwo Jima. Hayes may regard those fireworks as part of the farce of hero worship, but their morphing into the flares of battle suggests that, in wartime myth-making, each flash of light defines the other.

Here I wish to recall another image of a flashing light over a wartime Pacific sky, the flash that the boy Jim sees near the end of Steven Spielberg's *Empire of the Sun*. Within seconds, Jim learns that the flash he has just seen is the detonation of an atomic bomb over Japan. Part of that flash swirls, almost as if it were a northern-lights display, and Jim confesses that he had imagined it to be the soul of a woman companion "going up to heaven." He hears the truth of the flash's origin on the radio, a desultory luxury for a boy who is a prisoner of war, but the flash understandably fascinates him. This is a problem, however—for here Spielberg creates a romantic image for an atomic bomb. That, moments later, the young Japanese soldier whom Jim calls a friend is wantonly shot by a fellow prisoner cannot atone for

Spielberg's construction of an Asian enemy as deserving of annihilation by an atomic bomb, especially when that bomb's blast is beautiful. Neither the boy Jim nor the director Spielberg can imagine the souls of Japanese ascending to heaven in that flash of light—erasure is deserved and final. Eastwood's trading of fireworks for flares may be a conscious aesthetic device, but at least it points to war's ugly ambiguities, not to Spielberg's beautiful annihilations.[6]

Flags of Our Fathers moves across several temporal perspectives—the war itself, the years immediately following the war, and the younger Bradley's decades-later gathering of testimony from his father and from photographer Joe Rosenthal—which allows the emotional temperature to change too, from Hayes's rages and Gagnon's opportunism during the war to Hayes's decline immediately after and to the elder interviewees' reflections. But the film is based on the young Bradley's book written more than a half century after the war, and it shares many of the author's sentiments and reflections. *Letters from Iwo Jima* is largely based on letters written by Japanese General Kuribayashi before and during battle, letters that were discovered much later. Though Eastwood frames the film with the unearthing of the letters in 2005, still the range of perspectives is much narrower, and even episodes occurring beyond the witness of the general could still be contained in any letters his troops might have written. This is in some ways unfortunate. For example, while *Flags of Our Fathers* constructs a broad view of the battle, the war, and the myth from the perspective of an American half century, *Letters from Iwo Jima* must construct its characters' humanity in their moment of crisis, in the heat of battle. There is no long view from sixty years after. On the other hand, if *Flags* is largely concerned with the sixty-year-long process of piercing wartime myths, and if *Letters* is unconcerned with Japanese myths, then the shorter view may be justified in the later film. The building of myths is, after all, much less desirable in a nation that has just lost a war. A popular comparison of postwar Germany and Japan as peoples explaining defeat by constructing narratives of either guilt or shame must be regarded for what it is: the racialized gloating of a winner from the colonizing West. There is no gloating in *Letters from Iwo Jima*. Nor is there mythmaking, nor even the puncturing of myth.

Yet the absence of mythmaking and myth busting may still be a problem. The moral concern of *Flags of Our Fathers* is the task of honoring the flag raisers, and at the same time it is the task of piercing the myth of the flag raising. This is why one of the film's closing lines both elevates and drops myth: "Heroes are something we create. Something we need." Thus East-wood and the younger Bradley agree that the flag raisers must be believed when they claim not to be heroes and when they rage against the fundraising farce, yet they also agree with the politicians and the publicists who build sustaining myths by elevating nonheroes to the status of heroes. In this sense, *Flags of Our Fathers* promotes conservative lessons in both democracy and American exceptionalism. And the raced narratives of Hayes and Gag-non apply these lessons. For it was the mythic "self-made man" and lone, rugged, individual white American who decimated indigenous populations and, according to frontier legend, built the American West—and Hayes's refusal of hero status is a refusal of that individuated identity. It was a huck-ster, such as P. T. Barnum, who invented the myth of the "self-made man"—and Gagnon's opportunism and self-promotion, against the elder Bradley's humility and Hayes's revulsion, too eagerly, and perhaps too cynically, embraces that myth.

Myth does not feature in *Letters from Iwo Jima* either because there was no preexisting Japanese myth that could have transformed or been trans-formed by the war or because the lost cause represented by the island battle nullified the value of all myths. The "inscrutable Asian" stereotype does appear briefly in the film, as when a young soldier is labeled unpatriotic for refusing to obey an order to kill a barking dog, and the commanding officer who scolds him carries out the order;[7] and as when, in an early scene, Japa-nese soldiers and their commanding officers shout their exchanges, almost as if transported from a propagandistic wartime Hollywood film. Still, ste-reotypes are scarce here, and Eastwood clearly expects audiences to respect these soldiers. If a race problem exists at all, then it originates in Eastwood's eliciting of such respect by deracializing his principal Japanese soldiers. This is a variation on the liberal narratives of race to which I alluded earlier. Both General Kuribayashi and Baron Nishi have ties to the United States—ties made clear in conversations and in flashbacks—and they are both Western-ized and universalized by these ties. The Baron's horse, Jupiter, is killed in an air raid, and his love of horses is established in memories of his equestrian prowess in an Olympics hosted by the United States. He claims Douglas Fairbanks and Mary Pickford as friends. The general flashes back to a prewar visit to the United States where he is feted at state dinners; and when, in one of these events, he hazards a seemingly risky response to a question about possible conflicts between his nation's demands and his own princi-ples—"Are they not the same?" he asks firmly but deferentially—a white guest offers a hearty and conciliatory response: "Spoken like a true soldier!" Also, the general vows to march ahead of his soldiers, and an image of his leading his men across the island looks almost like a guerilla version of George Washington leading his troops. Thus linked to American sentiments and memories, Nishi and Kuribayashi are Americanized, and to be Americanized in colonizing Western culture is to be universalized. In this way, more than the other Japanese soldiers, they are deracialized. They lose much of their Japaneseness. Eastwood does not push this point very far—certainly not as far as he might have, nor as far as other directors such as Spielberg surely would have—and he attaches little of it to other Japanese soldiers. Still, the price of the film's compassion for the Japanese is largely paid with the extent of the Americanization and universalization of the baron and the general. The "yellow peril" has been blended in red, white, and blue. Eastwood's real achievement in this film is thus not his depictions of these two major characters but rather his depictions of the other Japanese soldiers, the frightened and quarreling young men whose humanity and whose deaths, with scarcely a filter of nationalism or colonization, are much more truly universal. This is no small achievement, either, given the "yellow peril" stereotype of Japanese as gladly forsaking their selfhood in the name of the Emperor.[8] Western audiences may not remember the names of these soldiers, but Eastwood individuates several of them sufficiently so that viewers may empathize with those young men who, terrified, rationalize their running from sure annihilation.

Of course, they are also running from self-annihilation. Eastwood shows some soldiers' suicides but neither praises nor condemns them. A more stunning self-annihilation occurs near the end of his 2008 film *Gran Torino*, in which protagonist Walt Kowalski, played by Eastwood himself, creates his own death trap so that a gang of violent Hmong teens might be arrested for his murder and removed from the neighborhood. Few American films in recent years have divided critics so surely along racial lines. Most mainstream reviewers praised it while most Asian American critics condemned it. Here I will cite some of those complaints, though I wish to focus more on the film's relationship to liberal clichés and stereotypes, especially as those stereotypes deny or at least constrain agency to an embattled community of color.

Though in its closing credits *Gran Torino* lists "Hmong Cultural Advisers," still Hmong critics have a long list of what Louisa Schein and Va-Megn Thoj call "cultural inaccuracies, exaggerations and distortions," at least a few of which bear mentioning: "the betel-nut chewing and spitting, . . . the obsequious making of offerings on doorsteps, inconsistent use of the two Hmong dialects within one family, the wearing of Hmong festival clothes to a funeral, the rape of a clan cousin . . ." (49). Defenders of the film might claim that, because Hmong culture is so unknown to mainstream audiences, some inaccuracies are unavoidable, but critics might charge that such inaccuracies are inexcusable *because* of the culture's unfamiliarity. Regardless, inaccuracies and distortions should be noted. A more serious charge is that the film "assumes the power of speech to define Hmong Americans," and that it attributes "hyper-violence to Hmong *as character*" (Schein and Thoj 1, 2; emphasis in original). In other words, despite the presence of Kowalski's peaceful but helpless Hmong neighbors—the family of the teen boy Thao whom he mentors—and despite the closing image of Thao driving the 1972 Gran Torino into the lakeshore sunset with Walt's old dog beside him, the overwhelming impression of Hmong people here is that, when they are not meek and helpless, they are murderously violent.

Gran Torino is a story of transformation, of "redemption and restorative justice," writes Debbie McBride, who adds that "just as relationships can develop, certain flaws can be accepted, lessons can still be learned and taught, and priorities can be shifted" (360, 361). In this reading, *Gran Torino* is much less the story of Hmong immigrants than it is the story of a grizzled and bigoted war veteran who, even as he turns eighty, learns to accept, even to honor, difference so much that he gives his life to serve it. In a similar reading, Gourlie and Engel argue that the film is a study in ritual and family, especially as Kowalski comes to serve as a father to Thao's family and as Thao's sister, Sue, comes to serve as a wife to Kowalski (268–70, 272).

Yet the illness—presumably lung cancer—that enables and motivates his self-sacrifice may be enabling the moral equivalent of a "foxhole conversion." More troublingly, Kowalski's transformation is only partial, as even the language of his will is peppered with the racial slurs that now define him in death as they defined him in life: viewers "feel okay about Walt because by the end, his behavior shows he has learned and grown away from his ignorance—his language may not have changed much, but his attitude has because now he uses it in the context of a caring relationship. Thus, we appreciate the curmudgeon and ignore the language" (Ward 388).

Fully transformed, Kowalski would abandon the slurs, and of course this might be too much to expect of his character, or of any character. Yet the film still expects viewers to assume that a bigot can reform even without dropping the discourse of bigotry. This is Archie Bunker logic—love the person, hate the person's language—that is most embarrassingly modeled in a scene in a barbershop in which Kowalski takes Thao for a lesson in "manning up," to learn "guy talk." Kowalski's barber-friend even points a gun at Thao to mock-reinforce a manliness defined by the language of racial slurs. But these are the racial slurs of white men, and in a city and nation being transformed by immigration these slurs will not serve Walt's mock-son in the future. Many activists and scholars of color, and even the president of the United States, have passionately argued for the difference between a white man's voicing the word "nigger" and a black man's voicing it, but this is a lesson that not even most liberal whites have learned, and Asian Americans' outrage over this barbershop scene indicates that Eastwood as a filmmaker has not learned it either. Conservatives in South Carolina have taken down their Confederate flag, having realized, after a century and a half, that whites' hate speech cannot be rationalized as symbolizing regional pride or wartime valor—it wounds its victims, and no truly antiracist white would utter it, not even in the interest of a filmmaker's remaining true to a character.

In Ly Chong Jalao's reading, Kowalski's transformation saves Kowalski himself more than it saves Thao and his family. Thus the film enacts conservative America's repudiation of defeat in Southeast Asia—it was the first President Bush who, sending troops to the Middle East, promised "no more Vietnams"—even if its message is subtler and looks more humane than the message in a Rambo film. Jalao argues that the film's plot "uncannily follows the broad outline of U. S. intervention in Southeast Asia. We have in Walt the well-intentioned American who lost his innocence in a foreign war, and we have in Thao an effeminate Asia in need of being saved from itself and from pathological interethnic strife." Further, Kowalski's "Christ-like posture in death assures us that while salvation is at hand for this American veteran, for his Hmong counterparts, the path toward legitimacy and legibility in America has been hallowed and made safe. But this comes at a cost to the Hmong" (Jalao). For this reason, "the most believable part of the film occurs when the gang members kill Walt at the end . . . because the gang members are the only characters in the film who exhibit the kind of agency that approximates the real possibilities and precariousness of life in a Hmong American community" (Jalao). Curiously, then, Hmong hip-hop artist Elvis Thao who plays a gang member who shoots Kowalski boasted online: "I shot Clint! Yeah, woohoo!" (Schein and Thoj 34). Schein and Thoj note that Thao said he had shot *Clint*, not Walt, and explain: "The agonism of masculinities is almost palpable—a younger man of color standing armed opposite a senior and unarmed white man of stature and narratively prevailing" (39, 35). If Kowalski first asserts his own troubled masculinity by killing Asians in a distant war, and if he later tries to redeem himself at least partly by teaching Thao the "safer" masculinity of white racial slurs, then what he may regard as self-sacrifice may be regarded by Asians as "chickens coming home to roost."

As Ly Chong Jalao argues, this is the logic of the narratives of colonizer and colonized. The so-called first Gulf War might not have become "another Vietnam," but the ongoing US presence in the Middle East has been as troubled as the US presence in Asia and in Asian wars. To the extent that Kowalski changes, he becomes a white liberal, but even that is not necessarily good for people of color. Those mainstream (white) critics who have followed Eastwood's work over decades note, and praise, a similar change in the director. But for every transforming Kowalski, there is an Eastwood narrating a television commercial for a Detroit automaker. And while artists of color have for decades constructed invisibility as a condition of racial marginalization, there is an Eastwood addressing an invisible Barack Obama at the 2012 Republican convention. In his review of Eastwood's *American Sniper*, Stuart Klawans praises the Iwo Jima films before zeroing in: ' People want *American Sniper* to come from the Clint Eastwood who directed *Unforgiven*, but it's made by the guy who talked to a chair at the 2012 Republican National Convention." This is why Elvis Thao relishes having shot "Clint."

The invisible Obama points back, however, to the most redeeming feature of *Gran Torino*. As the Hmong critics have argued, the film offers no Hmong voice. But at least their chairs are not empty. The Hmong are visible. Though Schein and Thoj gently accuse the young Hmong actors of equivocating, still they cite those actors' saying "that despite egregious malportrayals, *Gran Torino*'s focus on Hmong is unprecedented, that it is an opening, with a potential to make formerly untutored audiences curious to learn more about who the Hmong are" (41). Visibility may not be voice, and the years since *Gran Torino* have not witnessed a surge in Hmong media presence. Nor does *Gran Torino* partake of the majestic achievement of the Iwo Jima films. But it is also not the racial equivalent of *The Birth of a Nation* (1915). If this seems like faint praise, it should be noted that Spielberg opens *Empire of the Sun* with a narration that, even as it condemns the Japanese for waiting outside Shanghai for their attack on Pearl Harbor, gently describes the Westerners settling there "to live as they had lived since the British came here in the 19th century and built in the image of their own country . . . built banking, houses, hotels, offices, churches and homes that might have been uprooted from Liverpool or Surrey." Thus *Gran Torino*, like the Iwo Jima films but unlike Spielberg's film of an Asian war, at least recognizes the racial injustices of American incursions in Asia. Eastwood's solutions are not new or enlightened enough for the evolving needs of Asian Americans—may even aggravate existing problems—but at least he knows that the world demands solutions.

Notes

1. I use the first-person pronoun here and elsewhere because I am Japanese American.
2. For a sampling of revisionist histories of the Pacific War and its aftermath, see John Dower, *War Without Mercy: Race and Power in the Pacific War*, Pantheon, 1986; Yoshikuni Igarashi, *Bodies of Memory: Narratives of War in Postwar Japanese Culture, 1945–1970*, Princeton UP, 2000; and Lisa Yoneyama, *Hiroshima Traces: Time, Space, and the Dialectics of Memory*, U of California P, 1999. For populist revisionism, see Studs Terkel, *"The Good War": An Oral History of World War Two*, Pantheon Books, 1984. Senator Hollings told an anti-Japanese joke referencing the "mushroom cloud" of the atomic bomb. See "Japanese React Angrily to Hollings Remark," *New York Times*, 5 Mar. 1992: www.nytimes.com/1992/03/05/world/japanese-react-angrily-to-hollings-remark.html.
3. For an analysis of Malick's film, see my essay "The Greatest Generation Steps Over *The Thin Red Line*" in *The Cinema of Terrence Malick: Poetic Visions of America*, 2nd ed., edited by Hannah Patterson, Wallflower, 2007, pp. 141–51.
4. See Martin Edwin Andersen, "Flags of Their *Step*fathers? Race and Culture in the Context of Military Service and the Fight for Citizenship," in *Eastwood's Iwo Jima: Critical Engagements with* Flags of Our Fathers *and* Letters from Iwo Jima, edited by Anne Gjelsvik and Rikke Schubart, Wallflower, 2013. Andersen frequently cites Kenneth William Townsend's *World War II and the American Indian*, U of New Mexico P, 2000.
5. Another racial irony passes unnoticed in Eastwood's film. Hayes came from the Gila River Reservation, and in 1942, the year he enlisted in the US Marines, Japanese Americans living on the West Coast were removed by the US government to concentration camps in the interior West, and one of those camps was located at Gila River. In an irony of marketing, the DVD of *Letters from Iwo Jima* advertises the film *American Pastime*, a baseball story set in a Utah concentration camp in which Japanese Americans were imprisoned during the world war.
6. I am aware that Steven Spielberg is a producer of both Iwo Jima films, and that, as another producer, Robert Lorenz, says in a DVD feature, DreamWorks bought

rights to James Bradley's book, and only later did Spielberg offer the project to Eastwood.

7. Eastwood does not show the shooting of the dog. The sound of a gunshot is enough.

8. I recall watching Steven E. Ambrose saying on a cable show in the early 2000s that use of the atomic bomb was justified by the "fact" that Japanese civilians, including children, had been trained to kill invading American soldiers with even simple household items. I asked my mother, who was in her early teens in Tokyo in 1945, whether she had been so trained; and she said that she knew no one who had been. Her evidence may be scant, but I would argue that it is no less anecdotal than Ambrose's and, further, that it is not informed by racial stereotypes.

Works Cited

Bradley, James, with Ron Powers. *Flags of Our Fathers.* 2000. Bantam, 2006.

Empire of the Sun. Directed by Steven Spielberg, Warner Bros., 1987.

Flags of Our Fathers. Directed by Clint Eastwood, Warner Bros., 2006.

Gourlie, John M., and Leonard Engel. "*Gran Torino*: Showdown in Detroit, Shrimp Cowboys, and a New Mythology." *New Essays on Clint Eastwood*, edited by Leonard Engel, U of Utah P, 2012, pp. 266–76.

Gran Torino. Directed by Clint Eastwood, Malpaso, 2008.

Jalao, Ly Chong. "Looking *Gran Torino* in the Eye." *Journal of Southeast Asian American Education and Advancement*, vol. 5, article 15.

Klawans, Stuart. "American Shooter." *The Nation.* 11 Feb. 2015, www.thenation.com/article/american-shooter/?print=1.

Letters from Iwo Jima. Directed by Clint Eastwood, Warner Bros., 2006.

McBride, Debbie, and Lourdes Shahamiri. Reviews of *Gran Torino. Contemporary Justice Review*, vol. 14, no. 3, Sept. 2011, pp. 359–64.

Schein, Louisa, and Va-Megn Thoj. "*Gran Torino*'s Boys and Men with Guns: Hmong Perspectives." *Hmong Studies Journal*, vol. 10, no. 1, pp. 1–52.

Ward, Annalee R. "*Gran Torino* and Moral Order." *Christian Scholar's Review*, vol. 40, no. 4, Summer 2011, pp. 375–92.

7

Captain of My Soul
Inspiration in Eastwood's Films

John M. Gourlie

n "The Eastwood Experience," a short included in the bonus material for the film *Hereafter*, Eastwood himself remarks, "A story's happening here. The story's the king." I would like to suggest that a key element of Eastwood's storytelling is inspiration, both in *Hereafter* and elsewhere, even though that might not be the first quality most people would think about when any given Eastwood film is mentioned. The point is most clear in *Invictus* where inspiration is itself one of the film's major themes. The chief character. Nelson Mandela, seeks to inspire the Springbok rugby team to win the World Cup for South Africa. Mandela works primarily through the team's captain Francois Pienaar. At a key moment in the competition, Mandela hands Pienaar a copy of the poem "Invictus," a poem that has inspired Mandela himself to persevere in his darkest hours. The most famous lines from the poem are about a courageous stance amid life's punishing circumstances: "My head is bloody, but unbowed." Whatever "the Menace of the years," it "finds, and shall find, me unafraid." The poet roots that courage in his "unconquerable soul." Even in the face of death, life's final "Horror," he concludes, "I am the master of my fate: / I am the captain of my soul" (Henley).

Like the poem, Eastwood's storytelling emanates inspiration—not only in the form of the courage to meet the circumstances of one's life, but also in many other ways that touch the heart and soul. So in quite different ways, inspiration flows from four of Eastwood's films in particular: *Hereafter* (2010), *The Bridges of Madison County* (1995), *Gran Torino* (2008), and *Invictus* (2009). In *Gran Torino*, the priest specifically raises the issue of the meaning of our lives (and deaths) in his funeral sermons. Although not so explicitly identified in the dialogue, I would suggest that the other films we are discussing share life's meaning as their context too. For, directly or indirectly, Eastwood is exploring the meaning of his characters' lives in his storytelling—and by extension, the meaning of our lives. To see how Eastwood does so, we might group the films in pairs. *Hereafter* and *The Bridges of Madison County* deal with love—especially in the personal realm of how you deal with those who love you. *Gran Torino* and *Invictus* deal with love as well, but do so in a broader context of social and racial politics—how you deal with those who do not love you, in the main because of your race or ethnic identity. Whatever their differences, each film places love at the center of life's meaning, but it does so in the very specific vocabulary of its own story.

Hereafter—With the Touch of a Hand

In their separate ways, *The Bridges of Madison County* and *Hereafter* each transport us out of the confines of everyday life. *Hereafter* does so by virtue of a unique subject matter that places us at the very boundary between life and death. The French journalist Marie Lelay (Cécile de France) experiences this boundary quite literally when she steps over it into death during the recent Indonesian tsunami, only to be brought back to life by rescuers administering mouth-to-mouth resuscitation. The American psychic George Lonegan (Matt Damon) repeatedly crosses this boundary in intuitive flashes that allow him to communicate with "the Dead." The English schoolboy Marcus (Frankie and George McLaren) desperately seeks to communicate across this barrier with his twin brother, Jason, who was recently killed in a car accident. Starting as separate vignettes, the stories of these three characters spiral progressively closer until they intersect in London so that each character gains what he or she most wants. Marie and George find love in each other while Marcus communicates with Jason through George's gifts as a medium. As their paths cross, the spell of isolation each character has been living under is broken. The grief that Marcus experiences isolates him from his schoolmates and foster-care parents. The lingering effects of the near-death experience (NDE) that Marie underwent increasingly isolate her from her job as a star TV journalist and from her producer/lover, Didier (Thierry Neuvic). George's psychic abilities isolate him from the human beings around him, for even a casual hand contact can produce an intuitive flash through which he sees hidden family secrets. George's potential romance with Melanie (Bryce Dallas Howard) collapses, for example, when she pushes him into doing a reading and her father's abuse of her surfaces. Each of the characters becomes isolated from the immediate community around him or her. The unconventional drama of their lives removes them from the shared meanings ordinary social interactions would otherwise confer on them. Instead, they are each launched on an individual quest to find whatever hidden meaning life might hold for them—a meaning that must come from sources other than the commonplace, everyday interactions with family and the surrounding community.

Synchronicity, in the Jungian sense, is a major component of the inspiration in *Hereafter*. The structure of the film provides a map of the synchronicity. The film moves in repeated cycles of three vignettes each, one vignette for each character—Marie, George, and Marcus. Each turn of the cycle draws the characters into an ever-tighter circle until their paths finally cross. The characters start out widely separated: Marie first in Indonesia and then in Paris, George in San Francisco, and Marcus in London. But as the cycles of three vignettes progress, all three characters converge on London. Marie comes to promote her newly published book, George comes to escape from his life as a psychic, and Marcus is, of course, already there. They then all arrive at the London Book Fair: Marcus to visit his older foster brother Ricky who is working as a guard at the venue, George to attend a reading of Charles Dickens, and Marie to promote her book, *Hereafter: A Conspiracy of Silence*, about death, dying, and the NDE. As the vignettes circle ever closer, Marcus has the perseverance to stand vigil outside George's hotel room, and George has the compassion to reverse his ban on psychic readings for Marcus's sake. Even closer, Marcus calls George with the name of Marie's hotel. George writes her a personal letter. Marie reads the letter in her hotel room. Paths cross, destinies unite, life's promise unfolds. Marcus reunites with his mother at the rehab center. Marie meets George in the designated outdoor café. Synchronicity happens for Marcus, Marie, and George.

Visually, the glimpse into the hereafter is represented by a flash of white light. Sometimes there are blurred figures in the light, especially in the moments of Marie's near-death experience. For George, the very brief flashes represent his psychic contact, generally with the spirits of those who have passed on. George's flashes occur in a sustained pattern throughout the film, especially when he touches someone's hand, even in accidental contact. So the white light is an experience Marie and George share from the beginning. It is a visual clue that they will somehow be drawn together. It is also a strong visual expression of the hereafter's power both to compel attention and to isolate.

Various other motifs connect the vignettes. The lives of Marcus, Marie, and George contain certain pictures that both characterize them and provide subtle strands to unify the different vignettes. Marcus and Jason's photographic portrait is the most obvious. The photograph tracks Marcus's descent into misery as he first gives it to his mother as a gift and then carries it with him into a foster home after losing his twin to death and his mother to rehab. Likewise, outside her apartment, Marie passes large posters of her image promoting her and her TV show. Later at the book fair, we see a large poster promoting her as the author of her book. Similarly, family photos hanging on the wall of George's apartment figure in a conversation with Melanie, as does a photograph of Charles Dickens. Each of the characters is also characterized by items of clothing. Marcus wears Jason's baseball hat as a link to his dead twin. George dons gloves for his meeting with Marie to shield him from an accidental destructive psychic contact. Marie is notably associated with dressing, at the very beginning of the film and later before her parting dinner with Didier, both turning points in her journey. Finally, all of the characters are associated with rooms that express their isolation—none more so than George. He is seen after an encounter looking out the window, eating alone, or lying alone listening to recordings of Dickens. Usually, he is shown in deep shadow, especially when doing a reading—a stark contrast to the flash of white light in the psychic experiences themselves. Pictures, clothing, rooms—these are the vestiges of ordinary life, but that ordinary life has gone dead for the film's characters.

The moment of inspiration occurs in the final scenes where the characters' separate quests merge. Compassion wins out in George when he relents and grants Marcus a reading. Jason's communication with Marcus points Marcus to independence from his twin, to an acceptance of his own maturity and individuality. Although as a sign of this Marcus must stop wearing Jason's baseball cap, Jason meaningfully affirms that they are united as "one cell, one person." As a gesture of gratitude, Jason supplies George with the name of Marie's hotel. The letter George writes her demonstrates a new openness in George, albeit he is writing to someone he hopes will understand him. When George sees Marie in the outdoor café, he experiences another psychic flash. Only this time, it is a flash forward, not a flash backward. And it is not the momentary flash with blurry figures we have seen previously. The flash forward is a clear and extended image of George and Marie uniting in a kiss, with a significant close-up of their fingers intertwining as they join hands. The camera further unites them as it circles around them, as if caught up in the rapture of the loving moment. Compassion, kindness, gratitude, openness, union and reunion, renewal, love—life's blessings flood back into the characters' lives, and into ours insofar as we are attuned to the film.

The rapturous kiss is the emotional breakthrough point. In it, the film's emotion and inspiration soar to their highest pitch. The circling of the camera around the couple's embrace not only expresses the ecstatic swirl of their joy, but it also suggests that the cycles of the film's vignettes converge in this climactic moment. All the momentum of the film's dramatic energy explodes into this moment of fulfillment and promise, captured in a kissing embrace—heaven transfigures earth.

Eastwood's dictum "The story's the king" applies here. For the transformation of emotions signals a shift in felt realities. This moment happily reverses the chief polarities of George's life. It has been more of a curse than a blessing to have a foot in both worlds—ordinary reality and the hereafter. The film fully transmutes that curse in the climactic vision where he unites with Marie in a loving embrace. Immediately thereafter, he is able to remove his gloves and touch Marie's hand in greeting—an extraordinarily charged "you had me at hello" moment.

In the electricity of this moment lies the film's strongest argument and deepest inspiration. Perhaps we are intrigued by the film's depiction of an afterlife and the possibility of communicating with those who have passed over into it. For as most of us know it, life has many deep pits. High on that list is not only the fear of our own death but also our grief at the loss of our loved ones to death. We have neither Marie's near-death experience nor George's psychic abilities to assure us of continued existence in an afterlife. While some of us might find reassurance in our religion and our faith in its teachings, the film takes a secular approach to these questions. Most of the information on the NDE, for instance, is given by Dr. Rousseau when Marie interviews her at the hospice in its beautiful mountain setting. Dr. Rousseau prefaces her commentary by saying that she began as an atheist, but, contrary to her expectations, she found compelling evidence of the NDE and the hereafter in her work with the dying.[1] Paradoxically, knowing this, as Dr. Rousseau, Marie, and George do, makes one into more of a pariah than a prophet. And, like Marcus, if we search for this knowledge, we are most likely to run into a gauntlet of quacks, charlatans, and con artists. But, remarkably, the film treats Marie's NDE and George's communication with the departed as genuine. They are a given in Marie's and George's lives. Insofar as we join them emotionally in their visionary kiss, our realities shift too. Their reality and their experience/knowledge become our reality and our experience/knowledge. The emotional power of their kiss validates that reality in our hearts. The story is the king. It speaks to us of the meaning of life and death, but it speaks through the heart. The word it speaks of meaning and of reality is its visionary kiss.

The Bridges of Madison County—But Once in a Lifetime

Like *Hereafter*, *The Bridges of Madison County* suspends us in a loving moment set apart from the daily context in which it occurs. For four days, *Bridges* envelops us in the cocoon of a life-altering love that transpires in the midst of rural Iowa farmland and its traditional small-town mores. But it is a love that stands apart because of its secrecy, its brevity, and its intensity. As the punishing ostracism experienced by Lucy Redfield, the town's scarlet-letter woman, illustrates, the love between Robert Kincaid (Clint Eastwood) and Francesca Johnson (Meryl Streep) violates the mores of the community. While the covered bridges of Madison County are quite literal and Robert is there to photograph them for *National Geographic*, the love between Francesca and Robert acts as a kind of covered bridge that leads them across the Rubicon boundaries of their lives into a secret Eden. Their secret love is only revealed years later after Francesca has died. Among Francesca's effects, her adult children—Michael (Victor Slezak) and Carolyn (Annie Corley)—first discover evidence of Robert's existence, and then they read Francesca's journals, which detail her love affair with Robert. The frame tale that depicts the children's discovery of their mother's love affair serves as a crucial lens to view the story through. For when the story of Robert and Francesca's love unfolds before them, it transforms their lives in a way that confirms the continuing validity and power of that love.

Initially, Michael and Carolyn respond to their mother's request to be cremated with shock and refusal. Their views are the views of small-town

Iowa, the community they grew up in where everyone is buried—not "cremated." The mother's request makes them suspect that she has lost her mind, or, as Michael sputters in exasperation, "it's not Christian," so maybe "it's an Italian thing." How much more their sensibilities are shocked by the discovery of their mother's love affair: "Who knew that, in between bake sales, my mother was Anaïs Nin?" Robert's letters and Francesca's journals lead to the voice-overs and the extended flashbacks that constitute the central story of the film. Early on, their voices are incantatory, evoking the mystical power of their romance. Robert in a letter: "We're on separate roads. . . . I look through the lens of my camera and you're there. We're moving toward one another." Francesca in her journal: over the years, "one's fears subside. To be known becomes more important." Symbolically, the key that opens the mother's wooden chest opens into the deepest knowledge of who she has been—the story that has lived inside her for much of her life now emblemized in her remaining effects: Robert's camera, bracelet, and book; her cross, "wedding dress," letters, and journals.

Much of that story traces an argument between the rooted, small-town Iowa ways represented by Francesca's life and the wandering, "citizen of the world" ways represented by Robert's life. In evaluating their lives, Francesca praises the virtues of her farm life: people are quiet, they are nice, "they help each other out." But she has a major reservation: "It's not what I dreamed of as a girl." By his artistic life, but more essentially by the very nature of his being, Robert speaks to those dreams. It's as though he picked Francesca's dreams up by having stopped at Bari, her hometown in Italy and the place where she had earlier met her husband Richard (Jim Haynie). It's as though—in some behind-the-scenes dream world—time rewinds, Robert is placed on an equal footing with Richard, and Francesca again becomes the young woman she was back in that café by the railroad and church in Bari, the café where Robert also sat. And some parallel destiny has unfolded that brought Robert across all the world's paths to Francesca's home in rural Iowa.

In some mystical way, the possibilities of this other life ignite. Robert is the insertion point for the unspoken, dormant romance and possibility Francesca felt life might have contained but that had seemingly passed her by. Amid the romantic freedoms Robert embodies and gives voice to, the banked fires of erotic passion smolder into flames once more. He reenvisions her life, her home, and the countryside. He repeatedly sees the farmland as "beautiful" rather than dull and ordinary. When Francesca says she lives "nowhere," he sees the value: "This is your home. It's not nowhere." Later, he affirms her own depths as he tells her she is "anything but a simple woman." He reopens the doors to her life's possibilities: "I embrace the mystery." He invokes the romance of life—he is enthralled by the "beauty and magic" of Madison County: "It appeals to my Irish ancestry." After their first dinner together, he toasts "To ancient evenings and distant music" with his brandy.

In the evening of the second dinner, the romance of physical embrace, erotic fires, and soul-fusing passion consume the couple. They unfurl in a dance scene that is depicted in as lushly romantic a manner as anything in Eastwood's films. As they dance, Robert and Francesca gracefully move into union as a couple. Although darkened for night, the lighting has been warmed.[2] Soft, slow music plays on the radio, the lyrics expressive of their emotions intertwining: "If you could see the magic, if you could see too, there would be no tragic, in all my dreams of you." The inevitable first kiss comes but with such initial hesitancy and skittishness that it expresses all the vulnerability and uncertainty—even innocence—exposing oneself to a new love entails. But, defenses dropped, the floodgates of love open.

The film depicts the two days of romance in richly lyrical scenes of pic-nicking by the covered bridge, dancing at a jazz bar, and lovemaking in the nights. Both Francesca and Robert comment on their encounter. Francesca especially needs to understand what is happening to her and what it means, for Francesca can be destroyed in every way that matters to her by the affair. Robert realizes this too as he witnesses how the town treats Lucy Redfield in the luncheonette. But as they walk across a covered bridge within their lives into a landscape of love, Robert and Francesca come to perceive more and more deeply what that journey is. For Francesca, Robert's love grants her access to a greater and truer being. Lying together in a candle lighted bath, Francesca experiences a deeper, truer identity: "I had thoughts about him I hardly knew what to do with, and he read every one. Whatever I wanted, he gave himself up to, and in that moment everything I knew to be true about myself was gone. I was acting like another woman, yet I was more myself than ever before." But Francesca's doubts surface in multiple ways. Can she experience this love so fully that it becomes the equivalent of a lifetime? In the jazz bar, she wonders: "I don't know if I can do this. . . . cram a whole lifetime between now and Friday."

Even more, Francesca has doubts that Robert is a full partner in this compressed lifetime of love. At breakfast of their last day together, she wonders what the "routines" of their life might be once Robert has departed. Do they write? Is he going to be saying the same things to some Romanian housewife a few months from now? Feeling the way she feels about Robert, Francesca demands, "I just have to know the truth." Somewhere along the way, Robert has been going through the same transformation Francesca has. Coming along his own path, he has become a full partner: "If I've done anything to make you feel this isn't new for me. . . ." The experience is as unprecedented and as surprising for Robert as it has been for Francesca. It endows his life with a new meaning. All his career as a photographic wanderer has but led him to her doorstep: "When I think of why I make pictures, the only reason that I come up with just seems that I've been making my way here. It seems right now that all I've ever done in my life has been making my way here to you."

The garden of the house may grow many kinds of love, but covered-bridge love is not a compatible or sustainable variety. Both Robert and Francesca realize this, but they have different remedies. Robert wants Francesca to come away with him. Francesca realizes that her leaving will destroy everything—even the love in whose name they would be running away. Robert asserts the claim of love: "Do you think this happens to anyone? We're hardly two separate people now. Some search for it all their lives. Others don't even believe it exists." Francesca agrees, "You never think love like this is going to happen to you." But she realizes, "If we leave, we lose it." Her solution: "We have to hold on to it somewhere inside." Robert realizes he has lost the argument. He leaves holding on to the truth of his love, if not to Francesca herself: "I'll only say this one time. I've never said it before. This kind of certainty comes but once in a lifetime."

Earlier in the film, Francesca jokes that she is going to have some iced tea and split the atom. In the heart-wrenching door-handle scene, she does split the atom; she splits the emotional union she has with Robert, who is standing drenched in the street—alone, miserable, and now bereft of his covered-bridge experience save in memory and photograph. That this is the most emotionally powerful scene in the film testifies to the "reality" of their love. Although all seems lost in this separation, their split-atom parting fuels the nuclear fires of Robert's and Francesca's hearts. Their inner landscapes have changed. The very source of meaning in their lives has changed.

The structure of the film is crucial in demonstrating the ongoing power of their love. Scenes of Francesca's adult children discussing and reacting to her journals are intercut with the flashbacks portraying the actual love affair. Contact with their mother's love for Robert transforms their lives too. At the end of the film, they address the weaknesses in their own marriages. To his surprised wife, Betty, Michael reaffirms his commitment, "I want to make you happy more than anything." Likewise, seeking deeper integrity in her own self and in her marriage, Carolyn calls her husband, Steve, and says, "We have to talk," and lets him know she will be staying at the farmhouse for the time being. To this point, the children's lives are the vindication of Francesca's choice of her life of "details" with her husband, Richard. She has been the steady rock that has enabled them to grow thus far. But at this juncture, it is her love for Robert that brings them renewed inspiration in their own lives.

The fount of love at the center of Francesca's inner world transforms the world of detail in the end. Michael and Carolyn move from shock and refusal into renewed love and willing acceptance. They realize that Frances-ca's stance has honored and preserved both worlds. She has loved and cared for Richard in the world of detail until his dying day. But it was the power of her inner love for Robert that ultimately gave her the strength to sustain that life of detail. Her children come to realize this, and they honor her request to "give Robert what's left of me" by lofting her ashes into the air from the covered bridge that was the scene and genesis of their coming to know one another. Francesca has wondered in her journal about sharing her story: "Could anyone else have seen the beauty of it?"—the love whose "mystery is pure and absolute" and whose ways "won't obey our expectations." By the end of the film, Francesca's children have seen the beauty of her love, sustained in both worlds of her life, but especially as illuminated by her inner, covered-bridge world of love for Robert.

In Robert and Francesca, the film portrays the archetype of soul-mate love. The covered bridge of their love becomes a star gate. Love's power shoots through what starts as an ordinary encounter and transfigures it into a life-altering experience of such beauty and splendor that it transports the couple into a higher dimension of existence. Early on, we briefly glimpse Francesca sitting on her porch reading the poetry of W. B. Yeats. Perhaps we are reminded of Yeats's love for Maud Gonne. Beyond that are Romeo and Juliet, Sir Tristan and Lady Isolde, Catherine and Heathcliff, and a host of popular romance-novel couples. And further beyond that—soul mates or not—an endless stream of couples, real or fictional, whose love is denied, blocked, unfulfilled; or has simply failed to show up in their lives. We can all find ourselves somewhere on the spectrum if we care to look. The story of Eastwood's film allows us to look and, if we choose, to be inspired to love at a higher level—or perhaps even at our highest level. If so, the ultimate bridge of the film is the one where we experience the power of a transfiguring love flowing through us.

Gran Torino—I've Got a Light

In *Gran Torino*, the story again proves mightier than the sermon. The story is that of Walt Kowalski (Clint Eastwood), and the sermons are those of the priest, Father Janovich (Christopher Carley). The film opens with the funeral service for Walt's wife, Dorothy, at which the priest preaches a sermon about the meaning of life and the meaning of death from a Christian perspective. As the story progresses, it becomes clear that Walt tolerates the funeral and the dinner afterward for his wife's sake, but that his heart is not in them. More the opposite: Walt growls at his grandchildren and finds no rapport with his sons. As he slips out to the porch with his dog, Daisy, an even more distinct sign of life's decline appears to him when the Hmong family next door has visitors. Walt's rejection of his Hmong neighbors is evident in his derisive comment, "How many swamp rats can fit into one room?" Then, when the priest first visits, Walt rejects his desire to watch over him, especially over his spiritual welfare. Dorothy has charged the priest with getting Walt to confession, but Walt retorts: "I confess I have no desire to confess to a boy just out of seminary." Evidence abounds of Walt being an equal-opportunity insulter. In his commentary on the world around him, Walt seems to project a democratic disdain for all, and on the surface many of his words are those of actual prejudice and racism. Yet, as the film reveals, Walt's racism exists at some practical level—often grinding—of a functional social recognition of tribal identities. But it does not exist at the level of soul rot.

For the primary action of the film follows the arc of Walt's heart as it inscribes his increasing acceptance of Thao (Bee Vang) as a "son" and of the Hmong Lor family next door as his adopted family. With this growing acceptance, Walt's language of ethnic insult increasingly assumes the kind of dramatic irony it has with the barber Martin (John Carroll Lynch). Here the ethnic insult signifies deep friendship within a macho code that limits the forthright expression of emotion—especially in words of open love and affection. But in their first encounter, Thao's attempt to steal Walt's Gran Torino as an initiation rite into his cousin's gang ends in Walt's discovery of him in the garage and a wild shot being fired accidentally. When Thao's mother forces him to offer restitution for the family shame by working for Walt, Walt slowly begins to change his attitude toward "Toad" and his family. Walt's involvement is accelerated when he unwittingly rescues Thao from impressment by the Hmong gang in the famous "get off my lawn" confrontation—and, more wittingly, when he gallantly rescues Sue (Ahney Her) from harassment or worse at the hands of a black gang on the nearby streets. Walt is recognized by the Hmong community as a "hero," and he is inundated with gifts of food delivered by the neighborhood Hmong mothers and grandmothers. When invited to a Lor family celebration of a child's birth on his own birthday, Walt comes to appreciate their food, if also to encounter some of their different cultural ways regarding direct eye contact, touching a child's head, and smiling. But he is also able to assert his own cultural code as an old-school American male when he adjusts a wobbly dryer in the basement: "I fix things."

At the same dinner, deeper troubles raise their heads. When the Hmong shaman priest does a life reading of Walt, he gives him the diagnosis: "You have no happiness in life. You are not at peace." As the film develops, the theme of personal peace is elaborated in the continuing conversations between the Catholic priest and Walt. It becomes clear that the killing Walt participated in during combat in Korea still haunts him. Coupled with this inner malady is a deadly physical affliction that shows up in coughing fits causing Walt to spit up blood. Although not named, the diagnosis he most likely has received from Dr. Chu when he visits the clinic is lung cancer. Offsetting these maladies is Walt's renewed engagement with his Hmong neighbors and with life. It is one that no doubt surprises Walt as he comes to recognize, "I have more in common with these gooks than with my own spoiled family."

Walt's primary project, as he announces it to Thao, is to "man you up." Beyond the scenes of neighborhood repairs—roof and gutter repair, debris and brush cleanup, stump removal—during Thao's restitution work, scenes of neighborly help arise. Thao needs Walt's help to repair the kitchen sink and ceiling fan. Walt cannot make it up the cellar stairs with his old freezer without Thao's help. Walt introduces Thao into the world of tools. Walt has a lifetime collection of tools in his garage, but he starts Thao off with the three that can fix a majority of the problems: WD-40, vise grips, and duct tape. Even more, Walt seeks to save Thao from the "women's work" he is doing (dishes and gardening) by setting him up in a construction job, a man's work. Walt fronts Thao the necessary tools and, with the barber's help, teaches him how to talk like a man. Walt even offers Thao the use of his Gran Torino to take "Miss Yum Yum" out on a date. Seeing beyond his rough exterior, Sue affectionately recognizes Walt's true nature: "You're a good man, Wally." She even expresses something much deeper when she wishes that her actual father had been more like Walt—perhaps recognizing that Walt is beginning to play that role in her life.

But the destructive forces represented by the Hmong gang tragically interrupt Walt's plans. Earlier, when Spider and his Hmong gang cruise through the neighborhood, Walt realizes, "This kid [Thao] doesn't stand a chance." The "get off my lawn" moments escalate disastrously when Walt seeks to "fix things" after the gang has assaulted Thao on his way home from work, stealing his tools and branding his cheek with a cigarette. Walt severely beats one member of the Hmong gang both to exact vengeance for the assault on Thao and to scare the gang into leaving him alone. But the Hmong gang's reprisal greatly escalates the cycle of violence when they machine-gun the Lor home and then beat and rape Sue. In rage, frustration, and self-blame, Walt punches his fists through his glass kitchen cabinets, bloodying his own knuckles. And sitting in silence, he plots how to fix things beyond the cycles of vengeance that have only proved more and more destructive.

The great transformation that has been taking place in Walt over the course of the film reaches a culmination point in the scenes where he plots his next move. One sign is that the "no peace" burden now applies to Thao and Sue: "Thao and Sue are never going to find peace as long as that gang is around." Another sign is Walt's changed attitude toward the priest; he offers him a beer and says, "Call me Walt." The priest and Walt are united in an anger at what the Hmong gang has done, and they both seek a solution, if along different paths. As one of the many ritual preparations for his death (haircut, new suit, bath, lawn mowing), Walt goes to the priest for confession. Exiting the confession, Walt responds to the priest's benediction, "Go in peace," with the words, "Oh, I am at peace." While some of this peace does come from confessing his "sins" (kissing a woman at a Christmas party, failing to pay a tax, and not being close to his sons), Walt seems to have found a greater peace centered on deeper issues in his life. In some way not fully explained, the sacrifice of his life on behalf of his Hmong "family" seems to be balancing the PTSD guilt he experiences over killing Asians in the Korean War. This guilt seems to be set apart in Walt's psyche. He sees it as involving horrors beyond the priest's knowledge, and he does not confess it as a major sin. It seems to live in some other part of Walt's soul, and the iconography of Walt's death suggests that higher powers than those of the priest are involved in the resolution.

The final confrontation has aspects of a showdown in a Western. After the police have left, Walt calls the Hmong gang out in a magnificent tirade of personal and ethnic insult that includes the phrases "shrimp dicks" and "miniature cowboys." Walt gestures in the last of a series of pantomime shootings with his "finger pistol." Because he has backed these gestures up with his army rifle or his .45 caliber pistol before, we assume it is a gun when he makes his "draw" from beneath his jacket. Instead, he "draws" his 1st Cavalry cigarette lighter. He does so in conjunction with his utterance, "I've got a light." When the Hmong gang shoots Walt in a hail of bullets, he falls in a crucifixion pose, his lighter released from his hand while blood trickles down his wrist. The powerful mythic context suggests larger meanings. The climactic shootout, as in a Western, suggests that order is being restored and some kind of justice is being done. The personal symbolism of the 1st Cavalry cigarette lighter, which invokes Walt's Korean War guilt, perhaps suggests that sacrificing his life for Thao not only gives meaning to it, but that dying for an Asian somehow also atones for his own killing of Asians in the past. Walt draws the spiritual power of religious imagery into his own person. The iconography of the light and the crucifixion pose suggests some deeper spiritual way in which right and truth have been reestablished, sin has been forgiven, and grace has been bestowed.

The final scenes sustain the elevated level of things. The funeral service for Walt rounds out the film's structure as it echoes his wife's funeral with which the film began. Honoring Walt, Thao and Sue appear movingly in formal Hmong ceremonial dress. In his sermon, the priest expresses his gratitude for how much Walt has taught him about the meaning of life and death. In his will, Walt leaves his house to the church because his wife would like that, and the Gran Torino to Thao—because Walt would like that. In making Thao his true heir, Walt expresses the love of a father for his true son, transcending the facts of biology with the power of personal love. In taking Thao as a son, Walt enacts a deep dream of American democratic possibility in which races unite beyond bloodlines. When the film evokes the Western genre, it sets Walt's final actions in the context of our national myth, but it does so in a way that moves that mythology toward a level of racial harmony seldom attained by that genre in the past. When the film evokes Christian symbolism, it does so to suggest the presence of a transcendent spiritual power independent of specific doctrine. The crucifixion pose and the invocation of the light symbolically suggest that the power of spirit has touched Walt's death with sufficient benevolence and grace to cleanse and uplift his soul. At its very end, the film gently lifts into music. We hear Walt's voice singing the first stanza of the "Gran Torino Song" while Thao drives the car along the lakefront. Here Walt's gruff voice and the language of the film—formerly Walt's casual insult or masked affection in a dialogue of ethnic and racial epithets—are raised into the blessing of song. At whatever level one may choose—nurturing personal love, the unifying bonds of community, the grace of spiritual presence, or the gift of song—inspiration is there for the receiving.

Invictus—When Only Greatness Will Do

Inspiration is at the very heart of *Invictus*. The figure of Nelson Mandela (Morgan Freeman) embodies it, and he radiates it to all around him. The chief story of inspiration in the film centers on Mandela's engagement with the national rugby team, the Springboks, and particularly its captain, Francois Pienaar (Matt Damon). The tale is a true one, and it involves the fate of the nation of South Africa, newly emerged from apartheid and ruled for the first time by a member of the majority black population. Far more than the film itself indicates, it was a perilous historical moment. For the right-wing forces—both black and white—threatened to embroil the fragile democracy in civil war. Both Inkatha, the Zulu right-wing movement, and Volksfront, the Boer movement, threatened to plunge the country into violence. For the white Boer population, three symbols of apartheid days were especially treasured; two of those were their old flag and their national anthem, "Die Stem." The third symbol was the Springbok rugby team with their green and gold colors.[3] All three converged in rugby matches, and rugby especially was a deeply valued expression of the Boer culture. So in addressing himself to the Springbok rugby team, Mandela was communicating symbolically to the white population as a whole. The Springboks became an unusual but strong channel to communicate that he sought peace rather than vengeance—and as great a measure of national unity between the black population and the white population as could be achieved.

Several scenes in the beginning of the film indicate how great a gamble this Springbok "language" might be. At the very opening, for instance, we see the contrast between the well-to-do white youths playing rugby and the impoverished black youngsters playing soccer. As both rush to the fences at the edge of their playing fields when Nelson Mandela speeds by in a motorcade, the black youngsters cheer wildly while the white youths look on somberly. The white coach says, "It's that terrorist Mandela; they let him out.

Remember this day, boys. This is the day your country went to the dogs." In Francois Pienaar's family home, his father expresses the white fear about the blacks: they will "take our jobs and drive us into the sea." This mistrust is also expressed in the newspaper headline seen by Mandela and his security detail on their early morning walk: "He can win an election, but can he run a country?"—to which Mandela responds, "It's a legitimate question," speaking from an inner wellspring of peace, balance, and fairness none around him possess.

In instance after instance, Mandela must inspire an individual or a group to act in a manner that transcends the fears and negative expectations that otherwise govern their behavior. In almost every such encounter, Mandela speaks in words that transform the situation. These words come from a deep inner center within Mandela, seemingly his soul speaking through his heart. His words are invariably eloquent, inspiring, and filled with nobility, as is the figure of Mandela himself. Two instances occur in his first few days in office. One is the exodus of the office staff that has worked for the apartheid regime. Mandela appeals to them to stay, to "have no such fear" that they are not wanted. On the contrary, Mandela encourages them: "Do your work to the best of your ability and with a good heart" and "your country will be a shining light in the world."

The second instance concerns his bodyguards, and it cuts to the very core of the racial conflicts Mandela must make a thing of the past. When four white Special Branch officers show up to work as additional security officers for the president, Jason (Tony Kgoroge), the black head of security, goes to Mandela to protest. Jason's complaint is that these officers might be the very men who had been trying to kill them only a short time ago. Mandela's response is, "The Rainbow Nation starts here. Reconciliation starts here. Forgiveness liberates the soul. It removes fear. That is why it is such a powerful weapon." In this brief encounter, Mandela articulates the template that governs much of the action that follows. His mission is soul deep. He must find a way to liberate the souls in his nation—black and white—from the deep fears they harbor, especially of one another. The Springboks become his means of addressing and healing these fractured souls within his nation.

Mandela expands on his soul-changing template when he confronts the crisis created by the National Sports Executive Committee's vote to disband the Springboks. They have understandably voted unanimously to eliminate the Springboks, a hated symbol of the apartheid regime they are replacing. But in his argument to reverse the vote, Mandela explains how the conventional level of thinking and feeling must be raised to a higher level of consciousness:

> Our enemy is no longer the Afrikaner. They are our fellow South Africans, our partners in democracy. And they treasure Springbok rugby. If we take that away, we lose them. We prove that we are what they feared we would be. We have to be better than that. We have to surprise them with compassion, with restraint and generosity; I know, all of the things they denied us. But this is no time to celebrate petty revenge. This is a time to build our nation using every single brick available to us, even if that brick comes wrapped in green and gold.

So the continued existence of the Springboks conveys the compassion, restraint, and generosity of the Mandela government to the Afrikaner people. But the formerly oppressed that are now in power need to reach a level of grace within themselves whereby they are willing to forego revenge. They get there on Mandela's back. His aide Brenda (Adjoa Andoh) makes the risks of preserving the Springboks clear: "You're risking your political capital, you're risking your future as our leader." The courage of Mandela's leadership is in his reply: "The day I am afraid to do that is the day I am no longer fit to lead."

The next major facet in the unfolding template of leadership and inspiration involves the introductory meeting between Francois Pienaar, captain of the Springboks, and Mandela in the president's office for tea. The discussion between the two "captains" turns directly to the roots of leadership and inspiration. Mandela asks, "How do you inspire your team to do their best?" To which Francois replies, "By example. I've always thought to lead by example." Mandela continues, "That is exactly right. But how do we get them to be better than they think they can be? That is very difficult, I find. Inspiration, perhaps. How do we inspire ourselves to greatness when nothing less will do? How do we inspire everyone around us? I sometimes think it is by using the work of others." In this case, the "work of others" that Mandela wishes to use is the play of the Springboks. The greatness he wants them to rise to is winning the 1995 World Cup. The victory in sports will help inspire the nation's citizens to be better than they think they can be. During their meeting, President Mandela enlists Captain Pienaar as his partner in this endeavor to inspire the nation to greatness when only some form of greatness will do. It is not simply to fill the nation with whatever sense of greatness a prowess in rugby might bestow. Instead, Mandela seeks a level of spiritual greatness that will drain the swamps of fear, hatred, and revenge—a measure of spiritual elevation such that two races, now at war with one another, can find the ground to unite with one another in common cause.

Under Mandela's guidance, the Springboks take on the mission expressed in the motto "One Team, One Country." At first this guidance is indirect, and the Springboks are initially somewhat fitful about the new changes. They embark with grumbling, for example, on a public relations tour to offer coaching clinics in rugby to the black youngsters in the impoverished townships. Later on, Pienaar prompts them to learn the new black national anthem, "Nkosi Sikelel' iAfrica," and some players resist. But over time, the players come increasingly to recognize that they have "become more than a rugby team." Both Pienaar and Mandela articulate the changes in words that express the same thought. Pienaar: "Times change, and we need to change as well." Mandela: "If I cannot change when circumstances demand it, how can I expect others to?" The changes increasingly unify Mandela and Pienaar in the project of winning the World Cup and healing the nation.

In ways both direct and subtle, the poem "Invictus" expresses the men's growing unity. Mandela first mentions the poem in their initial meeting: "Just words, but they helped me to stand when all I wanted was to lie down." Later, as the competition for the World Cup becomes more intense, Mandela decides to visit the Springboks in practice and to give Pienaar a copy of "Invictus" that he has written out personally. He hands it to Pienaar with the words, "It has helped me through the years; I hope it helps you." Just before that, a player has given Mandela a Springbok cap, to which Mandela has responded, "I'm honored, truly honored. Your country supports you completely." With the cap, Mandela begins to don the uniform of the Springboks. In taking inspiration from him, the Springboks begin to don Mandela's spiritual mantle.

The Springboks gain deep respect for that mantle during the team's surprise visit to the prison on Robben Island before a crucial match. Many are affected by being in the same physical spaces as Nelson Mandela when he was a prisoner here for the last eighteen of his twenty-seven years of imprisonment. Although many members of the team in actuality experienced it, in the film we see the impact of Mandela's prison experience primarily through the eyes of Francois Pienaar. We see Francois measuring the confines of Nelson's cell with his arms. Later we see him stare into a trance-like vision of Mandela as a prisoner at his rock pile, and as Francois stares their eyes meet in a gaze that connects their souls. While this vision occurs, Mandela's voice intones the words of the poem "Invictus," and through these words, his soul pours into Francois. Later, we see Francois standing on his hotel balcony wondering to himself, "how [do] you spend thirty years in a tiny cell and come out ready to forgive the people who put you there?"

The team's visit drives Mandela's prison experience into the hearts of the rugby players. John Carlin's book *Invictus* underlines the intense emotional impact of the players' visit to Robben Island, and it makes clear that what the film shows happening to Francois actually happened in the deepest way to the team as a whole:

> "They [the prisoners] were happy to see us," Pienaar said. "Despite being confined here they were so obviously proud of our team. I spoke to them about our sense that we were representing the whole country now, them included, and then they sang us a song. James Small [Springbok player]—I'll never forget this—stood in a corner, tears streaming out." (Carlin 189)

Small remembered the episode:

> The prisoners not only sang for us, they gave us a cheer and I . . . I just burst into tears. . . . That was where the sense really took hold in me that I belonged to the new South Africa, and where I really got a sense of the responsibility of my position as a Springbok. There I was, hearing the applause for me, and at the same time thinking about Mandela's cell and how he spent twenty-seven years in prison and came out with love and friendship. All that washed over me, that huge realization, and the tears just rolled down my face. (Carlin 190)

As the World Cup competition continues, the symbolic exchange of the Springbok rugby cap and the poem "Invictus" gains weight as a deeper expression of how Mandela's spirit has infused the rugby players. The rugby players have become "my boys" to Mandela, the treasured human embodiment of those goals and values most dear to his heart (194). As the players become infused with Mandela's spirit, they become greater versions of themselves. In John Carlin's account, the team's manager, Morné du Plessis, makes it clear how Mandela's spirit inspired the team to win:

There was cause-and-effect connection between the Mandela factor and our performance on the field...

It was cause and effect on a thousand fronts. In players overcoming the pain barrier, in a superior desire to win, in luck going your way because you make your own luck, in all kinds of details that together or separately mark the difference between winning and losing. It all came perfectly together. Our willingness to be the nation's team and Mandela's desire to make the team the nation's team. (188)

The heart-pounding climax of this great unfolding miracle occurs, during daylong ceremonies, in the championship game of the World Cup in which the Springboks play against the New Zealand All Blacks with their unstoppable star Jonah Lomu (Zak Feaunati). Many elements converge in the miracle. But they are all encapsulated in Nelson Mandela's gesture when he appears wearing the green Springbok jersey with number "6" on its back, the jersey of the team captain, Francois Pienaar. The unity is complete. Pienaar is the rugby captain embodying Mandela's soul. In their hard-fought but clear victory, Pienaar and his Springbok team create a soaring moment of victorious joy, of racial embrace, and of unifying national glory. In one supernova moment, they make all of Mandela's dreams and visions for his country hyperreal, and they stamp them indelibly into South Africa's consciousness.

The rising arc of emotion is captured by many images but probably none so poignant as the scenes portraying the young black boy outside the stadium hovering near a police car to hear the game on the radio. The boy is treated initially with the customary hostility, suspicion, and "go away" attitude of the old South African white police. But as the game progresses, the boy is allowed to move closer and closer to the radio. By the time of the Springbok victory, the police are throwing the boy into the air in jubilation and anointing him with their caps. The boy himself is jumping and dancing at the Springbok victory—the exact opposite of black attitudes of the past in which they despised the Springboks and rooted for their opponents to win. The film shows variations of this scene throughout the stadium and particularly throughout the homes, bars, and meeting places of black South Africa. The reversal of attitudes seems all but universal throughout South Africa as the whites embrace Mandela and the blacks embrace the Springboks—all in the unifying joy of victory.

Near the beginning of the film, both Francois Pienaar and his wife

(Marguerite Wheatley) ask about Mandela, "What's he like?" The body-guard responds to Francois, "To him, no one is invisible." Later, Francois answers his wife, "He's not like anyone else I've met before." Perhaps a fuller response is encompassed in the Springbok victory if we see it as Mandela's identity writ large. To get at it, let us look at the experience of the captain (David Dukas) of the 747 that flew over the stadium just before the World Cup match. According to John Carlin, Laurie Kay (the actual captain, whom Carlin quotes in his book) had met Mandela only once when Mandela asked the captain for a favor to get his delegates into first class. Kay describes his experience:

> I'll never forget it. . . . The moment he saw me he stood up . . . and greeted me and shook my hand. It never, ever happened to me before or since with a passenger. For me it was transforming. The courtesy and respect of his gesture. . . . From that day on I was changed forever. He's a magician, no doubt about it. In my mind there is an aura about certain people. . . . Mandela has an aura of goodness. (217–18)

Carlin's book reports a similar transforming effect of Mandela's personal presence on most of those he meets face to face.

On the day of the match, Captain Kay flew the jet at only two hundred feet above the stadium—the wingspan of the jet—and at 140 knots, the slowest speed short of a stall. Because there were mountains immediately behind the stadium, Kay had to climb out at a steep angle under maximum power. Painted on the plane's underbelly was "Good Luck Bokke" (Boks). But that was not the complete message. As Kay describes the jet's climb out, "We revved up the engines, we really opened up to maximum sound and thrust so as to put as much noise and as much energy into the stadium as we could. . . . But above all I wanted us to send a message down to the stadium, that we were strong and we were going to win. And so, yes, we emptied all the power we could muster into the stadium." As Carlin observes, "Surprise and shock gave way to thunderous elation. That power Captain Kay emptied into the stadium electrified every soul present" (220–21).

The Springbok victory in the World Cup unleashes a force of joy among the South Africans—black and white—even more electrifying than the Jumbo Jet climbing steeply upward at maximum thrust two hundred feet above the heads of those in the stadium. And Nelson Mandela is, as it were, the captain unleashing this joy. So powerful is this joy that it sweeps all

South Africans—black and white, in the stadium and throughout the country—into a unifying state of euphoria. In this elevated state, if only for the moment of its duration, all the history of violence, oppression, and racial animosity is overcome. In this moment of joy, all South Africans are united as one people. It is a transcendent moment of joy and unity that exists at some miraculous level of reality—an incandescent reality of human brotherhood whose light reveals that the persistent shadows of everyday fears and discriminations are not the ironclad boundaries of darkness within which life must be lived, as much as they might seem to be so. In its consuming power, the ecstatic joy of victory annihilates all the lesser energies of life, if only for that magic moment of triumph. Though a lesser everyday reality might recede from this heightened glory, the revelation of that glory has been made. It has stamped its imprint into the annals of human consciousness. Nelson Mandela has called that revelation into being, and his soul has forged that stamp.

None bears the stamp of Mandela's soul more clearly than Francois Pienaar. In wearing Francois's Springbok jersey, Mandela symbolically states that the Springboks are now the team of all South Africa—black and white together. But with Mandela's blessing, it is Pienaar who acts to lead the nation. In the final moments of the World Cup match, for example, he rallies his team to give its greatest effort with the words: "Listen to your country. This is our destiny." The championship won, Pienaar continues to speak from the perspective of the nation. When told by a reporter that the sixty-three thousand fans in the stadium supported the team, Francois replies, "We didn't have 63,000 fans behind us. We had 43 million South Africans," meaning all the citizens—black and white—of South Africa. And finally, when Nelson Mandela presents him with the World Cup, "Francois, thank you for what you have done for our country," Francois responds, "No, Mr. President. Thank *you* for what you have done for our country." As Carlin describes the moment and as the film shows it, Morné du Plessis (observing and then commenting on that moment between Pienaar and Mandela) "saw Pienaar raise the cup high above his shoulders as Mandela, laughing, pumped his fists in the air. . . . 'I've never seen such complete joy. . . . He is looking at Francois and just, sort of, keeps laughing . . . and Francois is looking at Mandela and . . . the bond between them'" (242–43). It is the "Invictus" moment—suspended somewhere above ordinary time and achievement—in which Nelson Mandela and Francois Pienaar soar within an ecstatic realm of victory and joy, souls fused, on eagle wings that have lifted the nation into a newfound unity and common humanity—an absolutely improbable flight to all but unattainable heights.

Conclusion—Story Is the King

Eastwood has told us many a story—some as actor, some as director, and some as both. It might be that inspiration is an inherent trait in any tale where there is a hero of some sort at the center of it. Even the Dirty Harry films and the Westerns with some version of the Man with No Name offer the inspiration of an action hero who takes on long odds and deadly enemies. But I would suggest that there is a strong streak of inspiration in many of Eastwood's films and particularly in those we have just discussed—*Hereafter, The Bridges of Madison County, Gran Torino*, and *Invictus*. For in its role as king, story endows us with certain riches. Some of those riches are suggested by the poem "Invictus" whereby we are encouraged to maintain the heroic stance of being "bloodied, but unbowed." But even more, those riches, by many means, no doubt, are those that inspire us each to become, or to remain, master of our fate and captain of our soul. For in greater measure than we might suppose, Eastwood's stories speak to us—heart and soul—they speak in a language that inspires us to be that captain, and to be that captain so that the inner greatness of our spirit blazes through us with fires of such glory and power that they illuminate and transform the very lineaments of our lives.

Notes

1. A substantial literature exists supporting the validity of the near-death experience phenomenon. Scientific researchers such as Elisabeth Kubler-Ross, Raymond Moody, and Kenneth Ring have explored the subject and published numerous volumes on the NDE and its implications. An equally credentialed researcher, Brian Weiss, explores the continuity of the soul after life—indeed, through many lives—in *Many Lives, Many Masters* and his other works. Like George Lonegan in the film, the medium James Van Praagh, among others, seems to possess the ability to communicate with departed beings for the benefit of the bereaved. The most extended spiritual discussion of death that I am aware of is in Neale Donald Walsch's *Conversations with God* series, in the volume *Home with God in a Life That Never Ends*. It might also be relevant to note that Clint Eastwood himself is reported to be a longtime practitioner of meditation.

2. In the audio commentary for *Bridges*, the film's editor, Joel Cox, and its director of photography, Jack N. Green, discuss the way the lighting is controlled for emotional and other effects in the film. Meaningfully, they also observe that Eastwood was playing Robert Kincaid as himself.

3. The film *Invictus* is ultimately based on the book by John Carlin originally published in 2008 under the title *Playing the Enemy*. Where noted parenthetically, my

citations are from its reissue under the title *Invictus: Nelson Mandela and the Game That Made a Nation*.

Works Cited

The Bridges of Madison County. Directed by Clint Eastwood, performances by Eastwood and Meryl Streep, Warner Bros., 1995.

Carlin, John. *Invictus: Nelson Mandela and the Game That Made a Nation*. Penguin Books, 2009.

Cox, Joel, and Jack N. Green. Audio Commentary. *The Bridges of Madison County*. 1995. Directed by Clint Eastwood, Warner Bros., 2010, DVD.

Gran Torino. Directed by Clint Eastwood, performances by Eastwood, Bee Vang, Ahney Her, and Christopher Carley, Warner Bros., 2008.

Henley, William Ernest. "Invictus." Frontispiece for John Carlin's *Invictus: Nelson Mandela and the Game That Made a Nation*, Penguin Books, 2009.

Hereafter. Directed by Clint Eastwood, performances by Cécile de France and Matt Damon, Warner Bros., 2010.

"*Hereafter*: The Eastwood Experience." Bonus Material. *Hereafter*, Warner Bros., 2011, DVD.

Invictus. Directed by Clint Eastwood, performances by Morgan Freeman and Matt Damon, Warner Bros., 2009.

Walsch, Neale Donald. *Home with God in a Life That Never Ends*. Atria Books, 2006.

Weiss, Brian L. *Many Lives, Many Masters: The True Story of a Prominent Psychiatrist, His Young Patient, and the Past-Life Therapy That Changed Both Their Lives*, Simon and Schuster, 1988.

8

Cultural Hero-Systems in *Shane*, *Gran Torino*, and *American Sniper*

Glenda Pritchett

Central to mythologies the world over is the mythic hero. Cultural anthropologist Ernest Becker, in his 1974 Pulitzer Prize–winning book, *The Denial of Death*, describes human society as "a symbolic action system, a structure of statuses and roles, customs and rules for behavior, designed to serve as a vehicle for earthly heroism. What anthropologists call 'cultural relativity' is thus really the relativity of hero-systems the world over" (4–5). Writing in *American Scholar* in 1955, Harry Schein observed that while the mythological origins of Europe and the Far East are shrouded in the past, "the White man's America is no older than the Gutenberg Bible." Thus, the development of the novel in the eighteenth and nineteenth centuries coincided with North American westward expansion and the birth of a mythology and folklore ripe for the telling (405), one, it must be noted, that "freed the United States from a slavish imitation of Mother England" (Estleman i).

In these terms, the myth of the American West and the Western hero has created an aesthetic hero-system that has burgeoned in literature and film since the early twentieth century, and it continues in more recent cinematic endeavors that somewhat unexpectedly belie their genesis in classic Western achievements such as George Stevens's 1953 film, *Shane*, based on Jack Schaefer's 1949 novel of the same name. Of course Clint Eastwood's 1985 Western, *Pale Rider*, is heavily indebted to the film *Shane*, but, notably, so is Akira Kurosawa's 1962 samurai film, *Sanjuro*, which has been described as an "Eastern 'Western'" (Desser 54). Recently, David Sterritt identified the "Myth-movie" as a metagenre, which he defines as "centered on individual lives yet rooted in the collective American unconscious" (16), and which recurs in Eastwood's cinematic works. One can argue then that *Gran Torino* and *American Sniper*, two of Eastwood's most successful recent films with contemporary settings, in fact reflect key elements of the Western myth as portrayed in the film *Shane*. Upon careful scrutiny, it appears that Eastwood at the pinnacle of his career has not left the Western behind but rather has pressed it into service for the twenty-first century.

As recently as 2013, Michael Agresta opined that Disney's colossal flop *The Lone Ranger* marks "a decisive chapter in the sad story of how the Western was lost," and this, he argues, at a time when we need it most. After all, the Western was born in the early twentieth century and remained for much of that century "a reliable vehicle for filmmakers to explore thorny issues of American history and character," such that by the post-Vietnam era, cowboys more often than not were antiheroes. An examination of what might be called the essential Western and its appeal to filmmakers and audiences alike may allow for an enriched understanding of these exceptional Eastwood films that yet allow us to look in the mirror and see who we are as Americans, thorns and all.

Critics from Will Wright (1975) to Patrick McGee (2007) agree that "1939 initiated the 'renaissance' or 'golden age' of the Western" (McGee 39). And while not all critics share Wright's contention that the film *Shane* is "the classic of the classic Westerns" (34), there is consensus that Schaefer's novel represents the literary archetype, "the definitive formula Western" (Love 291).[1]

In Stevens's film, Shane arrives "in the summer of '89" (Schaefer 61) as an outsider, emerging on horseback from the Grand Tetons, and is first seen by Joey Starrett, the young boy who in the novel (as Bob) embodies the childhood memory of the adult narrator, while in the film he becomes a naïve observer of a complex adult world. Joe and Marian Starrett represent homesteaders seeking to legally put down roots, meaning fenced-in fields and cultivated farmland, whereas open-range ranchers represented by Rufus

Ryker and his clan are determined to maintain their rights to the open range by any means. Early in the film, Shane is revealed to have a gunfighter past that he is seeking to abandon, yet it is precisely this expertise that mesmerizes young Joey. And even though Shane is reluctant to return to his former vocation, he finds himself as the homesteaders' last hope in their confrontation with the unscrupulous cattlemen. In the end, Shane is the force that defeats the Rykers and their hired gun Stark Wilson, preserving a future for the Starretts and the way of life that they represent.[2] But the mythic hero is wounded and is not meant for this place. His exit is as providential as his entrance, and as powerful.

A central appeal of the Western, in both literature and film, is the heroic and the nature of the cultural or mythic hero. Of course, the usual attributes come to mind—courage, independence, seemingly superhuman skill—but the unique place and time must be considered as well, as Robert Mikkelsen observes: "Characters encounter situations demanding both moral and physical action, and their frontier environment allows them to act independently, guided by their senses of justice and decency" (306). Given these parameters, it is useful to consider Will Wright's "oppositional structure of the Western myth"—inside/outside, good/bad, strong/weak, and wilderness/civilization (49)[3]—as a means to examine narrative elements such as rites of initiation, the voice of the female, and the ambivalence of the mythic hero within the larger mythic structure, all of which may shed light on the Western cultural hero as perhaps Eastwood's shadow muse in *Gran Torino* and *American Sniper*.

Shane and *Gran Torino*

Whereas Shane enters the Wyoming valley as the archetypal loner and outsider, Walt Kowalski in *Gran Torino* is experiencing an inversion of what had been the comfortable inside/outside paradigm of 1950s America, and Detroit specifically. But with the loss of many US manufacturing jobs—automobiles in particular—the influx of Hmong immigrants into his neighborhood, and, at the opening of the film, the recent loss of his wife, Walt now feels like an outsider and very much a loner in what was and still is his home. Much as he tries to distance himself from the outsiders who now surround him and continually remind him of his unsettled past in the Korean War, his essence as hero comes to the fore as he steps in to protect the innocent from the evil gangs that have arisen with the influx of immigrants.

Like Shane, Walt initially is distrusted by his neighbors, though his own aversion to them is far more intense. But when he demonstrates the strength and courage to stand up to the various ethnic gangs threatening the neighborhood—and specifically Thao and Sue, the two adolescents living next door—he gains acceptance among the Hmong immigrants who recognize in him the mythic hero-warrior. Sue prevails on him to join a social gathering at which he becomes fully recognizable as the outsider, valued now because of his hero status. And just as we see Shane primarily from the point of view of the young boy Joey in the film, increasingly falling under the spell of the loner cowboy, so Thao and Sue's growing relationship with Walt becomes the basis for our understanding of Walt's gradual softening toward this social group that had previously been the target of his full-blown prejudice.

As Matt Wanat notes, "*Shane* [novel and film] doubles as a narrative of initiation" (299). In the opening scenes, a wide-eyed Joey, practicing with his unloaded gun, welcomes this enigmatic stranger, and the boy studies his every move throughout the film, ultimately coming to see him as "a knight errant destroying evil with a gun" (303).[4] His love and admiration for his father is constant, but in Shane he senses a different kind of role model. In *Gran Torino*, the adolescent Thao seems younger than his years and particularly vulnerable to the influence of his hypermacho cousins in the Hmong gang, so his forced (and botched) gang initiation, which involves stealing Walt's prized Gran Torino, sets the stage for his true initiation into not just manhood but what it means to be an American male, and in the end an American hero.

Referring to the role of guns in Westerns and gangster films, Robert Warshow writes, "Guns as physical objects, and the postures associated with their use, form the visual and emotional center of these films" (338). At the opening of *Shane*, Joey is sighting his rifle on a deer and through the antlers sees Shane riding in the distance. Later, we see that Shane is not wearing his holster, yet he startles, reaching for his gun, at the sudden sound of Joey cocking the unloaded rifle. At this time in his life, Joey's understanding of guns extends mainly to hunting and self-defense, but when he questions his father as to why Shane isn't wearing his gun, Joey adds, "It *goes* with him, though," as if sensing a shadowy yet prescient image of the gunfighter. When Marian objects to Shane giving Joey a shooting lesson, Shane famously schools her in the code of frontier justice where the marshal is two or three days' ride away: "A gun is a tool, Marian. No better and no worse than any other tool. A gun is as good or as bad as the man using it.

Remember that." In wishing nonetheless that there were no guns in the valley, Marian expresses a misplaced fear, according to Warshow: "Watch a child with his toy guns and you will see: what most interests him is not (as we so much fear) the fantasy of hurting others, but how a man might look when he shoots or is shot. A hero is one who looks like a hero" (350). With or without his gun, Shane is a powerful presence.

As with Western and gangster movies, both the good guys and the bad guys wield guns. Reflecting on Sue's remark that among the Hmong youth "The girls go to college and the boys go to jail," Walt gradually takes it on himself to mentor young Thao in the importance of honest, hard work. Otherwise, he concludes, "That boy doesn't stand a chance." In *Gran Torino,* Eastwood gives us alternating postures of Walt as a modern-day gunfighter, using a Korean-era rifle, a handgun, and, in a surprisingly effective gesture, simply his right-hand index finger aimed—childlike—as a pistol, sheer force emanating from his steely expression and growled commands. Like Shane, Walt has an unquiet past that haunts him in the present, and the ethos of the Western hero/soldier/warrior cannot be ignored.[5]

With the escalating gang violence threatening his young friends, Walt's heroic sense of right and wrong, justice and honor, is exposing the source of the guilt that haunts him. The initial incident that sparks the good will between Walt and the Hmong community is the gang's harassment of Thao in the yard next door, a fracas that spills onto his property. Walt points his rifle and growls, "Get off my lawn." When they try to dismiss him, he fires his verbal ammunition: "We used to stack fucks like you five feet high in Korea . . . use ya for sandbags." This time they listen. Sometime later, Father Janovich seeks out Walt at the VFW and a conversation on life and death ensues in which Walt reveals more about his war experience: "I lived with death for three years in Korea. We shot people, we stabbed them with bayonets, we hacked seventeen-year-old kids to death with shovels, for Christ's sake. I did things that won't leave me till the day I die, horrible things, things I have to live with." Finally, when Walt has tricked Thao and locked him in the basement, Thao asks what it's like to kill a man, to which Walt responds:

You want to know how it feels to kill a man? It feels goddamned lousy. And it feels even worse when you get a medal for bravery right after you mowed down some scared kid when he tries to give up. A dumb, scared, little gook, just about your age. I shot him with the same rifle you just held upstairs.

Walt is echoing Shane to Joey after the final shootout with Wilson and the Rykers: "There's no living with a killing, Joey. There's no going back from it." Walt has lived it and understands that in the twenty-first century young men on both sides—caught up in patriotic fervor and convinced that the enemy is evil—are sent to war and, if they survive, are often haunted by seeing themselves in the faces of their victims. Now his fervent hatred for a ruthless enemy is undeniably justified and heightens his resolve to put in place a plan that will capture the most gang members without endangering the innocent Thao, and moreover one that does not risk more killing of innocents. With or without his gun, Walt is a powerful presence.

The term "Western" denotes narratives set sometime between the Civil War and 1893—when Frederick Jackson Turner deemed the frontier closed from Texas to Montana and points west. These narratives are most often vague about specific location but breathtaking in the expanse of natural wilderness and raw beauty (Durham and Jones 2). The Western hero eschews the aristocratic trappings of the East, which are often represented by a woman (though not the prostitute of the saloons). Most often, "refinement, virtue, civilization, Christianity itself, are seen as feminine" while the West, "lacking the graces of civilization, is the place 'where men are men'" (Warshow 339). Much has been made of the suggestive relationship between Shane and Marian Starrett in both novel and film. However, the bond between Shane and Joe Starrett, symbolized in their joint attack on the massive tree stump, a proverbial man-against-nature tableau, highlights the degree to which Joe shares the very qualities that he senses and admires in Shane. On the other hand, as Forrest G. Robinson points out, the male-female relationships in the novel are dependent on language, which is shallow and inauthentic (81). Although in the film Marian's pleas that Joe not risk his life by going to town to face Ryker are clearly heartfelt, Jane Tompkins argues that Marian—despite being one of the few strong female characters in Western fiction—still "dissolves into ineffectual harangue at the end. . . . When the crunch comes, women shatter into words" (54).

The opening scenes of *Gran Torino* depict the funeral of Walt's wife, Dorothy, who before her death exacted a promise from Father Janovich to persuade Walt to go to confession. Father Janovich here takes on Dorothy's role of the feminine, using words not only to reach his flock in a eulogy about death being bittersweet, but also to reach Walt in an attempt to lift the burden that Dorothy surely felt he carried. In their conversation at the VFW about life and death, Walt drills the "padre": "What would you know about it?" Walt, like the Western hero, is a man of action, not words. When the gang brutally rapes Sue, Father Janovich, fearful of what Walt may be planning, comes to the house and Walt asks him what he would do, to which the priest replies, "What would I do? I'd come over and talk to you, I guess." So when Walt comes to the church to go to confession, Father Janovich knows in his bones that the time for talking has passed. And as Walt leaves, the priest's benediction—"Go in peace"—brims with irony. Walt's reply: "I am at peace." Just as Shane had to prevent Joe Starrett from laying down his life in a rigged shootout with a hired gunfighter, so Walt must forcefully save the innocent Thao from certain death in his crazed need for vengeance against the gang members. Walt, like the Western hero, "does what he 'has to do'" (Warshow 341), though his plan includes his own self-sacrifice. Walt finds peace on his own terms.

Shane and *American Sniper*

Though popular and especially critical response to *American Sniper* has been mixed, the issue that consistently dominates the conversation is whether Eastwood intended to make a pro– or anti–Iraq War film. Thomas Powers considers the film neither pro-war nor anti-war, but a film of "disciplined art and moral complexity" (8), while for David Denby it is "both a devastating war movie and a devastating antiwar movie" (151). Similarly, Mark Hughes in *Forbes* writes, "The film isn't about the war in Iraq. It's about the war every soldier fights, first to stay alive, then to reconcile their beliefs and illusions about their duty with the realities of war." Adeptly cataloging the objections of the critics who see the film as pro-war, Kyle Smith dismisses their stance as "infantile moral-equivalence arguments," and he concludes, "Eastwood hates the war. But he clearly loves the warrior" (51). This succinct observation raises the second hotly contested position: whether ace sniper Chris Kyle's portrayal is meant as that of an American hero. Chris Norris weighs in that such a film about "a slain war hero . . . risks becoming a Fallujah-set version of *Shane*" (69), a risk that in his estimation Eastwood deftly avoids. Granting this point, might *Shane* nonetheless contribute to these conversations in a way that allows for greater appreciation of Eastwood's artistry?

First of all, *American Sniper* is not a Western but rather a war movie, so of course guns and violence, revised credos of right and wrong, and modifications of civilized behavior are expected. At the start of Kyle's first tour, an officer announces, "Welcome to Fallujah, the Wild West of the Old Middle East." Here Eastwood is making explicit both the strangeness and the

familiarity of this place to the rodeo cowboy turned soldier. Warshow captures
the essence of this type of film in relation to the Western hero myth:

> In war movies, to be sure, it is possible to present the uses of violence
> within a framework of responsibility. But there is the disadvantage that
> modern war is a cooperative enterprise. Its violence is largely impersonal,
> and heroism belongs to the group more than to the individual. The hero
> of a war movie is most often simply a leader, and his superiority is most
> likely to be expressed in a denial of the heroic: you are not supposed to be
> brave, you are supposed to get the job done and stay alive. (349)

This analysis applies retrospectively to Walt's Korean War experience,
alluded to in *Gran Torino*, and to Chris Kyle's increasingly torturous experience as a Navy SEAL sniper. Both men are uncomfortable with the label
of hero, though Eastwood specifically delves into the bitter personal anguish
of the soldier that results from the violence of war. Such introspection is
critical to Walt's making sense of his part in the war and eventually taking
the actions that he does. Kyle's early indoctrination into simple notions of
good and evil, and justice and decency, are problematized by the reality of
war.

Kyle's boyhood past serves as an initiation into manhood that makes
him a candidate ripe for the military when he is emotionally moved by
attacks on the homeland. In a flashback just after the opening scenes of
American Sniper, he is poised to make his first kill as a young boy out hunting with his father. Like Joey in *Shane*, Chris is shown to be a sensitive,
impressionable boy who looks up to his father and seeks his approval. When
he kills his first buck, his father responds, "You've got a gift," which introduces the uncanny nature of the boy's abilities. At the same time, like Walt
instructing Thao about the value of tools and knowing how to use them, or
Shane pointing out to Marian that a gun is just a tool, Chris's father admonishes his son never to leave his rifle—his tool—in the dirt. In the next scene,
the family is in church, and as the minister intones that we cannot know the
glory of God's plan for us, Chris places a small Bible in his pocket, a physical
reminder of his destiny, a destiny he is unaware of at the time, and he keeps
the book tucked in his uniform throughout his deployments. Next, we see
the family at the dinner table on a day when Chris has fought a bully who
picked on his younger brother. An even greater impression results from the
father's declaration that the world is made up of sheep, wolves, and sheep

dogs, the last "blessed with the gift of aggression" and "an overpowering need to protect the flock." He turns to look at Chris: "You know what you are. We protect our own."

When the film returns to the adult Chris Kyle poised on the roof, he has in his sights a woman and a young boy walking toward the American troops. From beneath her clothing, she gives the boy a grenade and he runs ahead. Kyle tries to confirm over the radio what he is seeing but is told, "Your call." After seconds of deliberate breathing, he shoots the boy, and then the woman, who has retrieved the grenade and begun to run toward the Americans. The grenade explodes well out of range. Commenting on Bradley Cooper's performance as somewhat at odds with Chris Kyle's autobiography, Norris writes, "When a jarhead beside him slaps Kyle's shoulder in congrats, Cooper tersely backs him off, registering an ambivalence conspicuously absent from Kyle's account of the same incident" (70–71). Norris is attributing to Bradley Cooper—and by extension to director Eastwood—a depiction of Kyle's emotional and moral uncertainty that, according to Norris, is not true to the autobiography, as if Kyle had recounted the incident with bravado. But Norris fails to mention that the woman has the grenade, and Kyle has to be ordered repeatedly, "Take a shot. . . . Shoot. . . . Shoot!" (3). Upon stating that this is the only time while "on the sniper rifle" he ever killed anyone other than a male combatant, Kyle further reflects on the nature of this target: "The woman was already dead. I was just making sure she didn't take any marines with her. It was clear that not only did she want to kill them [marines], but she didn't care about anybody else nearby. . . . Children on the street, people in the houses, maybe *her* child" (3–4).

Eastwood opens *American Sniper* with this emotionally charged scene as if to engulf the audience from the outset in the split-second, life-and-death decisions that define war, and this war specifically. He returns to the dilemma of a child target—one that *is* in the autobiography—near the end of the film during Kyle's fourth tour in Iraq when he is noticeably disturbed by the war and his part in it. A young boy starts to pick up an RPG after the combatant has been shot, and Kyle, with the boy in his sights, says to himself, teeth clenched, "Don't pick it up." Finger on the trigger, his relief is visible as he chokes up when the boy drops it and runs away. Eastwood has drawn a dramatic arc from the film's opening scenes when Kyle reluctantly yet dutifully shoots a child—tragically as much a victim of his mother's ideology as of the sniper's bullet—to this one in which, like Warshow's Westerner, he exhibits self-restraint and independent judgment beyond that required by the rules of engagement, yet is sorely troubled that "whatever his justifications, he is a killer of men" (Warshow 342). As he shortly confides to his wife, Taya, "I'm ready to come home."

Shane rides out of the valley wounded, leaving behind a West that is forever changed but also an image of the cultural hero that resonates with lovers of Westerns the world over. Walt, haunted by his past, shrewdly determines how he might act independently of Thao, the police, and even the Catholic Church to bring justice and decency to bear, and to make amends to the former enemy who makes possible his act of redemption. Finally, like Shane, like Walt, even like Will Munny in Eastwood's *Unforgiven*, Chris Kyle expresses the hard-won moral lesson of the gunfighter: "It's a heck of a thing to stop a beating heart."

Notes

1. Critical of an "aestheticizing tendency" in certain Westerns, Robert Warshow writes that in *Shane* "the legend of the West is virtually reduced to its essentials and then fixed in the dreamy clarity of a fairy tale" (347).

2. Matthew J. Costello unconvincingly argues, "The failure to offer Ryker as truly evil is one of the great sources of ambiguity in the film" (264). While he cites Ryker's repeated claims to be "a reasonable man," he does not take into account that this exact claim is used to lure Joe Starrett into town where he will face the gunslinger Wilson.

3. Wright also identifies "sixteen functions" in the classic Western narrative, most of which apply to *Shane*, summarized here: the hero arrives, unknown, not fully accepted by the society, and is discovered to have an exceptional ability, which gives the hero status; because of a conflict of interest, villains threaten the society, which is weak, and endanger a friend of the hero; sometimes there is respect or friendship between a villain and the hero; reluctantly, the hero fights and defeats the villains, leaving the society safe and accepting of the hero; and the hero loses or gives up his status (48–49).

4. Wanat is addressing the novel. The romantic description, which exactly fits the hero worship of the boy in both novel and film, becomes richly problematic from the perspective of the novel's adult narrator.

5. John M. Gourlie and Leonard Engel also note "the ethos of the Western gunman and hero" in Clint Eastwood's portrayal of Walt (275).

Works Cited

Agresta, Michael. "How the Western Was Lost (and Why It Matters)." *Atlantic*, 24 July 2013, www.theatlantic.com/entertainment/archive/2013/07/how-the-western-was-lost-and-why-it-matters/278057/.

American Sniper. Directed by Clint Eastwood, performances by Bradley Cooper and Sienna Miller, Warner Bros., 2014.

Becker, Ernest. *The Denial of Death.* Free Press, 1973.

Costello, Matthew J. "'I Didn't Expect to Find Any Fences Around Here': Cultural Ambiguity and Containment in *Shane.*" *Journal of American Culture,* vol. 27, no. 3, Sept. 2004, pp. 261–70, doi:10.1111/j.1537–4726.2004.00134.x.

Denby, David. "Living History: *Selma* and *American Sniper.*" Review. *New Yorker,* vol. 90, no. 41, 22–29 Dec. 2014, pp. 150–51.

Desser, David. "Kurosawa's Eastern 'Western': *Sanjuro* and the Influence of *Shane.*" *Film Criticism,* vol. 8, no. 1, Fall 1983, pp. 54–65. *Contemporary Literary Criticism,* edited by Jeffrey W. Hunter and Timothy J. White, vol. 119. *Gale Literary Sources,* go. galegroup.com.libraryproxy.quinnipiac.edu/ps/i.do?p=GLS&sw=w&u=a13qu&v=2.1 &it=r&id=GALE%7CH1100004615&asid=a3e18f5b3a40ee18baac3bc03d7bf133.

Durham, Philip, and Everett L. Jones, editors. Introduction. *The Western Story: Fact, Fiction, and Myth,* Harcourt, Brace, Jovanovich, 1975, pp. 1–8.

Estleman, Loren D. *The Wister Trace: Assaying Classic Western Fiction.* 2nd ed., U of Oklahoma P, 2014.

Gran Torino. Directed by Clint Eastwood, performances by Eastwood, Christopher Carley, Bee Vang, and Ahney Her, Warner Bros., 2008.

Hughes, Mark. "*American Sniper* Says Much More Than You Think." Review. *Forbes: Arts and Entertainment,* 16 Jan. 2015, www.forbes.com/sites/markhughes/2015/01/16/ review-american-sniper-says-much-more-than-you-think/#6bc2a3c45eb1.

Kyle, Chris, with Scott McEwan and Jim DeFelice. *American Sniper.* Memorial ed., William Morrow / Harper Collins, 2013, pp. 1–377.

Love, Glen A. "Revaluing Nature: Toward an Ecological Criticism." *Old West—New West: Centennial Essays,* edited by Barbara Howard Meldrum, U of Idaho P, 1993, pp. 283–99.

McGee, Patrick. *From* Shane *to* Kill Bill*: Rethinking the Western.* Blackwell Publishing, 2007.

Mikkelsen, Robert. "The Western Writer: Jack Schaefer's Use of the Western Frontier." *Shane: The Critical Edition,* edited by James C. Work, U of Nebraska P, 1984, pp. 300–306.

Norris, Chris. "Review: *American Sniper.*" *Film Comment,* vol. 51, no. 1, Jan. / Feb. 2015, pp. 68–71.

Powers, Thomas. "The American Hero." Review of *American Sniper. New York Review of Books,* vol. 6, no. 8, 2 Apr. 2015, pp. 6–8, www.nybooks.com/articles/2015/04/02/ sniper-american-hero/.

Robinson, Forrest G. *Having It Both Ways: Self-Subversion in Western Popular Classics.* U of New Mexico P, 1993.

Schaefer, Jack. *Shane: The Critical Edition.* Edited by James C. Work, U of Nebraska P, 1984, pp. 16–274.

Schein, Harry. "The Olympian Cowboy." Translated by Ida M. Alcock. *Shane: The Critical Edition,* edited by James C. Work, U of Nebraska P, 1984, pp. 405–17.

Shane. Directed by George Stevens, performances by Alan Ladd, Jean Arthur, Van Heflin, Brandon De Wilde, and Jack Palance, Paramount, 1953.

Smith, Kyle. "*American Sniper* as Apple Pie." Review. *Commentary*, vol. 139, no. 3, Mar. 2015, pp. 50–52. *Literature Resource Center*, www.go.galegroup.com/ps/i.do?p=LitRC&sw=w&u=a13qu&v=2.1&id=GALE%7CA4137853027IT=r&asid=80ce0d69fb62bae72565835609b3bb54.

Sterritt, David. *The Cinema of Clint Eastwood: Chronicles of America.* Wallflower Press, 2014.

Tompkins, Jane. *West of Everything: The Inner Life of Westerns.* Oxford UP, 1992.

Wanat, Matt. "Writing Rhetorics, Reading Narrative." *"The River Is a Strong Brown God": Iconic Places and Characters in 20th Century American Cultures*, edited by Michael Connaughton, Suellen Rundquist, and Robert P. Inkster, St. Cloud State U, 2008, pp. 290–309.

Warshow, Robert. "The Westerner." *The Western Story: Fact, Fiction, and Myth*, edited by Philip Durham and Everett L. Jones. Harcourt, Brace, Jovanovich, 1975, pp. 338–50.

Wright, Will. *Sixguns and Society: A Structural Study of the Western.* U of California P, 1975.

9

"Life Takers and Heart Breakers"

Moral Injury in Clint Eastwood's War Films

Kathleen Brown and Brett Westbrook

"I am sick and tired of war. Its glory is all moonshine.
It is only those who have neither fired a shot
nor heard the shrieks and groans of the
wounded who cry aloud for blood,
for vengeance, for desolation. War is hell."

—William Tecumseh Sherman

During the course of his career, Clint Eastwood has made seven war films—where the action is set during wartime or the main character's status as a war veteran is central to the narrative. With Eastwood as either actor, director, or producer (or in some combination), these films include *Where Eagles Dare* (1968), *Kelly's Heroes* (1970), *Heartbreak Ridge* (1986), *Flags of Our Fathers* and *Letters from Iwo Jima* (2006), *Gran Torino* (2008), and *American Sniper* (2014). *Where Eagles Dare*, a Richard Burton vehicle, is action-packed, a straight-up war film. In his review titled "In the War Tradition," *New York Times* film critic Vincent Canby describes the movie as full of "almost constant destruction—vehicles, bridges, trees, faces, people, aircraft, with not much differentiation made among them." The main characters in *Where Eagles Dare* are not riddled with guilt about the startlingly high body count. A tree is the same as a human being to them. Similarly, *Kelly's Heroes* does not contemplate, as Pulitzer Prize–winning war correspondent David Wood put it, the fact that "success on the battlefield may call for the suspension of basic notions of civilian morality in order to accomplish the mission." The physical and psychological brutality of war—"the pools of blood and shattered bones and pain that are so funda-mental to the whole business of military-style conflict resolution"—gets no screen time in either movie (Halberstadt xvii). In *Kelly's Heroes*, for example, when two of the men are killed in a minefield, Big Joe (Telly Savalas) admonishes a grieving soldier: "They're dead, so forget it. Let's move."

The remaining Eastwood war films explore, deliberately and self-consciously, what happens to men who, in order to fulfill their military duty and simply to survive, manage to "overcome and neutralize [their] earlier resistance to violence" (Hendin and Hass 133). In these movies, the act of killing and the horrors of armed conflict are not, cannot, simply be forgotten and left behind after the soldiers move out. The war experiences of the major characters have left them damaged in ways best described as "moral injury," a term first used by army psychiatrist Jonathan Shay in 1991 in his ground-breaking article "Learning about Combat Stress from Homer's *Iliad*." Shay reads this famous piece of war literature as an "outstanding narrative of toxic combat experiences that appear similar to those reported by Vietnam veter-ans with severe, chronic post-traumatic stress disorder (PTSD)" (561). Vet-erans suffering from moral injury report the following experiences and emotional responses:

> [the perception of] a leader's betrayal of "what's right," blunted respon-siveness to any emotional, social, or ethical claims outside a tiny circle of combat-proven comrades, grief and guilt for death(s) in this circle, lust for revenge, renunciation of ever returning home, seeing one's self as already dead, berserking, dishonoring the enemy, and loss of human-ity. (Shay, "Learning" 562)

To Shay, the results of such "toxic" experiences constitute an *injury*, a "psy-chological injury," that has, like physical injury, severe complications, such as drug and alcohol addiction and suicidal tendencies ("Trials" 291). Kill-ing—the very essence of war—injures the killer. According to clinical psy-chologist Brett T. Litz, "killing, regardless of role, is a better predictor of chronic PTSD symptoms than other indices of combat, mirroring some of the results on atrocities" (697). And yet, as Shira Maguen so bluntly puts it, "military personnel involved in war kill as part of their mission," something they must be trained to do (21). The difficulties, sometimes extreme, faced by active service members and veterans expose the trauma of detaching a man from his moral center in order to transform him into a highly effective member—as clinical psychiatrist William Barry Gault puts it—of a "robustly homicidal combat team" (451). The characters in Eastwood's war films are all textbook cases.

Coming sixteen years after *Kelly's Heroes*, *Heartbreak Ridge* (1986) was the first war movie Eastwood made over which he had the kind of control he had wanted for *Kelly's Heroes*.[1] Produced by the Malpaso Company, the film features Eastwood as Gunnery Sergeant Tom Highway—a lifer, a gung-ho marine who saw combat in the US invasion of the Dominican Republic and served three tours in Vietnam. Korea, not Vietnam, however, was the crucible in which Highway's character was formed. In the Twenty-Third Infantry in Korea (not yet in the marines), Highway and his regiment were ordered to take what the men called Heartbreak Ridge. In six days of close fighting—"fixed bayonets, hand-to-hand combat"—he experienced "the actions, sights, smells, and images of violence and its aftermath" that put men at risk for moral injury (*Heartbreak Ridge*; Litz, et al. 696). In the chaos of battle, according to long-time friend Sergeant Choozoo (Arlen Dean Snyder), Highway "charged two machine gun nests by himself," holding off the "final human wave" of the counterassault "almost single-handedly" (*Heartbreak Ridge*). When it was all over, only Highway, Choozoo, and their platoon sergeant, Stoney Jackson, survived. Heartbreak Ridge indeed.

If the fictional Tom Highway could find himself under the care of the actual Dr. Jonathan Shay, the sergeant might have received a diagnosis of "berserking" for his pell-mell charge up Heartbreak Ridge. According to Shay, berserking is symptomatic of moral injury and usually emerges in the midst of high-intensity combat laced with desperation. Characteristics of the dissociated state of berserking include, among others, "loss of fear," "inattention to one's own safety," "superhuman strength and endurance," and risk-taking that amounts "to inviting death," all of which fit Choozoo's admiring description of the events on Heartbreak Ridge (Shay, "Learning" 570, Table 1). While such an event may seem to be an anomaly over the course of a war, Vietnam veteran and clinician R. Wayne Eisenhart argues that, in fact, military training practices deliberately link "military function with . . . the exacerbation and promotion of violence and aggression," and that the "repeatedly hammered ideal of seeking dominance at all costs . . . produce[s] in recruits a well-honed emotional edge" that can easily lead to the kind of frenzy of Highway's charge up Heartbreak Ridge (17). According to Shay, "berserking is highly valued by military commanders" because, in its ferocity, "it can completely reverse the outcome of a battle" (Shay, "Learning" 572). For his actions while in this state, Highway won the Congressional Medal of Honor, the nation's highest military honor. To the service member in that moment, however, heightened aggression is less a path to glory than a means to reduce fear—for oneself or for the lives of others (Hendin and Hass 27). The use of aggression to contain and cope with fear is certainly understandable in a combat zone. Aggression, however, is obviously maladaptive for a peacetime world. And while Tom Highway does not seem to be a version of what Eben J. Muse calls the "psycho-vet character" who drags war violence back home with him, Highway's continuing aggression off the battlefield does not earn him any medals on the home front and even threatens his career in the military (88).

The film opens with Highway smoking a cigar in the local drunk tank, filled with the usual assortment of tough-looking bikers and the one ingénue sitting close to the sergeant. Though many Eastwood films avoid exposition altogether, this scene sets up Highway's approach to the world with a great deal of cinematic economy. As Highway informs the captive audience, "I'm mean, nasty and tired. I eat concertina wire and piss napalm and I can put a round through a flea's ass at two hundred meters." The much larger biker threatens Highway and is promptly flattened by the veteran, who then picks up where he left off in his story about how he had been "pumping pussy since Christ was a corporal" (*Heartbreak Ridge*). This, then, is Tom Highway: highly sexualized, still highly aggressive, unflappable, and able to make good on his threats. He is also, apparently, routinely drunk. In court, *again*, as the judge (John Eames) makes clear, on drunk and disorderly charges, his only excuse for pissing on a cop car is that "it seemed like the thing to do" (*Heartbreak Ridge*). In an article on barriers to mental health care for veterans, Charles W. Hoge, psychiatrist with the Walter Reed Army Institute of Research, lists alcohol abuse and "impairment in social functioning" (among others) as symptoms of "deployment stressors and exposure to combat" (14). As the dialogue in the courtroom makes clear, this is not the first time that Highway has appeared before this judge who seems to understand the connection between war and Highway's behavior: "Just because there's no war going on it doesn't give you the right to start one every time you get drunk." The sergeant gets off—for the last time—with just a one-hundred-dollar fine. The local officer, Reese (John Hostetter), whose car was defaced is outraged at the outcome, demanding to know: "You think you can break our rules and just walk away?" (*Heartbreak Ridge*). He means *our* society, not

Highway's. Without a hot war to fight, Highway has no way to be in "normal" society. The aggression that served him so well through several tours of duty becomes a liability.

Highway's "impairment" also extends to functioning within the military itself. Having been "busted out" of his combat division "for insubordination, conduct unbecoming," Gunnery Sergeant Highway is assigned to a lowly base supply depot. When his request for transfer back to a proper combat unit is granted and he returns to the Second Recon Battalion, Second Marine Division, he encounters Major Malcolm Powers (Everett McGill), an Annapolis "football hero," according to Choozoo, a fact that leaves both non-com combat veterans singularly unimpressed. Powers shares Officer Reese's point of view that there is no place for Highway in the "new" marines as he aggressively assures Highway that in "the new Marine Corps . . . characters like you are an anachronism. You should be sealed in a case that says 'break glass only in case of war.'" Needing someone to whip new recruits into shape, Powers complains: "Division sends me relics," not marines. Both Powers and Reese see Highway's aggression and disrespect for "limp-dicked officers" of all stripes as threatening, certainly, but also simply out of place, not of this time (*Heartbreak Ridge*).

Highway fares no better on the domestic front, his wife, Aggie (Marsha Mason), having divorced him before the film opens. Highway would be home with her for a while, but then he would "volunteer for every damn war that came down the pike." Sergeant Choozoo pleads Highway's case with her: "He needs you, Aggie." She has been there before: "Until the next war" (*Heartbreak Ridge*). What Highway sees as his duty, Aggie sees as yet another abandonment. According to Kathryn Basham, professor of social work at Smith College, "lengthy separations and exposure to combat during deployment disrupt, and, at times, dismantle attachments among family members" (306). At the heart of the issue for Aggie is the agony of not knowing whether Highway is safe, or missing, or coming home in a body bag:

AGGIE. I lived in a rat hole when they were bringing those boys home in those flag-draped, metal coffins. I don't think I got a wink's sleep in '68. Do you remember that year?
HIGHWAY. Yes. I remember.
AGGIE. I'd turn on the TV in the morning, I'd eat dinner in front of it every night eyes glued, hoping to catch a glimpse of you on the news and then praying I wouldn't. Then I'd crawl into bed and wonder,

where were you? What were you doing? Were you alive? And I had no way of knowing. (*Heartbreak Ridge*)

Basham understands this conflict, the continuing difficulties between intimate partners, as "secondary trauma," a further complication of moral injury. In fact, according to Basham, "research data support the association between combat exposure," of which Highway has had quite a lot, "and heightened marital and family conflicts and serious levels of intimate partner violence" (307). In this fictional setting, Highway's aggression infects not only the relationship but even Aggie herself, who has previously displayed and continues to display aggression of her own:

HIGHWAY. Is there something you're afraid of?
AGGIE. Yes. I'm afraid I'll dent that thick skull of yours with this frying pan.
HIGHWAY. It wouldn't be the first time, would it?
AGGIE. No.

In a later scene, when she thinks Highway is trying to "outflank her," she hurls crockery at her ex-husband, and, out of frustration, fear, hurt, and anger, hits him repeatedly in another. As far as Aggie is concerned, "There is no room in my future for a marine" (*Heartbreak Ridge*). No room in the "new Marine Corps," no room in civilian society, and no room in Aggie's life.

Despite the ways in which military service and repeated exposure to combat seem to have eroded Highway's entire life, he is still served well by one marine mantra in particular: "Adapt. Improvise. Overcome." After having turned his platoon of malingerers into a disciplined and orderly fighting unit, they are deployed to Grenada to extract college students caught up in a civil war. Ordered to provide reconnaissance only, he and his men—along with their untried and bookish lieutenant, Ring (Boyd Gaines)—actually take the hill. They adapt to the facts as they are on the ground (Cubans armed with Soviet rifles). They improvise a solution to downed communications (one of the men uses his credit card to place a long-distance call). And they overcome the enemy. Major Powers is apoplectic. He wanted to take the hill himself, as if this were a mere war game. Colonel Meyers (Richard Venture), Powers's superior officer, helicopters in (very much a deus ex machina for the beleaguered Highway) and approves of the sergeant's and the lieutenant's actions: "Ring and Highway took a handful of young fire-pissers, exercised some personal initiative, and kicked ass! Good work, Lieutenant." He also calls the major a "cluster fuck as an infantry officer" and orders him back to supply. The initiative and aggression that had worked before in hot wars is apparently still needed—and valued—after all. And yet, after twenty-four years of service, Highway knows he is "coming to the end of it." As he tells the most recalcitrant recruit, Stitch (Mario Van Peebles), who has in fact re-upped: "No room in this man's corps for me now" (*Heartbreak Ridge*). His main concern before ending his career is the next generation of marines, who need to be trained into the level of aggression and solidarity that could keep them alive in combat. His unit suffered only one casualty, and some of his troops killed members of the enemy force. Of course, their efficiency in terms of the mission puts them at risk for moral injury, obviously not a problem on Highway's radar.

The gunnery sergeant deploys the marine mantra ("Adapt. Improvise. Overcome.") on the home front as well, obviously with modifications. He adapts to the fact that his devotion to duty came at the expense of his marriage. After hearing Aggie's sad, angry lament about not knowing, he realizes that "there are things that work harder on a woman than being shot at." When she slaps him and hits him in this scene, he first registers shock but does not respond—for once—with like aggression. He folds her into his arms and murmurs, "That's all right, baby. That's all right," while she weeps with anger, frustration, and a profound fear for his life. He also finds ways to improvise, mining women's magazines (a fact he denies to other men) for information about relationships. They talk about this at a military function:

AGGIE. Are you still reading them?
HIGHWAY. Affirmative.
AGGIE. What do they say about ex-wives?
HIGHWAY. Not too much. Just that sex is great because you don't have to establish a relationship or be meaningful.
AGGIE. You really are trying to understand us.
HIGHWAY. The best I can, yes. (*Heartbreak Ridge*)

In the end, as the men return from Grenada to cheers from friends and families accompanied by a military band, Highway seems to have "overcome" a reluctant Aggie, who greets him, tiny American flag in hand. They walk away together, sort of. They do not hug or kiss or even hold hands. Her presence there, her willingness to wait for this one last time, though, would signal at least some possibility for a future together.

Throughout the movie, Highway demonstrates many of the behaviors and symptoms constituting moral injury as described by Jonathan Shay. Highway abuses alcohol to the extent that he appears multiple times in court. He cannot sustain a long-term domestic relationship. With the important exception of Aggie, he exhibits a "blunted responsiveness to any emotional, social, or ethical claims outside a tiny circle of combat-proven comrades" (Shay, "Learning" 562). His aggression bleeds over into non-combat life in ways that undermine his professional life and infect his personal life. That he seems to have won a chance with Aggie is, according to Shay, Basham, Litz, and more, a positive outcome difficult to reproduce in an actual clinical setting. *Heartbreak Ridge* is the happy version of what happens to servicemen like Tom Highway.

In *Flags of Our Fathers* and *Letters from Iwo Jima* (both 2006), Eastwood examines what happens to the men who fought on and over those eight square miles of sulfur on the Ogasawara Archipelago during the waning days of the war in the Pacific. In comparison to Grenada—the "gray zone" conflict in *Heartbreak Ridge*—Iwo Jima was much more deadly, in reality and as depicted on film. US losses included 17,372 wounded and 5,931 killed (Nalty and Crawford 21). The Japanese suffered even greater devastation: 20,700 dead, with only a few over two hundred survivors (Dower). Both films depict the unfathomable depths of death and deprivation, a rain of blood and severed limbs. Within each film, men from both sides witness the sights, sounds, and smells of death—by grenade, machine gun, flame thrower, and mortar—exactly the kind of "toxic combat experience" that Shay and others argue puts men at risk for moral injury. Japanese and American service members alike react during near-continuous combat to the apparent certainty of death with the same complexity: shock, numbness, aggression, resignation, brutality, and berserk behavior.

In *Letters from Iwo Jima*, the viewpoint character, Katsuhiro Saigo (Kazunari Ninomiya) manages for a time to avoid a direct engagement with the act of killing, the principal function of combat soldiers. He is a baker whose goods, then his entire bakery, and then he himself, are pressed into service by the Imperial Japanese Army. Flashbacks reveal that Saigo's wife is pregnant and that he promised her he would come home to her and their child. On the island, he writes loving letters from the front lines and interacts with his fellow conscripts with humor and humanity. In particular, he develops a deep admiration and an affection for General Tadamichi Kurib-ayashi (Ken Watanabe). The general, who also writes letters from Iwo Jima, saves Saigo at several points in the film—from a beating and from decapita-tion by an overzealous officer obsessed with "honor" rather than the mission to hold out as long as possible. Saigo even avoids learning how to be a soldier. At target practice, he seems unable to keep his gun steady, jerking it when he pulls the trigger. Fellow private Kashiwara (Takashi Yamaguchi) specu-lates that after eighteen months in the service, no one can really be so bad. Saigo responds only that he has no aim, unable to bring himself to shoot even an inanimate target. Later, as the fighting intensifies, he is ordered to use his rifle. His bad aim, however, saves him. Labeled useless by the com-manding officer, he is sent off with a message for Kuribayashi instead. Saigo, in fact, rejects all identification as a soldier. After he manages a dangerous retreat from Mount Suribachi, the general compliments him, calling him "quite a soldier" for making such a journey. Saigo denies it: "No, sir. I'm just a simple baker" (*Letters from Iwo Jima*).

While *Letters from Iwo Jima* plays out entirely on the island, *Flags of Our Fathers* continues the story started on Iwo Jima, following survivors back to the United States, during wartime and beyond, focusing on three flag rais-ers: John "Doc" Bradley (played by Ryan Phillippe as a young man and George Grizzard in his later life) and two marines—Ira Hayes (Adam Beach) and Rene Gagnon (Jesse Bradford). Of these three, Gagnon was the most protected from risk of moral injury because he only carried messages between officers. The two who saw combat bore "witness to intense human suffering and cruelty" sufficient to rattle "their core beliefs about humanity" (Litz et al. 696). As hard as they wish it were possible, however, they cannot unsee what has been seen. These images as much as their own actions haunt them once they are stateside. The most significant emotion for both men is not abstract patriotism but rather the connections made with their comrades that were forged in the ferocity and intensity of the battle on Iwo Jima. Both men were fighting for much more than the flag. While Hayes fought to protect the men in his unit, Doc struggled to keep his wounded comrades, Iggy in particular, alive.

Only the politics of war could separate Doc and Hayes from their unit, only the accident of being in the wrong place at the wrong time: the moment Joe Rosenthal happened to snap a photograph of the second of two flag rais-ings on Mount Suribachi. To the men, raising either one of the flags was just a task to be carried out so long as no one was actually getting shot at. That was not an act of heroism; it was a chore. No one's life was at risk. At home, however, the flag was iconic, standing for all things American, and had been used for the duration to urge the public to cooperate with the war effort: sending sons to war, rationing food, and financing the conflict through war bonds. Wrapping that symbol around a group of fighting men produced a war-bond-selling machine. Once stateside, the men were packaged "as the heroes of Iwo Jima" and sent on tour to promote war bonds. Given the men's understanding of the flag raising as a mere chore, the business of being called a hero for it verged on obscenity. Even Gagnon, who enlisted for the snappy uniform and who seemingly enjoyed the bond tour, acknowledged that "the real heroes are dead on that island" (*Flags of Our Fathers*).

According to Litz, "social-cognitive theories of PTSD delineate how traumatic events clash with existing schemas that people hold about themselves and the world," including the belief that "the self is worthy" (698). Ira Hayes especially is haunted by the sense of unworthiness, that he in no way deserves to be called "hero." Hayes puts up great resistance to being sent back to the States. He understands his duty to be with his unit, in combat. The "real" heroes are found there, the men who fight and die. This character's actions on the screen (as well as those of the actual person) clearly exhibit symptoms of moral injury, particularly self-isolation, withdrawal, and alcohol abuse. Frequently drunk, he desperately seeks to numb himself to the throbbing dissonance between what he is told is his duty—to raise money—and where he feels his duty to be. Ultimately, he goes on a 1300-mile-long pilgrimage, an attempt to expiate the "sin" of having been forced to abandon his comrades-in-arms. Walking and hitchhiking, Hayes makes his way to Texas. According to Bradley's son, James Bradley (Tom McCarthy), Ira "found Harlon Block's father working his field. . . . And Ira told him the truth, that it had been his son who raised the flag with them, his son in the photograph. And then he just turned and walked away" (*Flags of Our Fathers*). While the parents are grateful to finally learn the truth, the act does not provide Hayes any relief from the incessant guilt and plaguing sense of unworthiness. Eventually, Private First Class Ira Hayes, the character and the man, veteran of one of the deadliest battles of the entire war, succumbed to complications of moral injury. He died of exposure in Sacaton, Arizona, at the age of thirty-two, a casualty certainly of Iwo Jima.

Doc Bradley also feels like a failure, not because he left his comrades but because he could not save them all. On the second day of the battle, Doc makes his way under heavy enemy fire to aid a wounded comrade caught in the line of fire. Doc patches him up and drags him to safety, saving the wounded man's life by placing his own in peril. For this act, Doc receives the Navy Cross, the second highest medal awarded by the military. His skill and courage are undoubtable. Understandably, however, Doc cannot save all the wounded. In particular, he cannot save Iggy. All Doc knows is that, when he goes to get a stretcher, he has to leave Iggy in a shell crater. When he gets back, Iggy is simply gone. Ultimately, Doc must identify Iggy's badly disfigured body, left in a cave by the Japanese soldiers who had bayoneted him to death. Like Hayes, Doc feels singularly unworthy to be called "hero." While his life takes on a more usual trajectory—marriage, children—he, too, exhibits symptoms of moral injury. Iggy's death is the stuff of his nightmares; he is plagued by a constant guilt that he did not do enough for his fellow service members. He never even tells his son about his role in raising the flag on Mount Suribachi. In the film, Doc and Hayes both struggle to make sense of their experiences, ultimately falling back on silence, living and dying with guilt and an undeserved, tragic sense of failure. All the men were subjected to the truly hellish conditions on the island: temperatures reaching as high as 130 degrees, the lack of a single source of groundwater or food anywhere on the island, and the constant venting of toxic sulfur fumes (Dower).[2] Neither *Flags of Our Fathers* nor *Letters from Iwo Jima* ends on a triumphant note, focusing instead on what one reviewer called the "chance, anarchy, absurdity, [and] the indifference of the war machine" on both sides (Bradshaw).

While Doc Bradley and Ira Hayes experience crushing guilt about being called heroes for the flag raising, they have a stable sense of themselves as nonheroic. Much of their interior agony turns on that cognitive dissonance between the way the world insists on understanding them—as heroes—and what they know to be true about themselves: that they are mere flag raisers.[3] Korean War veteran Walt Kowalski (Clint Eastwood) in *Gran Torino* (2008) also suffers from guilt about actions taken in combat. Those actions, however, and one in particular, have come to define him to himself. There is no cognitive dissonance, no play between outside perception and self-understanding. The film opens with Dorothy Kowalski's funeral mass being given by a stunningly young priest, Father Janovich (Christopher Carley). As with the drunk-tank scene in the opening of *Heartbreak Ridge*, this opening—also in a confined space, though a less physically violent one—functions as the exposition for family relationships. Walt is there for the sake of propriety, growling under his breath at grown offspring (who exchange smirking remarks about their father) and at grandchildren in clothes inappropriate to the occasion and place. He is alone there, isolated and embittered. Later, the house he shared with Dorothy is filled with people, but he suspects they showed up only because "they knew there'd be plenty of ham." He is as alone in a crowded house as he was in the church. In contrast, the Hmong who live next door celebrate a birth with singing, ceremony, and great affection. It is a happy noise, especially in comparison to Walt's growling "grr grr" at everyone (*Gran Torino*).

Even though he "survived the war, got married, raised a family," as he tells Father Janovich, he is still remarkably cut off from everyone around him. As he explains to the priest: "I lived there for almost three years in Korea with death. We shot men, stabbed them with bayonets, hacked seventeen-year-olds to death with shovels. Stuff I'll remember to the day I die, horrible things." Having promised the late Mrs. Kowalski that he would try to get Walt into the confessional, the good father offers the hope of forgiveness for "the horrible things you were forced to do": "I've seen a lot of men who have confessed their sins, admitted their guilt, and left their burdens behind them. Stronger men than you. Men at war who were ordered to do appalling things and are now at peace." Walt remains unconvinced: "halle-fuckin-lujah." Walt does confess to Father Janovich that he kissed a woman not his wife at the company Christmas party, that he made a profit selling a boat he failed to report to the IRS ("That's the same as stealing."), and that he was never close to his sons (*Gran Torino*). While the father is impatient with these items, they have been bothering Walt all of his life. These are transgressions, however, that Walt can live with.

For Litz, moral injury can be understood as the "psychological, biological, spiritual, behavioral, and social impact of perpetrating . . . acts that transgress deeply held moral beliefs" (697). The transgression that redefines Walt for himself is an act that took place in Korea; it is especially awful for Walt because it was one that he was not actually ordered to commit. As he explains to Father Janovich, that which "haunts a man the most is what he *isn't* ordered to do" (*Gran Torino*). Unlike combat events in which a service member is (naturally) afraid of a life threat, the events associated with moral injury are often based on "other affects and cognitions, such as shame" and guilt. The individual with such a moral injury "may begin to view him or herself as immoral, irredeemable, and un-reparable" (Litz et al. 698). This interpretation of events lacks an "appreciation of the unique context and contingencies in war" and can lead, often with tragic results, to "severe self-condemnation," feelings of being evil, feelings of worthlessness, and a sense that one is undeserving of forgiveness (Litz et al. 703).

There can be a route toward "moral repair and renewal," and Walt does seem to start down that path. In their plan for therapy for actual veterans suffering from moral injury and its complications, Litz recommends (among other steps) a "corrective life experience," one that will increase "positive judgments about the self by doing good deeds and positive judgments about the world by seeing others do good deeds." Also essential are "giving and receiving care and love." All of this will, hopefully, counter "self-expectations of moral inadequacy and the experience of being tainted by various acts" (Litz et al. 701). The first "good deed" comes at the end of a long gun, the one Walt carried in Korea. He breaks up a fight between one of his Hmong neighbors, Thao (Bee Vang), and some gangbangers, not because he intended to rescue the young man but because the fight tumbled over unto his lawn. After scaring off the gangbangers, he throws his neighbors off his lawn too. While Walt sees the event as merely troublesome, the Hmong express gratitude for his help and insist on leaving gifts of flowers, plants, and food on his doorstep. In her review, *New York Times* film critic Manohla Dargis notes that Walt "resists the family's overtures like a man under siege, walled in by years of suspicion, prejudice, and habit." He is also, to an extent, walled in by his understanding of himself as irredeemable. Still, the confrontation with the gangbangers and its aftermath establish a shaky bond with his neighbors. Sue, the likeably mouthy, young Hmong woman (Ahney Her), coaxes Walt over to their house during a party by proffering beer. He accepts (possibly) only because he has run out of beer. Sue provides a crash course in Hmong customs, such as never touching anyone on the head. Walt thinks they are all "nuts" but heeds the lessons. Most of all, he seems to enjoy the food, having had only "a piece of cake and some beef jerky" all day. The scene where Walt sits at a kitchen table surrounded by Hmong women pushing food at him, which he eagerly consumes, reveals another point of neighborly connection.[4] Eventually, after being reassured by Sue that the Hmong do not eat dogs (only cats), Walt invites his (mostly Hmong-speaking) neighbors into his yard, onto his lawn, where he grills burgers for everyone. While still drinking heavily, Walt does seem for a moment to be genuinely happy. For Litz, "forming connections with positive cultures and groups may be an optimal vehicle for transcendence—being part of something and being accepted by a group helps construct meaning and purpose that transcends the self" (704). For a brief moment, Walt seems to be in the midst of one of those "corrective life experiences" that can repair moral injury.

The violence of the gangs, however, disrupts this possibility. Thao is being threatened into joining the gang, and Walt seems helpless to prevent this. He tries to Americanize Thao, to butch him up some, teach him the distanced, rough banter that men sometimes have with each other. Walt coaches him, "Don't swear *at* the guy you're talking to, swear about another guy who ain't there." Walt vouches for Thao so that he can get a construction job, even stakes him to his first tool belt, trying to anchor him in what Walt understands as the American Way. It is useless. The gang jumps Thao, beating him and stealing the borrowed tools. Walt responds the only way he know how: with violence. He beats up one of the gang as a warning to back off of Thao. The gang retaliates, escalating the violence once again, shooting up the Hmong house and brutally beating and raping Sue. Walt understands that the violence will never end as long as his Hmong neighbors—his friends—are vulnerable to gang violence. Killing cannot "fix" anything.

In his article on moral repair, Litz warns therapists to be "mindful that this idea of making amends can sometimes be taken to an extreme; patients can come to feel that they, like Walt, must focus their lives only on activities that will 'right their wrong'" or expiate their sins (704). Walt meets with Thao, who believes they will ride off together to avenge his family. The young man picks up the rifle Walt had been cleaning and asks him what it feels like to kill a man. Walt's response is to lock Thao in the basement to prevent his act of revenge. Through the mesh door, like the partition in a confessional, Walt finally answers Thao's question:

> You want to know how it's like to kill a man? Well it's goddamn awful, that's what it is. The only thing worse is getting a medal of valor for killing some poor kid that wanted to just give up—that's all. Yeah, some scared little gook, just like you. I shot him right in the face with that rifle you were holding in there a while ago.

Thao screams to be let out, swearing to kill Walt, but the veteran is bent on saving him from himself:

> Not a day goes by that I don't think about it. You don't want that on your soul. Now I've got blood on my hands. I'm soiled. That's why I'm going it alone tonight. (*Gran Torino*)

Walt manages to find transcendence, just not the kind envisioned by Litz or his colleagues. He does go to the gangbangers' turf, leaving for this last mission unarmed, pistol and rifle still at home. With racist language—"swamp rats," "shrimp dicks"—he baits the gangbangers into shooting him as he pulls his trusty Zippo out of his jacket pocket (*Gran Torino*). Because he has no weapons on him, gang members cannot claim self-defense. They are herded into police vehicles and taken away. As Sue and Thao rush up on the scene, a Hmong officer lets them know that there are witnesses who will come forward and the bad guys will be put in prison for a long time. In the penultimate scene, the movie winds up where it began, at a funeral mass. This time, however, there are Hmong in the church.

In contrast to Walt's guilt over shooting an enemy combatant who was trying to surrender, Navy SEAL sniper Chris Kyle (Bradley Cooper) in *American Sniper* shows no guilt or remorse over the acts he committed on the battlefield. Unlike the other service members, Kyle has a clear framework for justifying the killings that would mark his military career. His violent and tyrannical father enforced with his belt an aggressive masculinity predicated on a triune world: the passive sheep, the protector sheepdog, and the predatory wolf. Determined that his boys will grow up to be neither sheep nor wolves, Kyle's father forces his young children to learn early on that their manhood depends on never walking away from a fight. Violence is not just an option in this world; it is the only option. Within this framework, joining the service as a Navy SEAL in response to the 1993 World Trade Center bombing is unproblematic.

Likewise, the brutality of basic training in the film simply reinforces the link between masculinity and violence. Vietnam veteran and clinician R. Wayne Eisenhart argues that military training consciously equates "military performance" and "military mission with raw aggression" (14). Eisenhart trained as a Marine in the 1970s in preparation for going to Vietnam. He describes an incident in basic training that involved the male sexual organ and the breech action of an M14 rifle. While such deliberate torture and mutilation of recruits is currently prohibited, the bar scene in *American Sniper* in which the men throw darts into each other's naked back indicates that the cult of masculinity and aggression persists.

For a sniper, "performance" means one-on-one killing from ambush. The sniper "sees the enemy in the scope," according to retired Marine Gunnery Sergeant Jack Coughlin in the foreword to *Triggermen*. "There is no guessing for" the sniper about who killed whom. As Coughlin explains, the "grunts on the ground" might be able to see "the fighter go down but not what the bullet has done to the human body." Through his scope, the sniper "may watch his target writhe in pain for long periods until he succumbs to the wounds" (Coughlin xii). The justification for this kind of deliberate, selective killing—for Coughlin and for the character Chris Kyle—is that snipers protect their fellow service members from harm. Taya (Sienna Miller), Kyle's girlfriend and eventual wife, asks him directly: "You ever think about what happens when it's a real person on the end of that gun?" (*American Sniper*). He does not think about it.

Like Tom Highway, Kyle cannot easily compartmentalize the linkage of aggression and masculinity. Further, this link is sexualized for Kyle. After watching his fellow SEALs deliberately puncture each other, Kyle turns from the game of "darts" to the game of seduction, picking up Taya in the same bar. The sexualized link between masculinity and aggression takes on more intensity when Kyle, in Iraq, listens to Taya, in San Diego, ask him if he wants her to "talk dirty" to him while he looks around for someone to kill. Home again, and apparently having regained some equilibrium, Kyle—with gun in hand—orders Taya to "drop those drawers." It is not Kyle alone who equates masculinity with aggression and guns. A veteran who has lost both legs responds enthusiastically to target practice: "Damn, if that don't feel like I got my balls back" (*American Sniper*).

His aggression and willingness to kill are put to the test when the United States invades Iraq. The combination of his father's emphasis on the moral necessity of the use of aggression and his SEAL training as a sniper result in his ability to kill anyone: man, woman, and child alike. Anyone who *appears* to threaten American or coalition forces becomes fair game to him. As barracks-mate Biggles (Jake McDorman) puts it, killing a child is justified because "that kid could have taken out like ten fucking marines." Through three tours of duty, behind his sniper's scope or leading a unit in door-to-door combat, Kyle appears to have no thoughts about the humanity of the Iraqis he encounters, no regrets at all about killing. His reliance on armed aggression only falters in his fourth tour when he is brought to tears by almost having to kill a four-year-old boy who picked up an RPG. His certainty of his righteousness allows him to serve four tours in Iraq, where he has over 160 confirmed kills. Asked by a VA clinician, "Do you ever think that you might have seen things or done things over there which you wish you hadn't?" Kyle denies any concern for or regret over his killing (*American Sniper*).

Among all the service personnel in war films directed by Clint Eastwood, Kyle fits most closely into army psychologist and historian David Grossman's description of someone with the "aggressive predisposition" of a killer. Lacking empathy for others, Kyle had no problem killing men, women, and children in Iraq. In Grossman's terms, the "presence of aggression, combined with the absence of empathy, results in sociopathy" (182). Grossman maintains that not all those who kill during military service, heedless of another's humanity, qualify as sociopaths. He asserts that some "armed and vigilant" men "would not misuse or misdirect their aggression any more than a sheepdog would turn on his flock" (183–84). Kyle's lack of empathy actually appears to protect him from the regrets and disillusionment faced by some of the other servicemen and veterans portrayed in the film—especially his friend Marc Lee (Luke Grimes), who is ultimately killed by the enemy sniper Mustafa (Sammy Sheik). Kyle blames Lee's death on the doubts he harbored about the validity of US involvement in the Middle East. For Kyle, doubt gets a man killed.

Like Ira Hayes and Doc Bradley, Kyle believes he should be with his unit even more than with his family. As Grossman points out, "veterans describe the powerful bonds that men forge in combat as stronger than those of husband and wife" (90). The quotidian now offends Kyle, whose focus is entirely on the men he believes he can and should protect: "There's a war going on and no one cares. There is a war going on and I'm headed to the mall. I am not supposed to be here, I'm supposed to be over there." The guilt that his absence from Iraq puts fellow marines at risk increases with each rotation home. Before his third tour, he appears to come completely unhinged when a nurse lets his newborn daughter cry. Like Walt Kowalski, Kyle is completely withdrawn, unavailable to his wife and children. As Taya explains to him, "Even when you're here, you're not here. I see you and feel you, but you're not here." Fearful for his life and for her family, Taya confronts him about what appears to her to be a death wish. Echoing Aggie's lament that Highway would "volunteer for every damn war that came down the pike," Taya demands to know why he continues on for a second, third, fourth tour of duty. Like Highway, Kyle cannot understand how his repeated tours affect his family. He falls back on the standard war rhetoric: "I do it for you, to protect you." She will have none of that: "No you don't. I'm here, your family is here, your children have no father." Just as Aggie was finally forced to leave Highway, Taya reaches the same conclusion: "If you leave again, I don't think we'll be here when you get back." Kyle may deny that war changes him, but his wife knows better: "You're wrong. You can only circle the flames so long" (*American Sniper*).

Guilt over "abandoning" his comrades prompted tours two and three; it is clearly vengeance that pulls him back for the fourth. Kyle's friend Biggles is shot in the eye. Before he succumbs to his wounds in a US VA facility, Biggles begs Kyle not to go back. For Kyle, however, failure to exact revenge would make him a sheep instead of a proper sheepdog: "You're my brother. They're gonna hafta pay for what they did to you." Kyle's quest for vengeance intensifies when his closest friend Marc Lee is killed by the same sniper. Vengeance shapes his every action on that fourth tour, ultimately impairing the overall mission. While in Sadr City, Kyle finally gets the opportunity to take a clear shot (albeit a mile away). Despite being ordered to stand down so as not to put his own men at risk, he chooses to kill. The shot discloses the unit's position, which is beyond immediate reinforcements and vulnerable to attack. It is only after he kills Mustafa that Kyle calls his wife and announces: "I'm ready to come home" (*American Sniper*).

According to anthropologist Pearl Katz, the "basic orientation of a military organization is toward the possibility of violence on the battlefield" (460). What this means is that men who fight and kill "are left with the dilemma of how to reconcile acts of behavior that in peacetime were regarded as among the most heinous of crimes, but for which they had been trained and then encouraged to perform" (Jones 246). As Grossman points out, "balancing the obligation to kill with the resulting toll of guilt forms a significant cause of psychiatric casualties on the battlefield"—a process identified by Jonathan Shay and others as moral injury (91). Those war movies directed by Clint Eastwood raise the most difficult of issues for the genre. When men kill other men, they do harm to themselves too. Such an act cannot be without consequences for the individual. As Dave Grossman, a former Army Ranger and retired lieutenant colonel, argues, "The dead soldier takes his misery with him, but the man who killed him must forever live and die with him. The lesson becomes increasingly clear. Killing is what war is all about, and killing in combat, by its very nature, causes deep wounds of pain and guilt" (93). Sending men into combat puts them in a morally untenable position: "If he overcomes this resistance to killing and kills an enemy soldier in close combat, he will be forever burdened with blood guilt, and if he elects not to kill, then the blood guilt of his fallen comrades and the shame of his profession, nation, and cause lie upon him. He is damned if he does, and damned if he doesn't" (Grossman 87). Jonathan Shay argues that it is the "enlisted ranks who pay the butcher's bill" for a nation's decision to enter into war ("Moral Injury" 187). Clint Eastwood's war films, though few in number, take the clinical research done by Shay and others within the Veterans Administration and project onto the screen the lasting, devastating damage done by moral injury.

Notes

1. In an interview with Paul Nelson, Eastwood noted that the original script, titled *The Warriors*, was "one of the best antiwar stories I'd ever seen." Scenes discussing "the whole deal about why and the philosophies of war," however, were cut, reducing it to a "shoot 'em up" and leaving it "completely dehumanized." Eastwood offered to recut the movie in order to "put back the values that were in the script." MGM refused. See Avery, *Conversations with Clint: Paul Nelson's Lost Interviews with Clint Eastwood, 1979–1983*, 51–52.

2. The name Iwo Jima means Sulfur Island.

3. It may be reasonable to argue that the men's actions, the risks they took to protect their fellow men, were heroic. The dissonance is produced by which actions of theirs specifically are labeled and trumpeted as "heroic." Raising a scrap of fabric on a pole was not one of those actions.

4. Manohla Dargis notes that "Mr. Eastwood's loose, at times very funny performance in the early part of the film is one of its greatest pleasures." Given that all the women in the scene were Hmong with no acting experience, one wonders whether a bit of Clint Eastwood's own delight may have slipped through the character of Walt Kowalski. It is the least cinematically constructed moment in the film and, in terms of the character, the most hopeful.

Works Cited

American Sniper. Directed by Clint Eastwood, Warner Bros., 2014.

Avery, Kevin, editor. *Conversations with Clint: Paul Nelson's Lost Interviews with Clint Eastwood, 1979–1983*. Continuum, 2011.

Basham, Kathryn. "Commentary on the Keynote Lecture Presented by Dr. Jonathan Shay, Friday, June 27, 2008, Titled 'The Trials of Homecoming: Odysseus Returns from Iraq/Afghanistan,' and Additional Reflections." *Smith College Studies in Social Work*, vol. 79, nos. 3–4, 2009, pp. 299–309, doi: 10.1080/00377310903152963.

Bradshaw, Peter. Review of *Flags of Our Fathers*. *The Guardian* [New York / US Edition], 22 Dec. 2006, Drama sec.

Canby, Vincent. "In the War Tradition, *Where Eagles Dare*." Review. *New York Times*, 13 Mar. 1969, www.nytimes.com/movie/review?res=9A05E6DA1039E63AB C4B52DFB5668382679EDE. Accessed 13 Jan. 2016.

Coughlin, Jack. Foreword. *Triggermen: Shadow Team, Spider-Man, the Magnificent Bastards, and the American Combat Sniper*, by Hans Halberstadt, St. Martin's Press, 2008, pp. xxi–xxii.

Dargis, Manohla. "Hope for a Racist, and Maybe a Country." Review of *Gran Torino*. *New York Times*, 11 Dec. 2008, Movie sec., www.nytimes.com/2008/12/12/movies/ 12tori.html?_r=0. Accessed 18 Jan. 2016.

Dower, John W. "Lessons from Iwo Jima." *Perspectives on History*, Sept. 2007, www. historians.org/publications-and-directories/perspectives-on-history/september-2007/ lessons-from-iwo-jima. Accessed 18 Jan. 2016.

Eisenhart, R. Wayne. "You Can't Hack It Little Girl: A Discussion of the Covert Psychological Agenda of Modern Combat Training." *Journal of Social Issues*, vol. 31, no. 4, 1975, pp. 13–23.

Flags of Our Fathers. Directed by Clint Eastwood, Paramount, 2006.

Gault, William Barry. "Some Remarks on Slaughter." *American Journal of Psychiatry*, vol. 128, no. 4, Oct. 1971, pp. 450–54.

Gran Torino. Directed by Clint Eastwood, Warner Bros. / Village Roadshow, 2009.

Grossman, Dave. *On Killing: The Psychological Cost of Learning to Kill in War and Society*. Little, Brown and Company, 1995.

Halberstadt, Hans. *Triggermen: Shadow Team, Spider-Man, the Magnificent Bastards, and the American Combat Sniper*, St. Martin's Press, 2008.

Heartbreak Ridge. Directed by Clint Eastwood, Warner Bros., 1986.

Hendin, Herbert, and Ann Pollinger Haas. *Wounds of War: The Psychological Aftermath of Combat in Vietnam*. Basic Books, 1984.

Hoge, Charles W., et al. "Combat Duty in Iraq and Afghanistan, Mental Health Problems, and Barriers to Care." *New England Journal of Medicine*, vol. 351, no. 1, 1 July 2004, pp. 13–22.

Jones, Edgar. "The Psychology of Killing: The Combat Experience of British Soldiers in the First World War." *Journal of Contemporary History*, vol. 41, no. 2, Apr. 2006, pp. 229–46.

Katz, Pearl. "Emotional Metaphors, Socialization, and the Roles of Drill Sergeants." *Ethos*, vol. 18, no. 4, Dec. 1990, p. 457.

Kelly's Heroes. Directed by Brian G. Hutton, MGM, 1970.

Letters from Iwo Jima. Directed by Clint Eastwood, Warner Bros., 2006.

Litz, Brett T., et al. "Moral Injury and Moral Repair in War Veterans: A Preliminary Model and Intervention Strategy." *Clinical Psychology Review*, vol. 29, no. 8, Dec. 2009, pp. 695–706.

Maguen, Shira, et al. "The Impact of Killing on Mental Health Symptoms in Gulf War Veterans." *Psychological Trauma: Theory, Research, Practice, and Policy*, vol. 3, no. 1, Feb. 2011, pp. 21–26.

Muse, Eben J. "From Lt. Calley to John Rambo: Repatriating the Vietnam War." *Journal of American Studies*, vol. 27, no. 1, Apr. 1993, pp. 88–92.

Nalty, Bernard C., and Danny J. Crawford. *The United States Marines on Iwo Jima: The Battle and the Flag Raisings*. History and Museums Division, Headquarters, U. S. Marine Corps, 1995.

Shay, Jonathan. "Learning about Combat Stress from Homer's *Iliad*." *Journal of Traumatic Stress*, vol. 4, no. 4, 1991, pp. 561–79.

———. "Moral Injury." *Psychoanalytic Psychology*, vol. 31, no. 2, 2014, pp. 182–91.

———. "The Trials of Homecoming: Odysseus Returns from Iraq/Afghanistan." *Smith College Studies in Social Work*, vol. 79, nos. 3–4, 2009, pp. 286–98, doi:10.1080/00377310903130332.

Where Eagles Dare. Directed by Brian G. Hutton, MGM, 1969.

Wood, David. "Moral Injury: The Recruits." *Huffington Post*, 19 Mar. 2014, projects. huffingtonpost.com/projects/moral-injury/the-recruits. Accessed 16 Jan. 2016.

10

Another Fistful

The *American Sniper* Franchise and Clint Eastwood's
Post-9/11 American War Film as Neo-Western

David Buchanan

Much has been said about the *American Sniper* franchise that Chris Kyle, Clint Eastwood, Jason Hall, and Bradley Cooper ushered into cultural significance in 2014. Yes, Kyle's service as a Navy SEAL began and concluded far before his "autobiography" (a book cowritten with Scott McEwen and Jim DeFelice) appeared in 2012, but the book, the lies Kyle told about Jesse Ventura, the extra Silver Star he dishonestly claimed, and the murder that ended his life all make Chris Kyle a troubling icon for America's post-9/11 wars. What is it about Kyle's particular war experience and the manner in which he reflected on that experience that led to the franchise's massive popularity, a popularity that exploded when Eastwood's film version of Kyle's book appeared?

The answer is troubling and elusive, but the debate that circles the *American Sniper* franchise is an important one, for the debate is about so much more than Chris Kyle. Not only does the franchise force many to consider the manner in which Americans care for and memorialize veterans, but it also asks us all to ponder the way military members conceive an enemy he or she is asked to kill on our behalf. At a minimum, Chris Kyle's story and the way Eastwood tells it forced many civilians, for the first time, to form and express opinions about a war that, in 2014, had become so easy to forget.

As far as Eastwood's film is concerned, however, the debate about *American Sniper* typically surrounds the dueling issues of authenticity, historiography, and the political moment that Kyle presents in his book and that Eastwood adapts to film. Sophia A. McClennen best summarizes the basic offensiveness of the *American Sniper* film. She writes:

> The logic of war is completely unquestioned, making this the most simplistic war film we have seen nominated for an Oscar in decades. But the fact that the film has no nuance, no context and no subtlety should not surprise us. . . . This is a movie that's not just about a sniper, but also about an attitude that threatens to destroy any chance in our nation for political compromise and productive debate. And that's what makes this movie really disturbing.

And disturbing it most certainly is. Both the book and the movie focus on Kyle's life before and during his service in Iraq, deployments that allowed this exceptionally effective and unapologetic Navy SEAL to amass a total of 160 confirmed kills as a sniper. So McClennen is right to say that the movie is disturbing. That phrase alone—160 confirmed kills as a sniper—should be enough to disturb anyone.

But, since the movie appeared, one thing has become fairly clear about the debates that circle Chris Kyle and the movie Jason Hall (the screenwriter) and Clint Eastwood ushered into existence: what disturbs one American doesn't always necessarily disturb any others. Indeed, some people aren't disturbed at all by the puritanical savage/civilian binary that Kyle explicitly invokes in his book, a binary he puts to good use as he justifies, defends, explains, and compartmentalizes the actions he took as a sniper. Here is Kyle in his book:

> Savage, despicable evil. That's what we were fighting in Iraq. That's why a lot of people, myself included, called the enemy "savages." There really was no other way to describe what we encountered there.
>
> People ask me all the time, "How many people have you killed?" My standard response is, "Does the answer make me less, or more, of a man?"

The number is not important to me. I only wish I had killed more. Not for bragging rights, but because I believe the world is a better place without savages out there taking American lives. (4)

It is important for Kyle that he maintains this binary, and his repeated utterance of such a Manichaean world view is sufficient fodder for most critics to, as Alex Trimble Young writes, "discredit the film's humanization of Kyle" and thereby "neglect the nuances of its plot and camera work."

Translating unvarnished reportage into nuanced art is a difficult feat, so Young is at least partially right. The film makes apparent—in ways that the so-called autobiography does not—that many Americans (not just Chris Kyle) accept the savage/civilian binary as reasonable and necessary in the way we fight war in a post-9/11 world. As Robert Ivie summarizes in his essay "Savagery in Democracy's Empire," "Although the trope of savagery is not unique to American war rhetoric, it is indigenous to it and deeply ingrained in the political culture" (52). Sociologically speaking, then, Kyle's book and Eastwood's movie prove that the trope of savagery is also deeply ingrained in American war culture and the American military. In his 2014 book, *The Puritan Culture of America's Military*, Ronald Lorenzo comes to the conclusion that, after an extensive analysis of US Army war crimes in Iraq and Afghanistan, there persists in the military what he calls a strain of "Puritanical revenge." He writes:

Instead of revenge, in its more traditional, and therefore authentic state, Puritanical revenge takes a form in which violence still exists but the existence of the emotion driving that violence is hypocritically denied. . . . [W]here traditional forms of revenge had a limit on deaths socially imposed by the community, there is an apparent infinite desire for revenge—and deaths—in the wars waged in Iraq and Afghanistan. (111)

As an officer in the military and a veteran of both Iraq and Afghanistan, I, too, am disturbed by the *American Sniper* franchise. I am, as are dozens of other critics, appalled when such attitudes are normalized in war and then reinforced in art. This is also why it is difficult for me to accept the canonization of such a man in such a film, especially if we read the film as just one more step in the construction of Chris Kyle's hagiography. I am also troubled by the enthusiasm of an American reading and viewing public that is hungry for narratives and films of this sort. Many seem too eager for the gore and the titillation that come from the easy consumption of vicarious war experience.

Despite what Kyle said and did, however, the ultimate question that remains about Eastwood's adaptation of Kyle's life to film is whether or not Eastwood blesses or subverts Kyle's uneducated and myopic world view. Where some see nuance and ambivalence, I see manipulation and glorification through elements of filmmaking that were carefully chosen to create an extensive scapegoat mechanism for an easily controlled audience. The resulting film doesn't challenge or question Kyle's puritanical narrative of war as much as it provides a vicarious purging for an audience's massive, collective war guilt, a guilt that perhaps shouldn't be so easily cleansed.

Early on in his book, Kyle questions the value of, as he writes, "publishing [his] life story" (5). This is the central issue of the franchise, as I see it. For one, this rare note of humility (just short of false modesty) claims the benefits that attend a memoir-styled war story like Kyle's. And it happily occupies that privileged space, a space cemented by the fact that many endow such tales with the epistemological strength that follows testimony and myth. Indeed, I would firmly fix both Kyle's book and Eastwood's movie as troubling manifestations of Gerald Vizenor's concept of "manifest manners" (3). Moreover, both are overt and rather bland expressions of what Tom Engelhardt describes as "the imperial unconscious," a master narrative of American war culture that has been renewed and invigorated through various forms of post-9/11 American war discourse (103). This is what makes the *American Sniper* franchise so problematic; it provides us another round of what Vizenor calls "the literature of dominance" (7). As Vizenor would quickly remind us, however, the literatures of dominance are not "cultural visions"; rather, they are simulations of, as he says, "vicious encounters with the antiselves of civilization, the invented savage" (7).

Kyle has little concern for such dialectic imagining in his book, and while I certainly hope his world view is different from that of the average American military member or civilian, the franchise he began with his "autobiography" presents the inherent issue that faces a biopic like the one Eastwood directs: to be successful and/or popular, the representative must be made both familiar and exceptional at the same time. The *American Sniper* movie is dripping with familiarity, and the title screams exceptionalism. As Lee Clark Mitchell writes in *Westerns: Making the Man in Fiction and Film*, a popular text or film should contain a "capacity" to "fulfill yet alter expectations, giving its audience a sense of novelty tinged by familiarity" (15–16). Or, as Mitchell continues, a film's popular appeal "lies in appearing to resolve cultural dilemmas in a way that satisfies disparate groups with opposed interests" (16). Since we must accept that the film version of *American Sniper* was a popular success—insofar as sales (it is the highest grossing war film of all time) and Oscar nominations (the film was nominated for six categories) reflect the relative appeal of the film—it is fascinating to reveal the manner in which its filmmakers achieved such popularity, such familiarity. Or, better yet, the scholar is practically dared to trace the ways in which Eastwood and Hall *appear* to "resolve" the "cultural dilemmas" (or, rather, the dilemma of culturally sponsored violence) that face the agents of post-9/11 war.

There is, of course, the added sadness that attends Kyle's life, and there is the fact that, in the end, his skill with a rifle and his savage/civilian perspective failed to bring him or his family protection from the ravages of war. Yet the "autobiography" Kyle wrote and the life Kyle lived must have presented Eastwood and Hall with rather tricky material to adapt into film. The simplistic perspective of the book fits the metanarrative, but Kyle's testimony follows no narrative arc. Indeed, with some effort, one could read Kyle's "autobiography" as nothing more than a firsthand account of SEAL training and war as told by a writer with the diction and narrating capabilities of a man who spent a large portion of his life being guided by the inertia of a career in the military while acquiring little or no formal education beyond high school. In small chunks of text, Kyle describes barroom fights, weapons, encounters with his future wife, and combat, all with the same matter-of-fact tone. When he does discuss the political realities of the war in which he fought, he sounds like a man repeating intelligence briefings he received while he was deployed to Iraq. When he describes punching a guy in a crowded bar in Steamboat Springs, Colorado, his narration differs very little from the way he describes shooting a man with an AK-47 in Ramadi, Iraq. This is the narration Hall and Eastwood had to reshape when they got ahold of Kyle's story.

There may have once been a clear line between Chris Kyle the man and Chris Kyle the character, but the various versions of the man who reached the reading and viewing public made that line an indiscernible one. It was blurred by the self-deceptions of the author, the manipulations of the screenwriter, the filmmaking experiences of the director, and the expectations of a war-weary public in need of a purge. This is where and how Eastwood's politics, career, and filmmaking techniques found particular purchase with the puritanical revenge metanarrative Kyle embraces. But Eastwood couldn't quite make it all work without—as Young points out in his *Salon* piece about the film—translating Kyle's "facts" into cinematic fiction with countless book-to-movie divergences and a number of outright inventions. While I agree with Young that it is rather "remarkable" that many critics "treat a carefully engineered Harper Collins bestseller as an authentic account of its putative author's inner life," I do draw forth a slightly different lesson regarding Eastwood and Hall's specific manipulations. Young argues that Eastwood's adaptation is "not a war movie: it's a classic revisionist western." Because the hero dies, Young suggests, Eastwood delivers a "subtle critique on frontier justice and hyper-masculinity." By revealing the incongruent ironies in Kyle's life, so goes Young's argument, the Western-styled tropes and plot structure of the movie make it easy for us to recognize Kyle's world as a "deliberate collision of liberal humanism with frontier violence," a collision that highlights how "the tragedies perpetrated and experienced by men like Kyle are not a conservative problem; they are an American problem." Richard Brody, for the *New Yorker*, argues something similar, that Eastwood's film, "without expressly challenging so-called American values, raises the question of the abuse of those values in a system that lets armchair warriors send real ones to destruction in vain."

Both Brody and Young are right to alert us to the Western shape of Eastwood's adaptation. Indeed, we've long been trained to look for the Western in modern war stories. As Richard Slotkin writes in *Gunfighter Nation* (1992), "the readiest ways to modernize the frontier hero was to militarize him" (88). This seems especially true in post-9/11 war culture. One might even argue that the inverse of Slotkin's statement is more accurate today: the readiest way to popularize a contemporary military hero is to expose him (or her, think Jessica Lynch) to frontier conditions. Bradley Cooper (who plays Kyle in the film and convinced Warner Brothers to purchase the movie rights to the autobiography) noted in an interview with National Public Radio's Terry Gross in early 2015:

> I love the idea of framing it as a Western. I thought that could be very sort of cinematically viable—ripe for cinema—to have this story. And that this guy happened to be incredibly charismatic. . . . You have a guy going into a town, and there's his equivalent on the other side— another sharpshooter. He's a sharpshooter. You end it in, you know,

tumbleweeds. At the dust storm, there's a showdown. This sort of, you know, one man and his sort of pursuit—that idea. Framing this genre within a Western construct was sort of something that I thought would be interesting. (Cooper)

Indeed, according to Cooper, it wasn't until he and Hall "framed" Kyle's story "as a Western" that the studio "went for it." As Danny Leigh writes in his review of the film for *The Guardian*, "when in doubt, make a Western."

Thus, the critic is left with the nagging task of figuring out what to do with a war film that cements its narrative strength within the seductive—yet dubious—metatestimonial construct on which the *American Sniper* franchise capitalizes. Plus, we must account for what it is about the film's biographical source that makes the story so perfectly suited for generic mash-up. Ultimately, then, it is difficult to agree with Young that Hall and Eastwood's book-to-movie fabrications offer a "subtle" critique on much of anything. Rather, I argue that it is far more fruitful to examine this contemporary war film and the reasons *why* the Western so easily delivers the gratification for which the public hungers. Whereas some may read Eastwood's adaptation as a revealing indictment of the myth-making moment that is so repetitive in other representations of post-9/11 combat, I read his additions as symbolic manipulations that do little beyond deepening Kyle's fitness to serve as our convenient scapegoat. Eastwood and Hall use Kyle's service, his tragic end, and his conventionally racist perspective to turn a veteran into a little bundle of trauma for us all to pity. The result is more reverent than subversive, more cleansing than questioning. Kyle's world view is never exposed as untenable or unhealthy; it merely deepens his victimhood.

In his 2009 essay for *PMLA*, which is dedicated in its entirety to war, Fredric Jameson points out that there are often formal elements in representations of war that "are content to confirm the stereotype" of traditional aesthetics (1533). Jameson goes on: "Indeed one often has the feeling that all war novels (and war films) are pretty much the same and have few enough surprises for us, even though their situations may vary. In practice, we can enumerate some seven or eight situations, which more or less exhaust the genre" (1533). I agree. Very little material within the growing body of contemporary war literature and film is worth a second look or a closer read. Violence, instead of being shaped into pictures of depravity or narratives that explore man's capacity to visit inhumanity on his fellow man, often ends with repeated pleas for pity for war's agents, following a somewhat automatic assumption of the savage/civilian binary. This soldierly impulse in witness-based war narratives is what Paul Fussell describes as the "*versus* habit" (86; italics original). While such a narrative habit doesn't always result in pictures that wallow in patriotic splendor, such narratives do often allow viewers a chance to respond in conventionally moral terms. Peter Berg's film *Lone Survivor* (2013), for instance, which was also based on another Navy SEAL's cowritten autobiography, presents one small slice of the war in Afghanistan in such a way that it elicits little more than the vicarious thrill drawn from the spectacle of four Americans fighting a horde of brown people. True empathy is nowhere in the equation, for neither the American heroes nor the Afghani people who save the "lone" survivor. Such representation can be thrilling to behold, but this is also probably why so many of our contemporary war narratives land with a muted sound of rote.

So yes, the complementing genres of war writing and war film do indeed seem exhausted. Jameson lists eight "narrative variants" that drive war's representation in fiction and film, and, since 9/11, popular war narratives rarely escape the solipsism of the very first one he lists: "the existential experience of war" (1533). This is perhaps why these narratives test our patience at times. In the case of the *American Sniper* franchise, the movie not only deploys the narrative variants of one exhausted genre but blends the master tropes and plot structures of *two* exhausted ones. After all, Kyle's book was far easier to ignore before the movie came out even though it graced the *New York Times* best-seller list for months before Kyle's death and years before the movie was released.

As Cooper reported in his interview with Terry Gross, *American Sniper* the film isn't a biopic; it's a Western. He and Hall set out to create it as such far before Eastwood even signed on as the director. However, different lessons can be drawn about that creation when we compare the film Eastwood made to other popular Westerns. Young draws a parallel between *American Sniper* and John Ford's *The Man Who Shot Liberty Valance* (1962). Brody compares it to Ford's *The Searchers* (1956). Stevie Howell does the same with elements from *Unforgiven* (1992). None of these analyses, however, sufficiently explain the filmmakers' manipulations of Kyle's "autobiography" as they created this Western and dressed it up as war reportage. The easy redemptive payoff and the scapegoating process that Eastwood's film completes is quite obvious, however, when we compare it to the Western that made Eastwood famous, Sergio Leone's *A Fistful of Dollars* (1964).

Camera angles, the establishment of setting, the introduction of the hero, the generic context from which it emerges: Eastwood's contemporary war film shares much with his first Western. As Will Wright (in *Sixguns and Society*), Christopher Frayling (in *Spaghetti Westerns*), and Lee Clark Mitchell (in *Westerns*) all suggest, Leone's film ushered in the "Spaghetti Western" genre by challenging the genre itself. Along with Sam Peckinpah, Mitchell writes, Leone "turned the genre . . . inside out" in such a way that "not only did violence no longer offer moral resolution, it also served only marginally as closure to western plots now loosely defined" (224). With the Spaghetti Western, Mitchell suggests, Natty Bumppo's "hectoring expert" was replaced by a "degraded version of the stalwartly moral Westerner whose vision now extended no further than his own well-being" (225). *American Sniper* does the same thing, in reverse. And it takes no leap of the imagination to see that the hero that Hall and Eastwood created is far more similar to Cooper's Natty Bumppo than he is to Leone's Man with No Name. Indeed, *American Sniper*'s plot follows the dictates of a narrative that couples certain moral dogmatizing and a clear redemption cycle. For these reasons, I submit that instead of operating as a revisionist Western, Eastwood's *American Sniper* reverts to a genre of war films that predates the Spaghetti Western, Vietnam, and postmodernism. It not only reverts to a pre–Spaghetti Western message but it does so by using many of Leone's cinematic formal innovations.

Both *American Sniper* and *A Fistful of Dollars* accompany their opening credits with music, but each one follows a slightly different aural path: non-diegetic, sentimental music in the Western, a lone muezzin calling the faithful to prayer over a static-y speaker with the easily recognizable "Allahu akbar" in *Sniper*. In each case, the music characterizes the space and the hero. For Leone, Ennio Morricone's score, as Mitchell writes, gives "acoustic definition to personalities who seem visually two-dimensional. Compensating, as it were, for the silence of the characters, the music offers an external, sonic expression to attitudes felt otherwise unexpressed, even unfelt" (231–32). In the *Sniper*'s opening, as the call to prayer crystalizes, the hero is introduced as no empty moral shell. We never wonder what the Sniper is thinking or how he will respond to his environment. And, as we soon find out, he will often express, with zero ambiguity, his stark us-versus-them moral attitude. This is what the call to prayer signals: there will be no absent dimensions of personality to fill once we meet Eastwood's one-dimensional Sniper. The 'Allahu akbar" prayer-chant lands hard on one side of the binary oppositions and moral certitudes that will fuel the Sniper for the rest of the film.

As the opening credits of each film roll and the opening music fades, new sounds grow louder and become more distinct: the hero has arrived. For *A Fistful of Dollars*, the clippety-clop of the horse, carrying the hero, is dominant. The frame focuses on a patch of arid desert ground before the horse's hooves cross the screen. In *American Sniper*, the creaking iron tracks of an American tank invade the soundscape. Like Leone's opening, Eastwood's camera focuses on the tank's tread as it rolls into the frame and across destroyed and lifeless ground. With both films, the ground the hero must traverse to join the narrative is infertile and devoid of life, places in need of the hero's assistance. In Leone's film, one horse carries one man, but Eastwood's film requires a more substantial vehicle. Nothing smaller than a tank can carry the burden that the Sniper will soon shoulder on our behalf.

In each movie, the camera next pulls back to a position of moral high ground, up and behind the heroes, so that we can join our gaze to theirs as they survey the destroyed landscapes. And, in both films, the hero is somewhat precariously or uncomfortably perched there. The Man with No Name seeks a drink of water from a nearby well, silently, as a boy appears and nondiegetic cartoon sounds follow the boy's scamper across the scene. The Sniper suffers the heat as well, but his duty prevents him from seeking water. Instead, he searches for targets through his rifle's scope as sounds of war (radios, calling soldiers, the tank) establish the security of his moral high ground while simultaneously threatening his physical security. The worlds of both films need help, we are to assume, but the urgency differs between the two as the cameras switch to closeups of the heroes' faces. We study each one as each studies "them," but again the filmmakers establish the character of the hero in slightly different ways. In Leone's film, No Name shows nothing through his personality-erasing mask; we can't be sure whether he is going to growl or whether he is going to laugh. Of course, he does neither, and the effect is such that, as Mitchell writes, No Name seems "deprived of life altogether" while his "profound detachment and silence . . . seem the result of an emptying out of emotions *into* the world . . . giving the sense that emotions and world are in a kind of symbiotic relationship with one another" (233, 232). This is most certainly not the case for the Sniper and the world he surveys. No Name's face shows nothing, but the Sniper's is troubled by the onerous radio call he has to make when he finally finds his target (a man on a rooftop staring at the American patrol advancing down the road below). A voice on the radio clears the Sniper to shoot, but before he can pull the trigger the man disappears behind a wall. The ordered world on the other side of the radio slows the certainty and speed of the Sniper's work; the threats may be everywhere, but the Sniper's personal ethics are trumped by more onerous, official, detached ones. The Sniper returns to the scope, his face full of moral resolve. No Name, on the other hand, just observes, alone, bound only by his own set of ambiguous ethics.

Both opening sequences close with the hero watching a boy fall prey to the forces that rule the liminal spaces the heroes will soon enter. No Name watches two villains chase a boy out of a building with kicks and gunshots. A scantily dressed woman watches from a window, with slight concern, and the boy's father pulls the child back into a nearby shack. No Name smiles ever so slightly at the woman, but she slams the door in his face as a bell begins to beckon him deeper into this unknown town of unknown moral codes. The Sniper, too, spies a boy and a woman, but he watches them from afar, through his scope. No Name is recognized but denied involvement in the scene he observes while the Sniper is hidden but forced to intervene. The woman hands the boy a grenade, and the Sniper has no choice but to save his boy and his team of Americans from clear evil. No Name's boy is saved by his father; the Sniper saves his boy by shooting him.

But first, the Sniper reports the woman and the boy over the radio, and a voice responds, "You know the ROE [rules of engagement]. Your call" (Hall 3). The Sniper does pause and ponder his place and the call he must make, and Hall slightly complicates the ethical situation by inventing a line for Kyle's spotter: "They fry you if you're wrong," the youngster whispers. The Sniper's deep breathing slows in preparation for the shot, and the spotter repeats the sentiment: "Send your ass to Leavenworth" (3). But these bothersome ethics will cost him a target for the last time, so we know he won't fail to send his bullet downrange to kill this child. He may be aware of the moral difficulty of his role, but the rightness of his place on his high perch is secure throughout.

A fan of the film and Kyle's book may be quick to point out that Kyle's book opens with a similar anecdote, that Eastwood is merely shaping bland reportage to Oscar-worthy cinema, merely translating the textual into the visual. However, the movie adaptation takes considerable license with the source material in the opening scene and so many others. As many have pointed out, these additions humanize Kyle and clearly establish a level of ambivalent morality in the film narrative that simply doesn't exist in the book. As I see it, however, the movie fabrications don't exactly introduce a

healthy ambivalence; rather, they deepen the Sniper's fitness as our convenient scapegoat. In one scene, toward the middle of the movie, the Sniper is
on his way back into combat in Iraq when he passes his brother (a soldier in
the US Army) who is on his way home. One disillusioned brother passes an
illusioned one, and the brother says, "Fuck this place," as they part. The
Sniper is startled but unruffled by his brother's cynicism. So, unlike the
carefully constructed ambiguity that follows No Name in Leone's film, this
American Sniper scene, like the opening sequence, shapes the Sniper into a
vicarious vessel for a viewer's cathartic purgation. We don't pity the brother;
we pity the Sniper. We don't pity the child he shot; we pity the Sniper for
having to shoot him on our behalf.

This is why Hall and Eastwood's book-to-movie manipulations deserve
closer attention. Neither the exchange with the brother nor the killing of the
child ever happened. The tank from the opening is a movie invention as well.
In the book, Kyle does open with an anecdote about his very first "kill" as a
sniper, a shot that kills an Iraqi woman who sets a grenade ahead of a line of
marines in a manner similar to the movie's opening sequence. And, as Kyle
reports, "It was the first time I'd killed anyone while I was on the sniper rifle.
And the first time in Iraq—and the only time—I killed anyone other than
a male combatant" (3). But this wasn't enough for Hall and Eastwood; they
had to put the grenade in the hands of a young boy and make him Kyle's
first "kill." Indeed, in the film, this "kill" is paired with the Sniper-as-a-boy
shooting his first deer back in Texas. The boy-Sniper's father proudly
announces, "you got him," predicting that the boy is "gonna make a fine
hunter someday" (Hall 4). In his book, Kyle doesn't reflect on his first deer
at all, nor does he ever quote his father making such a prediction. In fact,
Kyle has little more to say about his first kill (a woman, not a boy) beyond
using the anecdote to segue into his explanation of the savage/civilian binary,
essentially the only rule that will guide him for the rest of his life.

"He had to do it," a student of mine once commented after reading the
opening pages of Kyle's book. I don't dispute such an argument at all. After
all, the book as a whole operates the same way, as one big shrug following
an extensive reportage of massive amounts of violence. What the film didn't
have to do, however, was to recast the Sniper as a victim. It didn't have to
turn "autobiography" into hagiography. The utter absence of ambiguity
leaves the viewer little room for a response other than pity, pity for the
triggerman instead of the dead child, pity for the men in the tank rather
than the people who live on the ground it crushes. When the invented boy

charges the invented tank with the grenade held high, Kyle justly shoots him for us. Thus, the film makes war easy. It makes it easy for us to forget the destroyed city in which other children live and die. It allows us to be refreshed and cleansed by the unburdening of war's guilt onto the shoulders of a vengeance-seizing scapegoat. Hall and Eastwood's fabrications don't critique the frontier justice that guided Kyle's life or the invasion of Iraq; they celebrate it.

The Spaghetti Western forced the genre to emerge from the stock plots of the traditional Western, plots shaped around the redemption of the hero. Eastwood and Hall's manipulations follow the same generic tradition closely, but they do so by disguising Kyle's redemption (and ours) within the innovations of Leone and Peckinpah. The Sniper dies, of course, but the additions and fictions they bring to the film ensure that his demise will provide the watching public a corresponding vicarious redemption. Indeed, the cinematic fictionalization of the Sniper is completed with a plot that rather closely follows Will Wright's "vengeance variation" of the stock narrative structure of the traditional Western, a structure that Wright argues guided the production of Westerns between 1949 and 1961 (all of the films he examines predate *A Fistful of Dollars*). Wright outlines this structure: "Unlike the classical hero who *joins* the society because of his strength and their weakness, the vengeance hero *leaves* the society because of his strength and their weakness. Moreover, the classical hero *enters* the fight because of the values of society; whereas, the vengeance hero *abandons* his fight because of those same values" (59; italics original). A few more examples (there are too many to be comprehensive) of the film's departures from the book are enough to show how Eastwood and Hall shaped a shapeless book into a plot that follows the structure of a traditional Western quite closely.

The Sniper is alternately part of society and outside society (both elements of Wright's vengeance plot) as he moves back and forth from his life at home with his family to the war in Iraq (Wright 69). In Iraq, as Wright's plot dictates, the Sniper, who "is revealed to have a special ability," is able to bring his sniping skills to bear on evil Muslims as he "seeks vengeance" on behalf of a society that is "unable to punish the villains" itself (69). But this skill comes at a price. In the movie, the Sniper's wife begs him to stay home, not to deploy to Iraq for a fourth time: "I need you to be human again," she says. Taya, the wife, is far more eloquent and introspective than the Sniper, and this is probably why the cowriters of Kyle's book encouraged Taya to contribute her own first-person commentaries to the "autobiography." In a number of them, she does repeatedly express her wish that Kyle would stay home, but that rather emotional line—"I need you to be human again"—exists nowhere in the book. Not only does it hit a rather striking emotional cord, it further shapes the Sniper into the hero of Wright's vengeance structure of the classic Western. As Wright puts it, after "society recognizes a difference between themselves and the hero . . . the hero is given a special status" (69). Kyle (in the book) and the Sniper (in the movie) both bear the nickname "The Legend," but Taya's comment cements his special status through displacement, distance from his family, and distance from his former humanity. This invented line also fits with Wright's eighth step of the vengeance structure in which "A representative of society asks the hero to give up his revenge" (69) since Taya repeatedly pleads with her husband to leave the navy and come home to his family. Yes, Kyle and the Sniper both come home, but the movie can't let the Sniper off so easily. He must first get revenge.

Thus, in the movie, after Kyle kills the boy with the grenade and the film flashes back to his upbringing and his failed rodeo career, Hall and Eastwood invent an extended revenge tale beginning in an invented bunkhouse. Kyle's friend Biggles hears of Kyle's proficiency with his rifle, and so he asks, "Did you pop your cherry?" Kyle responds, "It was evil, man. That was hate like I've never seen before." Kyle goes on to say that all his kills that day were "righteous. Like God was up there blowing on my bullets" (Hall 35, 36). In the book, Kyle does use the phrase about God's breath (I assume it is common among American snipers, or at least the Christian ones), but it is occasioned by his description of one of his "longest confirmed kills in Iraq," not his first "kill" as a sniper (179). The word "righteous" is also a movie invention. Thus, before the Sniper can end his vengeance, he must, as Wright's structure suggests, fight and defeat the evil villains before he can heed his wife's call and give up his "special status" (69).

As we know, Kyle killed 160 "villains" in real life, and the movie obliges by showing us a few of them. Of course, in the book, Kyle does not so clearly describe or establish the villainy of many of his kills, so the filmmakers do it for him. At one point in the movie, the Sniper is leading a group of marines through a section of Ramadi when they discover a frightened family. After a tense struggle, the father begs them all to come in from the alleyway: "please tell the others to come inside," he says. "If you are in the street, *he* will know" (Hall 45). This old man, it turns out, is right to be afraid. "He" is a particularly sadistic man who has been terrorizing the entire city, and, as we learn more about this horrible person, "he" clearly qualifies as an example of the specific vision of evil Kyle claims that he can see everywhere in Iraq. This man carries the nickname "the Butcher," and he punishes disloyal Iraqis by doing horrible things with a handheld drill. All of it—the old man, the butcher, the drill, the evil—are movie inventions.

Still, the butcher is not the Sniper's ultimate villain, an evildoer whose death is necessary for the prerequisite vengeance so the hero can give up his special status and reenter society. That role is played by a terrorist sniper named Mustafa who matches, as he must, the Sniper's skill with a rifle. Mustafa was even an Olympic marksman for Syria, and so the nature of this equally matched fight takes over the arc of the entire film. As the end of the movie and the Sniper's death near, this fair fight becomes the only thing to be examined as the Sniper becomes increasingly obsessed with killing his man. The Sniper speaks of him often to his superiors, and he is asked to head up a big mission specifically designed to kill Mustafa. And, as any good traditional Western should, the entire movie culminates when the Sniper finally kills the villain from the rooftop of a crumbling building. As a sandstorm bears down on the Sniper and his buddies from one side and a wave of brown people flows toward them from the other side, the Sniper kills Mustafa with a mile-long shot (not unlike the shot No Name takes to free Tuco from the noose at the end of *The Good, the Bad and the Ugly*).

But this is all movie magic. The villain in *American Sniper*—no, the entire narrative arc of the film—correlates with nothing in the book or, we can fairly assume, with Kyle's war. According to Kyle, nothing close to it ever happened to him or any other sniper. In the book, Mustafa is only mentioned once, in passing, and Kyle never mentions him again. Kyle even says that other snipers in the US military were rumored to kill this rumored man, but Kyle doesn't even know their names. The vengeance variation of the traditional Western must be completed, however, so the fabrications don't end there. After the Sniper shoots his villain, he rolls over and calls his wife on his satellite phone and tells her he is coming home. Again, nothing similar ever happened to Kyle in his life or in his book. In the book, he does mention that he often called his wife during various operations, but no conversation close to the one that closes the movie is recorded anywhere in the book. And while Kyle also mentions sandstorms in his book, not once does a sandstorm ever bear down on him or any American in any combat situation.

One could argue that many of the additions and narrative tweaks that the filmmakers deploy in *American Sniper* can be dismissed as little more than cheap additions of military kitsch needed to base a film on a "true story." And, to be fair, Hall and Eastwood's film does manage to follow the lead of the Western and create, as Mitchell describes the Western genre as a whole, "a formal tension between the self-confirming and self-contradictory" (21). Thus established, however, *American Sniper* departs sharply from the innovations of the Spaghetti Western to cement its fictional story with tired, repetitive, and predictable forms. In the work of Sam Peckinpah and Sergio Leone, Mitchell argues, one is left with a "joint sense of belatedness, of needing to revive the Western at a moment when it had come to seem exhausted as a form" (226). This is at least partially true of the *American Sniper* franchise. Eastwood, Hall, and Cooper are all driven by a similar sense of "belatedness" in relation to the post-9/11 American war story that was, and still is, fraught with unoriginality. For this reason, perhaps, they turned to the stock characters of the pre–Spaghetti Western in order to satisfy the easy payoff of the easily fabricated purgative war story. Mitchell suggests that *A Fistful of Dollars* "prompts a viewer to ask if the whole is to be taken straight or tongue-in-cheek" (227), but *American Sniper* carries no such parodic implication. There may be a few contradictions sprinkled throughout the film, but they pale in the shade cast by the scapegoated hero. The film, then, overtly confirms, for a complicit and easily rewarded viewing audience, that post-9/11 Americans still live in a just and ethical war culture.

Of Stephen Crane, Mitchell writes that fiction "reveals how tenaciously life imitates art and how historical facts therefore always need interpretation according to the conventions, clichés, and expectations established by legends that people believe" (21). Eastwood and Hall know this, and their knowledge of what made (and makes) Westerns so popular served them well when they fictionalized Chris Kyle's life. And that is, in this final assessment, the most disturbing part of the *American Sniper* franchise. Eastwood may have injected his narrative with a bit more ambivalence, but those injections did little more than neatly complete a well-worn cycle of American war and redemption via vicarious entertainment. As our morally overburdened scapegoat, Eastwood's *American Sniper* shows us in glaring detail how easy it is to turn war reportage into war legend, and, after the purge that the hero's death brings, leave a society ready to begin such a cycle again. The home footage of Kyle's funeral at the end of the film is Eastwood's final pandering gesture to such a society, one that wants little more than pictures explaining how a society can create a soldier, use that soldier as a tool of

aggression, and then purge any feelings of guilt through a vicarious experience of that soldier's death. When we are presented with Kyle's casket, sitting
squarely before the big blue star on the fifty-yard line of the Cowboys' home
in Texas Stadium, we can sigh with pity-filled relief. America's Sniper fits
well inside the home of "America's Team," and America is granted its purge.

We should feel uncomfortable with Kyle's existence and death and the
movie that portrays him, not necessarily because of what he did or what he
said, but because we needed him to exist at all. No matter how one feels
about Kyle's service, his lies, his portrayal in the film, or the brutal reality of
war of which he was an agent, nothing about that catharsis should leave us
undisturbed about America's relationship with war.

Works Cited

American Sniper. Directed by Clint Eastwood, screenplay by Jason Hall, Warner Bros.,
    2015.

Brody, Richard. "*American Sniper* Takes Apart the Myth of the American Warrior." *New
    Yorker Online*, 24 Dec. 14, www.newyorker.com/culture/richard-brody/american-sniper-
    takes-apart-myth-american-warrior.

Cooper, Bradley. "Bradley Cooper: *Sniper* Controversy Distracts from Film's Message
    about Vets." *Fresh Air*, interview by Terry Gross, National Public Radio, 2 Feb. 2015,
    npr.org/templates/transcript/transcript.php?storyId=383062401. Transcript.

Engelhardt, Tom. *The American Way of War: How Bush's Wars Became Obama's*. Haymar-
    ket Books, 2010.

A Fistful of Dollars. Directed by Sergio Leone, MGM, 1964.

Frayling, Christopher. *Spaghetti Westerns: Cowboys and Europeans from Karl May to Ser-
    gio Leone*. Revised ed., I. B. Tauris, 2006.

Fussell, Paul. *The Great War and Modern Memory*. 25th Anniversary ed., Oxford UP,
    2000.

Hall, Jason, screenwriter. *American Sniper*. By Chris Kyle with Scott McEwen and Jim
    DeFelice, 17 July 2013, pdl.warnerbros.com/wbmovies/awards2014/pdf/as.pdf.

Howell, Stevie. "America's Sniper." *Partisan*, 16 Apr. 2015, partisanmagazine.com/blog/
    2015/3/16/americas-sniper.

Ivie, Robert. "Savagery in Democracy's Empire." *Terrorism and the Politics of Naming*,
    edited by Michael Bhatia, Routledge, 2008, pp. 51–60.

Jameson, Fredric. "War and Representation." *PMLA*, vol. 24, no. 5, Oct. 2009, 1532–47.

Kyle, Chris, with Scott McEwan and Jim DeFelice. *American Sniper: The Autobiography
    of the Most Lethal Sniper in U. S. Military History*. HarperCollins, 2012.

Leigh, Danny. "American Sniper: An Old-Fashioned Western in Military Uniform."
    Guardian, 29 Jan. 2015, theguardian.com/film/2015/jan/29/american-sniper-
    old-fashioned-western.

Lone Survivor. Directed by Peter Berg, screenplay by Berg, based on the book by Marcus
    Luttrell with Patrick Robinson, Film 44, 2014.

Lorenzo, Ronald. *The Puritan Culture of America's Military*. Ashgate, 2014.

McClennen, Sophia A. "*American Sniper*'s Biggest Lie: Clint Eastwood Has a Delusional Fox News Problem." *Salon*, 16 Jan. 2015, salon.com/2015/01/26/american_snipers_biggest_lie_clint_eastwood_has_a_delusional_fox_news_problem/.

Mitchell, Lee Clark. *Westerns: Making the Man in Fiction and Film*. U of Chicago P, 1996.

Slotkin, Richard. *Gunfighter Nation: The Myth of the Frontier in Twentieth-Century America*. Macmillan, 1992.

Vizenor, Gerald. *Manifest Manners: Narrative on Postindian Survivance*. U of Nebraska P, 1994.

Wright, Will. *Sixguns and Society: A Structural Study of the Western*. U of California P, 1975.

Young, Alex Trimble. "*American Sniper* Is Not a War Movie: It's a Classic Revisionist Western, and One of Eastwood's Finest." *Salon*, 19 Feb. 2015, salon.com/2015/02/19/american_sniper_is_not_a_war_movie_its_a_classic_revisionist_western_and_one_of_eastwoods_finest/.

11

The Legend

Situating *American Sniper* in Clint Eastwood's Canon

Landon Lutrick

Most books about Clint Eastwood's career contain an early paragraph dedicated to the diversity of his work. This is often accompanied by praise for his evolution as a filmmaker—from star to director to Academy Award winner. This praise is sometimes tempered with a mild critique of his early acting ability or of his centrist politics that, by contrast with much of Hollywood, look rather conservative. The challenge of fully defining Eastwood's career has only become more demanding because of Eastwood's increasingly deft filmmaking as well. Jim Kitses best describes the difficulty of classifying Eastwood, calling him, "a juggler, a tightrope walker, a trade-off artist . . . , a gentle revisionist, [who] revels in contradiction and bedeviling classification" (292). When attempting to organize Eastwood's work, thematic analyses of his core concerns have served many critics well because the most interesting points about Eastwood's career are made by contextualizing his evolution as a filmmaker within the larger evolution of American cinema. Take, for example, the role Eastwood has played as both an actor and a director in the postmodern deconstruction of the Western. His characters, especially the ones he has played himself, both usher in order and resist authority, and the stories he directs frequently embrace heroic archetypes while simultaneously questioning their efficacy.

Eastwood's growth in stature among critics has developed largely because of his inquisitive approach to cinematic themes such as violence, heroism, and masculinity. Questioning such popular themes in American cinema, especially within the genres he primarily engages—the crime drama, the war film, and the Western—cleverly satisfies a range of viewers who may hold differing views about those themes. Eastwood's recent film, *American Sniper* (2014), draws from a memoir of the same title written by Navy SEAL sniper Chris Kyle, and the film follows Kyle through his four tours in the Iraq War. Upon its release, *American Sniper* inspired fervent responses ranging from praise for the film's portrayal of an American hero to condemnation for its glorification of xenophobic attitudes and gun culture.[1] Eastwood has a long history of being viewed warily by the left, but two issues on which he has repeatedly positioned himself as a centrist are violence and the role of the myths associated with the American West. Rather than raising questions about the efficacy of violence, which I argue that the film does, the debate focused more on whether the film gave an accurate treatment of its source material. The debate was further complicated by the film's use of imagery and ideology associated with the Western genre, namely Kyle's (Bradley Cooper) beginning as an amateur cowboy and the climactic showdown between snipers as a stand-in for a shootout among Western gunslingers. Writing for the *New York Times*, A. O. Scott argues that *American Sniper* is surprisingly devoid of the politics surrounding the Iraq War, and that it "can be seen as an expression of nostalgia for [George W. Bush's] Manichean approach to foreign policy." Scott's argument typifies the liberal disgust caused by a reading of *American Sniper* that misses its critique.

In *American Sniper*, the Western's influence and the historical setting in Iraq bring to mind the two streams of Eastwood's films as identified by David Sterritt. The first is the myth movie that focuses on individual lives rooted in the American unconscious. In this case, Eastwood draws on the myth of the frontier in which violence is used to establish law and order. The second is the history movie that revises the grand narratives of the distant and recent past, in this case focusing on the Iraq War (Sterritt 3). Keeping these two branches of Eastwood's work in mind, I draw from William Beard's breakdown of classical heroism. Sterritt and Beard are especially helpful for examining the postmodernist disavowal of such heroism as I bring to light the film's problematic reception in contrast with my reading of *American Sniper* as a film that critiques Kyle's Western mentality and the motivations for starting the Iraq War. Such a critique fits with Eastwood's previous political positions and artistic choices. True to form, his use of myth to interrogate recent American history is gentle, but it is there. Beyond that reading of the film, I argue that Eastwood's coupling of the myth movie and the history movie is a new development in his career that exposes how the Western mythos comes to bear on American culture.

Eastwood's Politics

Eastwood has faced criticism for his perceived right-wing leanings, a political position with which many left-leaning critics seem uncomfortable, especially considering his stature in Hollywood. That critique is best exemplified by Pauline Kael's now infamous labeling of Eastwood's work as fascist. However, Eastwood's biographer, Richard Schickel, optimistically proclaims that the early suspicion bordering on distrust has largely diminished, only remaining in a few centers of cultural power that are largely academic (17). Such reactions may be due, in part, to Eastwood's widely acknowledged intelligence coupled with his lack of desire to be perceived as intellectual (Schickel 4). It is also due, at least in part, to some recent support for Republican presidential candidates. His support of John McCain in the 2008 presidential election—along with his performance at the Republican National Convention in 2012 in which he directed pointed questions to an empty chair meant to represent President Obama—understandably makes Eastwood seem more conservative, even if John McCain was famous for bipartisanship and considered too liberal by many Republican voters. Nevertheless, with that endorsement Eastwood once again drew the ire of his critics, possibly costing him an Academy Award nomination for his acting in *Gran Torino* (Sterritt 227). Critical displeasure had not yet subsided by the time of *American Sniper*'s release, and it colors the film as an overly conservative view of Kyle and the Iraq War, a perception that is problematic in that it does not correspond to what we know of Eastwood.

Keeping in mind critics' recurrent misunderstanding of Eastwood—"even sophisticated people understand [him] too quickly"—I would point out that Eastwood has addressed many of the recurrent arguments about his politics (Schickel 3). A closer inspection reveals that rather than a pat right-wing doctrine, Eastwood follows a libertarian philosophy, and libertarianism is hardly without points of contention with the far right to which Eastwood is perceived to belong. Such libertarian ideals lead him to be fiscally conservative, especially when it comes to promoting business, but he is also quite progressive in regard to social issues such as gay rights and abortion. Most pertinent for this paper, Eastwood, while fairly neutral about the Iraq War, came to detest George W. Bush's policy that led to the war's inflated budget and to the inescapable mire that the war turned out to be (Sterritt 220). While the standard political critique of Eastwood has been that he is too conservative, Eastwood has also been accused of being too liberal.[2] His attention to the "changing social milieu in which the Western had to make its way" and his understanding that "one could not simply reproduce old certainties,"—needing instead to "show that it (the Western) was aware of its own past and in touch with the present"—make up the bulk of his originality (Buscombe 16). Eastwood's willingness to engage both perceptions of the Western mythos frustrates people who view that mythos as contributing to problematic world views. Likewise, there is no shortage of the opposite view—that Eastwood's tampering with the Western damages an important tradition.

Despite the roller coaster of critical perception, Eastwood's interrogation of violence has remained consistent since the early 1990s. The artistic potential that Eastwood sees for violent genres like the Western and the war film speaks less to a faulty preoccupation with violence and more to a critically minded perspective. Eastwood likes to make the audience think, but he avoids being condescending (Sterritt 5). His ability to see multiple sides of a story and his willingness to explore those sides in a way that is not demeaning enables a deeper discussion of social issues. Furthermore, that attitude allows him to deliver critically minded filmmaking to a wide audience—an approach that is no easy task for any film director, and that has contributed to the criticism lobbied from both sides of the political spectrum. Interestingly, Eastwood's broad appeal is not diminished by his complicated politics; they may even add to it. Economic motivations notwithstanding, an artist being criticized as both too politically conservative and too liberal suggests that the artist demonstrates a more complete understanding of cultural currency than would an ideologically cooperative filmmaker.

Thematic Analyses

As a way to order Eastwood's career for the sake of making all-encompassing arguments about it, critics have identified several themes that run throughout his work. Many of these themes are examined in relation to "the Eastwood persona," the laconic and cool character Eastwood brings to his portrayals of

Western heroes. Attending to the characters that surround his monolithic persona, Sara Anson Vaux notes that such figures are, in fact, more interesting than the Eastwood persona anchoring their respective films. Furthermore, she insists that Eastwood as a director is more interested in those everyday characters than in his own acting persona (5). This interest in the "regular folks" is also noted by Drucilla Cornell who argues that Eastwood explores the complicated, and realist, perspective that evil is a possibility for everyone, a potential countered by Eastwood's interest in the power of moral repair (7). These themes play an important role in *American Sniper*'s conflict, as Kyle struggles between two sets of responsibilities: his duty to "protect" his fellow soldiers by fighting in the war, and his responsibility as a father and husband, an obligation that demands he return home. Kyle's struggle as he carries on a relationship with his wife, Taya (Sienna Miller), largely via telephone, adds significant tension to the war drama that makes up the bulk of the film. Even so, the domestic struggles deepen the film's realism, as does Cooper's powerful portrayal of Kyle's psychological trauma.

The trauma that Kyle endures during and after his tours of duty darkens his personality considerably, to the point that viewers question not only his well-being but his soundness of mind. Character development through a struggle with trauma is another recurrent theme in Eastwood films (Cornell 5), along with Vaux's overlapping theme of tortured consciences. Those mental and emotional challenges are caused, at least part of the time, by the characters having been "deceived by the 'conquest of the West' mythology" (Vaux 7). Whether tortured by past behavior or traumatized by the ever-present violence in Eastwood's worlds, his characters are frequently darkened by the events of the narrative. Kyle's volatility brewing just below the surface as he watches a blank television screen—and the eruption of that volatility in his violent attack on the family dog—gestures at the strain carried over from Iraq in the form of PTSD. These homelife complications raise two issues that are important for my argument. On one hand, they complicate Kyle as a heroic figure fully confident that he is doing the right thing by carrying on his fight. On the other, these scenes add to the realism that makes Kyle come across as an uncomplicated classical hero—a perception that I argue is done purposely in order to question the Western mythos that drives Kyle's heroic actions.

Classical Heroism

Part of the appeal that *American Sniper*'s authenticity holds is its reengagement with classical heroism that "works with the dominant ideology in order to justify it" (Beard 3). Eastwood's engagement with the classical heroic mode near the beginning of *American Sniper* moves through two transitions that open up that mode for critique. First, it sets Kyle up as a classical hero only to problematize him as a hero. As Kyle's heroism is dramatized, the film tests the viewer's allegiance to Kyle as the protagonist.[3] The realist approach paints an initial picture of Kyle as classically heroic in the way that William Beard argues has been defunct since the days of John Wayne. Kyle's difficulty in reconciling his relationship to the war and his moral dilemmas when faced with killing—along with earnestness and steadfast belief that he is morally right to defend his country and promote freedom abroad—hearkens back to Wayne's classical heroism. Kyle's motivation for joining the military and continuing to go to war is naïve in a way that makes some modern-day viewers uneasy. As Beard explains, the years that separate modern audiences from John Wayne's heyday brought about significant changes in the cinematic landscape. As an actor, Eastwood was savvy enough to recognize the unbelievability of characters like those Wayne played, but Eastwood cleverly held on to them in appearance while simultaneously withholding subscription to self-sacrifice for the greater good (Beard 7).

Though some viewers welcomed the resurgence of classical heroism in *American Sniper*, those still skeptical of such a thoroughly debunked model argued that it glorifies a racist murderer and lets Kyle off the hook for his wartime misconduct and his despicable stereotyping of the Iraqi people as "savages." While I find those critiques of Kyle's xenophobia apt, I argue that Kyle's vocabulary is an important way that *American Sniper* challenges Kyle's heroic integrity. The word "savage" carries significant baggage in American culture because of its historical use in labeling Native Americans as both hostile and primitive in contrast with the Americans of European descent seeking to overspread the continent. Kyle's use of that term, coupled with his Western persona, draws attention to a problematic world view at work in his reasoning. It also oversimplifies the moral challenges of war, clearly demarcating good from evil in a way that is too tidy to support the film's claim to realism. It is true that Kyle's language and demeanor are despicable, and they are meant to be. Eastwood frequently encourages "our allegiance with a skilled, (sometimes) morally superior hero and our opposition to the criminal and the corrupt," but he also willingly challenges that allegiance as he did in *Unforgiven*, clearly rendering William Munny's humanity and deep flaws (Plantinga 71).[4] Exposing Kyle's flaws does the same thing, and it speaks to what Beard labels the "artifice" or impossibility of Eastwood's heroes, including his own performances ("Lies" 224). During the 1960s, postmodernism thoroughly purged that kind of heroism from American cinema, showing "that the paradigm of classical victory has not only disintegrated, but has been replaced by an anti-type of equally systematic and certain failure," such as the narratives in films like *Midnight Cowboy*, *McCabe and Mrs. Miller*, *Deliverance*, and *Chinatown* (Beard 5). This era, according to Beard, was represented by actors like Dustin Hoffman, Warren Beatty, Jon Voight, Jack Nicholson, Al Pacino, Gene Hackman, and Elliott Gould—all actors whose non-heroic appearance and nervousness stand in stark contrast to the Eastwood persona (6). The persona Eastwood built throughout this period was one that abandoned the "charade of official morality" and "saw through the tired old shibboleths of self-sacrifice and devotion to the common good" (Beard 7). By carrying on postmodern skepticism, *American Sniper* refutes Kyle's individual fight with his adversary as a potential resolution to the greater conflict.

Shootout at the AK Corral

Structurally, *American Sniper* shifts between motivations for its protagonist who is much like the hero in early Westerns. Kyle begins by wanting to enable a better society, a desire that fails tragically when an ally Iraqi family is killed while Kyle watches helplessly. Having failed to promote the good society, Kyle becomes motivated by revenge when an enemy sniper named Mustafa kills Kyle's friend Biggles. Many have noted the parallel with the Western genre in that two equally skilled gunfighters are drawn into battle as part of a quest for revenge. If this were executed true to form as a Western, Kyle's personal battle with his adversary would carry over to benefit the region with his victory. While the final shootout with Mustafa satisfies Kyle's need for revenge, the proceeding analysis will indicate its problematic culmination, adding to the debate about Kyle's heroism by questioning his effectiveness as a hero, in addition to the problem of his xenophobia.

The scene begins with an aerial view of the building Kyle's unit occupies as their base of operations for the mission. From that aerial view, the frame is marked with various data points and targeting lines, quickly recalling the view from a surveillance drone camera. The drone's perspective emphasizes the group's isolation and precarious position surrounded by insurgents, and, because this bird's eye perspective is enabled by new technology, it highlights the complex nature of modern warfare, especially in contrast with the simplicity of a Western high-noon-style showdown. The contrast between the scene's cinematography and its showdown theme reveals the mismatch between the attitudes about how the battle is being planned and the actual situation the soldiers are in. As a group of army engineers is assailed by Mustafa's sniping, the camera cuts to the view from Kyle's spotting scope, revealing very little detail—only a potential sniper's nest obscured by heat waves. A series of slow cuts mirrors the Western showdown formula, as close-ups of Kyle are countered with medium shots of Mustafa straight on, putting the audience in front of his rifle. Kyle somehow knows both that he has discovered the sniper's vantage point and that the sniper in question is Mustafa. Despite being far out of position and surrounded by insurgents, Kyle decides to take the shot anyway. While Mustafa does pose an ongoing threat to the soldiers Kyle wants to protect, the scene is tinged with Kyle's reckless-ness in taking the shot. The final confrontation between Kyle and Mustafa satisfies the heroic standoff model and is a satisfying conclusion to the film's most pronounced conflict. Outside that formula, though, there is something deeply illogical and, consequently, unsettling about Kyle's decision to take the shot that simultaneously is the finest of his career and endangers the entire group accompanying him. The momentary relief afforded by Musta-fa's death is immediately undercut by an Army Ranger's admonishment, "You just fucked us, Legend," and by the chaos that quickly follows.

After the formulaic duel, the slow cuts back and forth between Mustafa and Kyle are immediately replaced by quick cuts as the insurgents surround-ing the American unit respond to Kyle's gunshot. Two formal choices help Eastwood convey the challenge to Kyle's heroic authority in this scene. As the fight continues, the camera angles slowly move from a low perspective on the American soldiers to a high perspective on them, suggesting their loss of power to the enemy combatants. Immediately following Kyle's shot, the Americans have the high ground, making use of it as they fire at Iraqis on the ground across the street and on the first floor of the building they occupy. The camera angles then move to an even field, in which the fighting takes place on the same plane, as the insurgents make their way to the roof of the Americans' building and to the adjacent rooftops. Finally, their situations are reversed as Kyle's team is forced to retreat into the street below, surren-dering the high ground and the cinematic power to the enemy. The compo-sition of the shots in this scene reinforces the challenge to Kyle's heroic efficacy made by the choice of camera angles. Cuts—dramatically juxtapos-ing one-shots or two-shots of Americans with multiple insurgents suddenly appearing in the frame as they either shoot back or run toward the American stronghold—add to the sense of urgency as the Americans are overrun. The camera angles and composition of the frames emphasize the waning power of the Americans in this scene. Moreover, all this happens in the midst of a raging sandstorm that obscures the scene to near darkness: a powerful metaphor equating the lack of visible clarity in this scene to the lack of moral clarity not only in this scene but in the entire enterprise of American forces in Iraq—a clarity that an old Western shootout, no doubt, would have provided.

The loss of power conveyed by the camera angles and composition is remarkable given the expectations set up by the duel. Even more remarkable is Kyle's demeanor as the shootout intensifies. There is no proud acceptance of his successful role in ushering in law and order. Instead he calls his wife in the middle of the firefight, blubbering that he wishes to come home. Then, after narrowly escaping the rooftop, he loses his rifle in the middle of the street—a surprising castration of his masculine power rather than a reaffirmation of it following the killing. The scene ends with a shot of Kyle's abandoned rifle in the street obscured by the all-encompassing sandstorm. The combination of Kyle's reaction to his successful shootout and the formal choices in filming the aftermath of the duel provides a surprisingly chaotic counterpoint to the law and order that should follow the shootout. By drawing on the heroic model Eastwood has honed over the course of his career, *American Sniper* is able to question that model with an even more violent firefight as a result. Kyle's authority as a Western hero is challenged by the reality of war, which, in turn, challenges American conceptions of the world that are filtered through the frontier myth. By confronting recent historical events, specifically the Iraq War, and by using a mythic hero like Kyle, Eastwood exposes the myth for what it is and exposes how it comes to bear on our engagement with the rest of the world.

Beyond Realism

The real-life footage from Kyle's funeral as the credits roll can easily lead to the conclusion that the film primarily justifies, even glorifies, Kyle's actions. As the film blurs the lines between realist fiction and real life, it complicates my reading of the film's critical view of Kyle. The funeral footage, accompanied by a lone bugler, adds even more to his heroic stature. Though the bugler isn't playing "Taps," the track is reminiscent of the classic military elegiac music. The soundtrack and the footage of fellow Navy SEALs pounding their pins into Kyle's casket understandably give the sense that the film honors Kyle more than it criticizes him. However, the funeral footage takes on a different meaning when we keep the earlier challenges to Kyle's heroism in mind. As an Eastwood film is apt to do, *American Sniper* satisfies the heroic efforts Kyle made while exposing how heroism is constructed. The critical understanding of Kyle's character makes the funeral seem overwrought—too heavy-handed for Eastwood's subtle style of directing. Even if one agrees with everything Kyle says and does, this footage illuminates how a person like Kyle takes on mythic proportions. In other words, the funeral scene cements Kyle's development into a legend, but because it does so self-consciously after having challenged the Western mythos, the scene uncovers the mythmaking process for viewers as an undeniably complicated character becomes immortalized as "the Legend." Rather than saying, "Here was a great hero," *American Sniper* says, "Here is how a great hero is made." Reconsidering the funeral footage in this way fits with Eastwood's interest in uncovering how myths—especially those associated with the American West—are constructed, and how they can be deployed in a narrative that simultaneously investigates their construction. Reading the film as a combination of Eastwood's myth and history movies reveals the particularly interesting development in Eastwood's career that *American Sniper* represents.

History and Myth

Susan Kollin launches her collection *Postwestern Cultures* with an anecdote about George W. Bush and the backlash he received when calling for Osama Bin Laden to be brought to justice dead or alive. From that interview, Bush learned the power of words, especially those we often take for granted in the Western, prompting Kollin to pose the question: "What does it mean for critical regional studies when the popular idioms that have often defined the American West in narrowly conceived ways are called into question in such a public manner?" (x). *American Sniper* joins in that questioning of the frontier mythos while posing a larger challenge to American attitudes typified by the description of Iraq as the "new wild West in the old middle East" that Kyle learns upon arrival in the country. This kind of challenge is characteristic of Eastwood, and Kyle's recklessness in the shootout mirrors George W. Bush's haste in waging the Iraq War. Rather than focusing the film on the grand narrative of the Iraq War or even the grander one about "the war on terror," Eastwood focuses on Kyle's story. He then incorporates the myth and exposes how that unconscious is at work in our recent history. More specifically, by painting Kyle as a Western hero in a recent historical set of events, *American Sniper* exposes the problems carried over from the Western influence on American thinking in regard to foreign affairs. This challenges the heroic model Kyle subscribes to and runs counter to Scott's assertions about *American Sniper*: that it ignores the politics of the Iraq War and that it is "an expression of nostalgia for [Bush's] Manichean approach to foreign policy." Though Eastwood did not speak for or against the war in Iraq, the deficit caused by the war and Bush's policies earned President Bush no fan in Eastwood (Sterritt 22). In other words, *American Sniper*'s interrogation of the Western mythos carries over to the politics surrounding the Iraq War.

Conclusion

Keeping Eastwood's libertarian political beliefs in mind, it seems unlikely that he would create a war film that uncritically glorifies a soldier like Kyle, as so many have argued. Given his opinion of George W. Bush's motivations for going to war with Iraq and his belief that violence is not something to be exploited for entertainment, one can see how the film warrants a more critical look than one that dismisses it as glorification of a controversial figure at best, and as right-wing propaganda at worst. In *American Sniper*, Eastwood carries on several themes that he has explored in previous films, especially the everyday complications of life, made more difficult in this film by military life and Kyle's struggle with PTSD. But the primary development and focal point of my paper is Eastwood's marriage of myth and history in the film. The Iraq War has long been tinged with Western overtones—possibly caused by George W. Bush's affectation of a Western persona—but by complicating the Western shootout formula and using it to usher in more chaos rather than law and order, Eastwood points out the problematic attitude American officials have toward war and, specifically, the ineffective way the frontier mythos leads characters like Kyle to think about their actions. Like many of Eastwood's films, *American Sniper* has run aground on critical suspicion. That is due in part to an impulse to read Eastwood as a conservative hero, but that impulse should be overridden by an understanding that Eastwood is not simplistic, only complex and subtle. Once viewed with an eye toward Eastwood's inquisitive style, a much different, more thoughtful film emerges—one that is legendary and challenges the nature of legends.

Notes

1. Some of the more amusing review titles from IMDb range from praise ("Brutal and Powerful: *American Sniper* Ranks among the Best of the Year") to the

hilariously skeptical ("Good Ol' Murican Propaganda" and "Anyone Remembers [sic] Nazi Sniper from *Inglourious Basterds?*") to the morally outraged ("This Is a Disgrace of a Film").

2. Christopher Orr points out the many perceptions of Eastwood over the years in his article for *Salon.com*, "Dirty Harry or P. C. Wimp?" Orr recalls Pauline Kael's well-documented fascism accusation along with Ted Baehr's claim that *Million Dollar Baby* supported euthanasia.

3. For a more detailed explanation of viewer allegiance, see Carl Plantinga's article in *Cinema Journal*, "Spectacles of Death: Clint Eastwood and Violence in *Unforgiven.*"

4. My reading of the shootout scene draws from Alex Trimble Young's reading in his review of *American Sniper* for *Salon.com*. In his review, Young points out the critical point that Kyle's shootout fails to usher in law and order; I agree with Young and build on that reading here.

Works Cited

Beard, William. "Lies of Our Fathers: Mythology and Artifice in Eastwood's Cinema." *New Essays on Clint Eastwood*, edited by Leonard Engel, U of Utah P, 2012, pp. 224–48.

———. *Persistence of Double Vision: Essays on Clint Eastwood*. U of Alberta P, 2000.

Buscombe, Edward. *Unforgiven*. BFI, 2004.

Cornell, Drucilla. *Clint Eastwood and Issues of American Masculinity*. Fordham UP, 2009.

Foote, John H. *Clint Eastwood: Evolution of a Filmmaker*. Praeger, 2009.

Kitses, Jim. *Horizons West: Directing the Western from John Ford to Clint Eastwood*. BFI, 2004.

Kollin, Susan, editor. *Postwestern Cultures: Literature, Theory, Space*. U of Nebraska P, 2007.

Orr, Christopher. "Dirty Harry or P. C. Wimp?" *Salon*, 24 Feb. 2005, www.salon.com/2005/02/24/eastwood_2/. Accessed 6 Jan. 2016.

Plantinga, Carl. "Spectacles of Death: Clint Eastwood and Violence in *Unforgiven.*" *Cinema Journal*, vol. 37, no. 2, 1998, pp. 65–83.

Schickel, Richard. *Clint Eastwood: A Biography*. Knopf, 1996.

Scott, A. O. "Review: *American Sniper*, a Clint Eastwood Film with Bradley Cooper." *New York Times*, 25 Dec. 2014, www.nytimes.com/2014/12/25/movies/american-sniper-a-clint-eastwood-film-starring-bradley-cooper.html. Accessed 6 Jan. 2016.

Sterritt, David. *The Cinema of Clint Eastwood: Chronicles of America*. Wallflower Press, 2014.

Vaux, Sara Anson. *The Ethical Vision of Clint Eastwood*. William B. Eerdmans, 2012.

Young, Alex Trimble. "*American Sniper* Is Not a War Movie: It's a Classic Revisionist Western, and One of Eastwood's Finest." *Salon*, 19 Feb. 2015, www.salon.com/2015/02/19/american_sniper_is_not_a_war_movie_its_a_classic_revisionist_western_and_one_of_eastwoods_finest/. Accessed 6 Jan. 2016.

12

With Some Trepidation, I Suggested That We See *American Sniper* Together

Dennis Rothermel

We had agreed to see a film, and we selected a night. Josie asked me to choose, averring considerately to see films that interested me and avoid those—mostly mainstream Hollywood films—that did not.[1] With some trepidation, I suggested that we see *American Sniper* (2014) together. I wasn't sure that I wanted to see it—not because I avoid movies about war and soldiers, and not because I don't care about Clint Eastwood films. I've written about films about war and soldiers—certain ones, that is, and I've written about films that Eastwood has directed ("Anti-War War Films," "Eastwood's Treatment of the Life of Creativity and Performance…," and "Mystical Moral Miasma in *Mystic River*"). But I wasn't sure I was going to like it. I feared it would disappoint; I feared that I would dislike it immensely—just because of what I've written about war movies and Eastwood movies.

Eastwood is not easy to write about. He is broadly and sorely misconstrued. It's his own fault and, really, his own intention. He speaks from far, far back behind the screen and in a soft voice, uninflected, and rarely with anything dramatic to say. He just shows us something to see, something to interpret. Reading Eastwood, you need constraint—not to presume too easily that you've caught his message. Having a message may not be his purpose. He may not have a message to deliver. Oliver Stone, for example, is his opposite in this regard. Stone's voice is unmistakably clear in every frame. It's all assembled in detail to intone that message from start to finish, compiling comprehensive evidence in support of the ultimate conclusion that was evidently coming all along. With Eastwood, you can hardly detect that voice or know for sure that it's there. It's all in what he shows, in the showing of it, and that's what he has to say.

Eastwood speaks within the vernacular of American cinema, which is to say, indistinguishable from the conventions of style, dramatic construction, and montage of Hollywood movies. But just as there is nothing blatant or ostentatious in his cinematic constructions, there is also nothing vulgar. There might be humor but rarely cartoonishness. There are characterizations readily accessible to comprehension but no facile heroization. In contrast to the films he starred in directed by Don Siegel and Sergio Leone, there are also no facile villainizations in most films that Eastwood has directed. He is, first and foremost, an actor—an actor who has become a director. He learned by paying attention during those early years as a TV cowboy, by studying the history of cinema and international cinema, and then by doing it—as soon as he could wrangle it. He is still the actor, with the actor's passions and the actor's purposes. He looks for material that gives actors the chance to immerse in what enlivens and enthralls the actor. He looks for character and story, that is, complex character and nuanced story. He is an actor become director, an actor/director who thrives in being an actor's director. The nonflamboyant, cinematic voice is precisely suited for that purpose—not to distract from how good actors have the chance to sink their teeth into a rich character.

He is an actor, a capable actor, an actor with much more accomplishment than he's ordinarily credited for. He's not an actor who disappears behind a role—not an Anthony Hopkins or Daniel Day Lewis or Dustin Hoffman or Meryl Streep or Helen Mirren or Kate Winslet. He's an actor with the limitation of an unmistakable physique, face, voice, and screen presence that won't easily allow him chances at lavish impersonation of characters much different from how he looks and speaks, where extensive makeup and costume embellish the extraordinary dramatic invention of the virtuoso actor. He plays with a different instrument and knows his capabilities well, which isn't to say that he plays type but that he plays within a range of possibilities. So he's not given due credit, and his character is easily taken as the idealization of the actor/filmmaker's personal moral world view. People take it as given that Eastwood plays himself in all his films, but Eastwood simply assigns himself the roles—quite distinct roles—that he, as filmmaker, sees sensible to cast himself in (Kapsis and Coblentz 33, 87, 114, 118; Wilson 51, 80, 137). There's more variance than people see, and they don't see the acting, which is what actors want—not for the acting to be seen (Kapsis and Coblentz 51, 80, 137). Oddly, the somewhat belabored effort to effect the distinctive diction of John Huston in *White Hunter Black Heart* (1990) was important not to showcase his talent but to undermine the association of the role with the screen persona that the culture has bestowed on him. We can see this distance between characterization and actor in the early roles and what happens to those characterizations—Blondie, the Man with No Name, and Dirty Harry. "It's remarkable how much he's *not* Dirty Harry." He's the actor who plays that role. As grateful as Eastwood is for what Don Siegel and Sergio Leone gave him the chance to do, once those two roles were his own to direct and mold, they became different, more nuanced, less heroicized, less flat. See in particular *High Plains Drifter* (1973), *The Outlaw Josey Wales* (1976), and *Sudden Impact* (1983).

We have an early installment of Eastwood's audio commentary for *American Sniper*—about the scene in the bar where Chris Kyle sips a beer, alone and despondent, recently returned from his fourth and last tour in Iraq (Mekado Murphy). At one far end of the bar, there is a small group of patrons conversing privately. At the other far end, a TV is tuned to a basketball game. Kyle glances at the TV indifferently, without any sign of interest. For one who has seen and participated in military combat, there is little attraction in the cultural emulation of that in popular sport. He appears to have a need to talk with someone but makes no effort to find someone to talk to. There is no one there who would be ready for what he needs to talk about. His phone rings. It is Taya. Where is he? Still abroad, on his way home? He's in the States, but not home yet? Why? Come home. Almost tearfully, he avows that he wants to come home. And so he will, but still without finding the opportunity to talk about what he needs to talk about. Eastwood explains how he set up the scene and then let Bradley Cooper simply do it. They had worked on the project together for some time. Cooper is a fine actor. "I try not to say too much," Eastwood says. "I like to set things up and then see what happens." That's Eastwood the noninvasive director of acting. He gathers a talented cast and then lets them do it, preferring the first take when the approach is unstudied, even a bit raw. He doesn't rehearse. Actors who know that will set up rehearsals the night before the next day's shoot. Sometimes an actor will want to work through a scene or a take on the set before shooting. Fine, Eastwood says, and he'll shoot that informal walk through, and often it will be the take that he uses (Kapsis and Coblentz 52, 82, 155; Wilson 159, 186, 184, 211).

What he says about directing an actor—which is virtually indistinguishable from not directing an actor—that's Eastwood's filmmaker's voice (Kapsis and Coblentz 57, 89, 191). It's all we can detect of that voice far, far back behind the screen—"I don't like to say much. I like to set things up and then see what happens." He wants to see what an actor can create; he wants to see what that actor with that script can show us; he wants to see how the story will materialize—and this, too, is an example of what it is to be human, entirely idiosyncratic, rich in contradictions and inexplicable behavior, aspects of personality not reducible to common traits, without explanation, without justification, and without vindication. It tells us something about the world, about people and how they cope and create. It's not to endorse or to condemn, or to judge at all. It's to understand.

Eastwood has undertaken to film the story of a Navy SEAL sniper who was phenomenally efficacious during deployments in Iraq. Eastwood is concerned first and foremost with character and story, but in a way that consistently slips by critical reception of his films. He speaks very softly and from a standpoint far, far back behind the screen. This could be trouble, and hence my trepidation. What will he have done with this material? Regardless of what he will have done with it, how will people perceive it? I had resolved not to see it—to just wait until the initial flurry of reactions subsided and see it later, months later, maybe years later. But then I read Mick LaSalle's review in the *San Francisco Chronicle*, which I read regularly ("Clint Eastwood Aims for a Little Nuance"). LaSalle reviews films within the scope of the popular mainstream, most of which I don't bother seeing. LaSalle sees a film once, writes about it, and never sees it again. I see a film that interests me multiple times and then write about it after it simmers in my thoughts for a considerable amount of time. LaSalle sees that his primary role is to judge a film, and to explicate and justify the criteria underlying his judgments. I tell my students to forestall judgment; the mind snaps shut once judgment is made, and further understanding—particularly of complexities and nuances—is curtailed. LaSalle does what he does, and I do what I do. If I had to watch and write about movies I didn't like, it would make me cranky, and I would likewise find it necessary to justify my reactions, which would be tedious and thus amplify the crankiness. But LaSalle is a keen observer and for me a useful sounding board, which results in an odd alignment on a couple of rare films—Roman Polanski's adaptation of *Carnage* (2011) and John Wells's adaptation of *August: Osage County* (2013 ["Ask Mick LaSalle: *Carnage* Wasn't Funny"]). Precisely LaSalle's reason for disliking these two films was what I found interesting in each one. For my part, I'm giddily content with the role I've finagled for myself—I teach film and I write about film as part of my role as an academic. But I don't have the obligation to write film reviews, and I'm not in a film-studies program. I've not been hired for or assigned a research agenda to address some narrow range. "What's your specialization?" people ask me at film-studies conferences. I say, with unsuppressed delight, "Whatever I like."

LaSalle is a keen observer of acting, character development, story, and cinematic authorial voice. He can offer me an initial vantage point before I see a film—not necessarily expecting to agree or disagree overall. And then, these startling remarks in his review of *American Sniper*:

> Clint Eastwood has made a sneaky, complicated film that takes the form of a rousing war movie but whose ideas are almost subversive, or at least too provocative to state overtly.
>
> For that reason, "American Sniper" is bound to be misunderstood even by those who admire it. And it will definitely be misunderstood by people who don't like it, who might wonder why they didn't walk out inspired by the story of a real American Hero. ("Clint Eastwood")

How prophetic! Within two weeks, a review appears by John Powers for NPR, one of just a few (including LaSalle's) that come close to getting it, and there's a mountain of wildly misconstrued reaction.

> Of course, given today's polarized politics, the film has spawned the usual knee-jerk squabbling. Put crudely, its detractors argue that *American Sniper* is a right-wing movie that ducks essential questions—such as whether the Iraq war was a righteous one—and glorifies a remorseless sniper who killed somewhere between 160 and 250 people. Its defenders on the right accuse such critics of hating America and our troops. The left fret that *American Sniper* is so popular because it lets viewers stay in denial about Iraq—it doesn't say that the invasion was

wrong, wrong, wrong. The right thinks it's so popular because it celebrates good, old-fashioned patriotism. (Powers, Jan. 28, 2015).

And, so, trepidation modestly assuaged, I suggested to Josie, let's go see
American Sniper, an Eastwood film about a Navy SEAL sharpshooter. We
got seats at a theater on San Pablo Avenue, where you order a meal that they
bring to you at the beginning of the showing, thus combining the time
commitments of dinner and a movie. The place was packed. We got the last
seats, in the front row way over to one side. "For extreme close-ups, we'll be
able to see up the actors' nostrils," I joked. People around us explained that
to get decent seats, you need to come an hour earlier, which sort of defeats
the attraction of dinner and movie together, especially since the fare was not
terrific. Josie had a hummus plate and I ordered a Greek salad (a dish that's
not easy to screw up), and I didn't bother applying the dressing since I figured most of it would wind up on my shirt if I did. Maybe ours was an
unusual perspective. Maybe the action scenes lacked tumultuous effect seen
that way. But those weren't the scenes that interested me. Josie and I stole
glances at each other during the quiet scenes, the scenes in between Chris
Kyle's deployments, and that's where Eastwood did the more interesting
work. Josie is a psychotherapist; her insights are keen, and I've come to listen
to her carefully. So, okay, I wanted her to come along with me on this little
trepidatious venture. At the end of the film, Josie turned to me and said, "it's
an anti-war film." I hadn't said a word, I hadn't indicated any expectation,
but, yes, that's what I had come looking for, and that's what I thought, too.

It's an anti-war film and, more specifically, an anti-war war film. It's not
about Iraq. It's not about politics. It doesn't glamorize war. It doesn't hero-
icize Chris Kyle nor even purport to be a factually accurate depiction of the
actual person and deeds of Chris Kyle, though certainly Eastwood, Jason
Hall, and Bradley Cooper were assiduous in capturing the character of the
real man and not denigrating him (Hausam; Myers; Baker). The film doesn't
demonize Iraqis or Muslims. It doesn't glorify Americans or American military incursions. It doesn't justify the American military activity in Iraq—
nor condemn it. It doesn't promulgate a position on the Iraq War. It does
show the experience of soldiers, and of one in particular. Showing the experience of soldiers in war is what an anti-war war movie can do. And specifically not glamorize that experience. Other sorts of films that can accomplish
an anti-war perspective can do other things, and mostly this will be a project
for documentary films.

Hilarious Film Reception

But the broad culture isn't ready for this, which is really the source of my trepidation. The most telling insight in the vortex of virulent pontifications in response to the film comes from a hilarious incident. Seth Rogen, who bears no resemblance to a filmmaker with a political agenda, idly tweets that Kyle's efficaciousness as a sniper as depicted in the film reminded him of the film *Pride of the Nation* that Nazi leadership watches during the penultimate scene in Quentin Tarantino's *Inglourious Basterds* (2009 [Rogen]). A German sniper kills American soldiers by the dozen. The Nazi audience hoots and cheers with each new kill as the tally mounts. The sniper shows no relish in what he does. In the film, that is, *Inglourious Basterds*, he's portrayed by the very same German soldier whose exploits the film within the film, *Pride of the Nation*, depicts. He's not Rambo with bulging muscles wielding a heavy machine gun in one arm, bullet bands draped around his neck, teeth gritting, muttering invectives to his army of enemies who all fall flailing and tumbling to his personal firestorm. The German sharpshooter is a gentle man, angelic, and anything but proud of what he does. He was in a position to do that, and he did, without relish, without exultation, but not without remorse. He's called a German Sergeant York, but the more obvious model is Audie Murphy translated willfully anachronistically into a fictitious context of WWI German cinema. Audie Murphy played himself in a Hollywood glorification of his exploits and then acted in a series of war and Western films that extended that persona. It was a fate he could never reconcile to, which compounded his severe PTSD (Audie Murphy). Now, Tarantino contracted Eli Roth to shoot *Pride of the Nation*, and to do so *exactly* in the manner of Hollywood movies about WWII—Audie Murphy's story only a bit hyperbolized. Only with this one change: swap the uniforms. It's the kind of hilarity that Tarantino delights in—in this case, reverse the empathy and catharsis in heroism in combat that Hollywood war films have cultivated over decades so as to place them on the other side of the battle, against American soldiers. See if anyone notices. It's not the only nose tweaking that Tarantino does in that film—the commando heroes manage their way into the theater, machine-gun as many of the unarmed Nazis as they can, and then detonate the explosives strapped to their bodies underneath their clothes. This makes them suicide terrorists who, in disguise in civilian clothing, murder soldiers and officers, and civilian men and women, before immolating them all in gory explosions. The heroes employ the exact equivalent of suicide-terrorist tactics against American soldiers in Iraq and

Afghanistan. Only they're American commandos obliterating the Nazi high command. It's hilarious with the sort of wry, biting cultural humor that delights Tarantino, including the joke delivered by a German officer about *King Kong* and American racism earlier in the film:

> I am from the jungle. I came to America by boat, not voluntarily but in chains, and I was displayed in chains upon arrival, which is either the story of the Negro in America or King Kong.

What obscures the hilarity is the camp tone of fabulous Spaghetti Western outré scenario transposed to WWII.

But this hilarity is lost upon the torrent of incensed responders to Seth Rogen—how dare he compare Chris Kyle to Nazis! And so the hilarity is compounded. The dummkopfs don't get Tarantino's joke nor its implicit critique of Hollywood's emotional, manipulative practices, particularly in war movies. Rogen immediately apologizes profusely—he was only pointing out a parallel, he says, nothing else! And that compounds the humor still more. This is too wild—you couldn't make this stuff up. It's hilarious, and troubling—how much shallow reactions to films permeate the culture and its public discourse.

The Genesis of *American Sniper*—
The Person, the Book, the Script, the Film

Some reception has focused upon discrepancies between the film and Kyle's coauthored autobiography, as well as discrepancies between the book and actual events. Bradley Cooper explains, "We did take liberties with the book. It's a movie" (Myers). That is, a fiction film, not a documentary, not a dramatization, and not journalism. Fiction film means telling what is not necessarily factually true. In the genesis of the film, we know that Jason Hall and Bradley Cooper worked with Kyle while he was still alive (Cooper and Taya Kyle). Hall reports that there were details in the book that were changed subsequent to review by the military, specifically the opening incident of the film in which Kyle kills first a boy and then a woman (Ito). That a child was his first kill was suppressed in the book. That Taya Kyle had considerable effect upon Hall's script before and after Chris Kyle's death Hall cites as the cause for the alternating structure of the narrative between war scenes in Iraq and home scenes in which Taya's relationship with Chris becomes increasingly tormenting. Chris and Taya alternate testimony about their lives in the book, so there had been that material for Hall to work with (Kyle).

What is interesting in film adaptation is what a filmmaker—or filmmaker team of writer, director, and actor(s)—does with the source material. What is retained? What is omitted? What is altered? What is invented? These are the interesting questions. There is, in fact, precious little in the book that's retained in the film, which makes the film interesting to study. Of the differences is this one, wholly missed by those who have commented on the contrast: Kyle's understanding of the purpose of the United States military incursion in Iraq. In the film, Kyle recites astoundingly trite explanations of how, if not there, we'll have to fight them in San Diego and New York. These people are evil savages. He's fighting to protect Taya and their children. These remarks fall on dumbfounded ears in each case. In the book, Kyle reports that his duty is to serve, and, if the country's leadership sends him to a foreign country to carry out the nation's interests, he will do that. If you don't like that, vote in different leadership (Kyle 341). That might be among the revisions encouraged by the war department review, only it's a sentiment that Taya Kyle reports as Chris Kyle's belief (Cooper and Taya Kyle). The long letter that Kyle's comrade Marc Lee wrote two weeks before his death gets unreserved praise in the book (Kyle 414). Just a few sentences arise in Lee's mother's recitation in the scene of his funeral in the film, sentences which, along with doubts that Lee had shared with real-life Kyle, the movie Kyle cites as the real cause for his death. Lee harbored severe doubts about the mission in Iraq, and that loss of focus was the cause of his dying. Taya is dumbfounded. Chris Kyle's views about the war he fought are jingoistic in the film but moderately removed from personal endorsement in the book. What is common to both is the soldier's primary motivation of protecting fellow soldiers in harm's way. It is his ardent motivation, which is particularly evident in the film's depiction.

Eastwood, of course, was incensed at the entrenched political reception to the film (Howell). An affront equally to both leftist criticism and rightist adulation, Eastwood proclaimed these reactions stupid and the film to be anti-war. He, too, is anti-war. Carefully, though, his articulated reasons for opposition to the wars in Afghanistan and Iraq are particular—these wars are not in the best interest of this nation (Feinberg). His is not an absolutist conviction founded upon articles of faith or philosophical principles. He has, though, opposed every American war subsequent to WWII. His purpose in *American Sniper* was to show the experience of a soldier enduring war, and the impact of that war on the soldier's life and family (Dockterman). Hall and Cooper echo this focus on a universal story rather than on the political circumstances of the US incursion in Iraq (Suebsaeng; Johnson).

Commentary on the film subsequent to the initial frenzy has included recognition of the film's content independent of political perspectivism (Rich; Page; Smith; Lisi). It stands as a single decisive aspect of the film's reception—those who insist upon a national, political agenda misconstrue the film; those who eschew that context come closer to comprehending the film. The perception of political intent uniformly assumes that a movie's protagonist is meant to be taken as heroic, virtuous, admirable, and good, and that the protagonist's contrary is meant to be taken as villainous, soulless, despicable, and evil. The expectation for a mainstream Hollywood film is that it gratify the culturally conditioned (by Hollywood) expectation for these cardboard characterizations to be reasserted. And good wins out over evil. Liberal critics of the film presume this selfsame structure of the common cinema narrative but decry the choice of what is good and evil. Conservative responses make that same presumption but endorse the supposed choice between good and evil. But, of course, these are traits of literature appropriate for children's stories. Hollywood thus sustains the juvenilization of the country's viewers. It is an intellectual—or, better, an anti-intellectual—orientation that dominates the national cultural and political discourse, atrociously evident in the 2016 presidential campaign. Hollywood is at fault for that, and not just from its war films. What Eastwood has done in this film is to supply a litmus test of not just cinema sophistication but also political sophistication. His cinematic style is subdued and sufficiently within the cultural vernacular, but his subjects wander beyond the boundaries of Hollywood's careful artifice of simplistically vague ideological accommodation.

Eastwood calls himself a libertarian somewhere between left and right ideologies. He says he's a social liberal and a fiscal conservative (Dawson). And opposed to every foreign war since 1950. That does make sense, both on the basis of nonintrusive government and on the basis of government's not incurring the enormous expenses of wars—expenses that make socially liberal programs fiscally infeasible. Libertarians tend to have a puzzling mixture of views on national issues (Eastwood, "1974 Playboy Interview"). Eastwood abhors violence and supports laws restricting gun ownership. He supports gay rights, conservation of the nation's natural preserves, and sustainability. As odd as his surprise appearance and clumsy attempt at stand-up satire was at the 2012 Republican National Convention, his points are telling (Eastwood, "Transcript"). He criticizes Obama for there still being twenty-three million people unemployed. He praises Obama for being against the war in Iraq but criticizes him for still waging war in Afghanistan. He echoes Mitt Romney's charge, "Why are you giving the date out [for withdrawing from Iraq] now? Why don't you just bring them home tomorrow morning?" But whereas Romney had meant that sarcastically, Eastwood meant it seriously. Eastwood could not have done Romney's campaign any good, though perhaps any such effect was mitigated by what everyone took to be an incoherent ramble. In August 2016, Eastwood indicated—when asked—that he would be voting for Trump in spite of the dumo things Trump has said, but hardly indicating enthusiasm, and indicating little enthusiasm for the choice (Hainey). His complaint against Obama is that he hasn't been able to work with a Republican Congress to get the business of government done. The advantage he sees for a Republican President would be to break the deadlock.

Among the inventions of the film are the adversaries the Butcher and Mustafa. The latter gets but brief mention in Kyle's book, and there is no evidence that the two men were ever within shooting distance of each other. It was Steven Spielberg who injected the development of the exact contrast of the two artful and intrepid snipers in the screenplay (Baxter). Eastwood assumed the project after Chris Kyle was murdered, and after Spielberg had dropped it (Galloway). Eastwood says that typically he waits for the director of photography to light a set prior to shooting a scene, and then he goes around and turns off some of the lights (Kapsis and Coblentz 56, 143; Wilson 94–95, 188). The clean coverage in light that typifies Hollywood production values is lost ever so slightly in that adjustment, though it falls short of the other extreme: sharp film-noir chiaroscuro. It's symptomatic of how Eastwood works on the edge of the cinema vernacular—and yet self-effacingly, if not entirely undetectably.

One can see something similar in how the script evolved into the film. The contrast between the two snipers is retained in an accessible version of the screenplay dated "(03.18.14)" (Hall). In that version, and as emerges in the film—though we know much more about sniper Kyle than about sniper Mustafa—the two soldiers are in all respects identical. The script has both men whisper a brief prayer before firing, and this does not happen in the film. The small Bible that the boy Chris Kyle lifts from the bracket at the back of the pew in church becomes his talisman as a soldier. We understand, in the film, that he has it in his shirt pocket next to his heart, but it is mentioned only once, in a conversation with Marc Lee who notes that he never sees Kyle read it. In the script, Kyle takes the Bible out, along with an American flag, and lays them out next to him while in his overwatch sniper position. This ritual evocation of religious and nationalist purpose does not happen in the film. In the last combat sequence, as Kyle discards equipment and body armor, rushing to catch up with the personnel carrier, he leaves behind the Bible, the flag, and a toy tin soldier that had adorned the dresser top in his childhood bedroom. This, too, does not happen in the film. Rather, what he leaves behind in the film in that rush is his sniper rifle, binoculars, and helmet.

The script delineates in a succession of two sequences the (purely fictitious) encounter with the man and family whom Kyle coerces into agreeing to finger the location of the Butcher. The latter half of these scenes shows Kyle confronted by an angry Muslim cleric who upon a subsequent event comes to appreciate that the American soldiers are his protectors against the genuine evil of the Butcher and al-Qaeda in Iraq. This latter part is excised from the film, which is significant since this scene alone would impart at least modest justification for the methods of the American military in its incursion in Iraq. These several points, along with some pop-culture references and numerous small detail close-ups designed to solidify the narrative—especially the scene with the cleric that would justify the American incursion—are typical of a Spielberg film. Spielberg packs his cinema with completely digested moral and political judgment. The evolution of the script shows the difference between the two filmmakers. Eastwood pares away the details that judgmentally solidify narrative, leaving a story left to viewers to interpret actively. And so Eastwood speaks to us from far back behind the screen. If Oliver Stone shouts at us in every shot, Spielberg speaks gently but with presumed authority to show us how to think about what we see.

American Sniper is the second war film that Eastwood says he got as Spielberg's leftover (Galloway). The first was *Flags of Our Fathers* (2006), which became the first of Eastwood's pairing with *Letters from Iwo Jima* (2006). How different *Flags of Our Fathers* is from *Saving Private Ryan* (1998), and exactly in the way that we can trace the evolution of the script of *American Sniper*. How well I remember a student telling me how impressed he was with the courage of a Japanese soldier in *Letters from Iwo Jima* who, upon exhortation from his companion, blows himself up with a hand grenade rather than let himself be dishonored with capture or surrender. An innocent young man, the student, not obviously prone to militarism and not altogether different from the young soldier who had a life and family to return to. Courageous?? Horrifying!! That young soldier and that young student were both innocent and earnest, and equally duped into a moral fantasy of military heroism. Eastwood's diptych, like *American Sniper*, is about the experience of soldiers, their plight, and how what happens to them affects those they hold close. The two Iwo Jima films don't simply show the battle from both sides, thus giving us a balanced view of it. They show the experience that soldiers suffer, and that happens to be set in two different armies on opposite sides of a horrifying battle on an island. These are nondidactic presentations. They are meant to show us the way it happens for soldiers, show us without overriding judgment, but in a way that ought to be sufficient to foster adequate reflection on how cautious a nation ought to be regarding sending youth to serve, suffer, and perish on behalf of the nation's perceived interests. That my unassuming student would react that way—to valorize a soldier's acquiescence to senseless sacrifice for the sake of honor—shows the efficacy of the simplistic notions of valor and courage that the image industry has inculcated, particularly in the young.

Multiple Themes

So, how to read this film, *American Sniper*? Eastwood backs the film away from the political context of the wars in Iraq and Afghanistan. Taking some cues from Chris Kyle, Jason Hall has taken the material part way in that direction, but Eastwood takes it further. Substitute any nation, real or imagined, for "Iraq" in this film, and the film is unchanged. To get at how it's a story independent of historical context, we can take a cue from a few thoughts that Gilles Deleuze provides in an essay, "Literature and Life."

> Health as literature, as writing, consists in inventing a people who are missing. It is the task of the fabulating function to invent a people. We do not write with memories, unless it is to make them the origin and destination of a people to come still ensconced in its betrayals and repudiations. . . .
>
> The ultimate aim of literature is to set free, in the delirium, this creation of a health, or this invention of a people, that is, a possibility of a life. To write for this people who are missing . . . ("for" means less "in the place of" than "for the benefit of").

The possible people will include those whose induction into horrors need not be required by the nation they live in. Subsuming Kyle as representative of the virtues of the national character, instrumental to its righteousness, emblematic of its greatness, takes Kyle standing in place of a generality. Taking Kyle invented as a possible people understands him as *a* man, with *a* wife, with *a* buddy to protect, as *a* soldier. Strip away the names, and one has the genuine story of *American Sniper*. It is a story of complexities, and a characterization fraught with contradictions. Understood this way, the film explicates numerous themes, in nonnarrative order, that articulate a soldier: the gun, the Bible, the woman, the boy, the sheepdog, the butcher, Mustafa, the eye, the breath, the call, the calling, the job, the weight, the reflex, the denial, the other, the sacrifices, the doubt, the tactics.

Never lay your gun down on the ground, the father instructs his son. It's a sternly imparted lesson, one pertaining to respect for the power of the weapon, and respect for safety. The obedient boy accepts it without diminishment of his excitement from his first hunting prize—a young buck deer. The deer is another young boy—innocuous and peacefully vegetarian. The father compliments the boy's handling of the gun and ability to shoot; he has a gift for it, for shooting and killing live targets. Our view at the time of the shooting is from the angle of the deer, looking directly at the gun leveled in our direction and at the father standing attentively behind the crouching boy. This is an alignment that reverses the opening image of George Stevens's *Shane* (1953), which we know Eastwood is familiar with since he did *Pale Rider* (1985) as his own version of *Shane*, though with extensive alteration of the story and devoid of that opening image. In that image in *Shane*, we view from behind the boy, who handles a child-size rifle, aiming at the young buck gently grazing beyond. The deer casually raises his head and then lowers it again calmly, revealing the man on horseback wearing fringed buckskins and approaching from that direction. As the man approaches, he has a gentle verbal exchange with the boy, somewhat taking the threat the boy posed more seriously than need be, a gesture meant to bolster the boy's self-esteem. The boy's father approaches and assures the man in buckskins on horseback that the boy isn't allowed to handle a loaded gun.

The sniper lies comfortably prone, his cheek cradling easily on his long rifle, as he scans a desolate urban scene below him. He communicates with off-site command, reporting what he sees: a woman who holds a grenade under her robe, how she hands it to the boy she leads by her side, and how the boy runs forward toward approaching soldiers, intending obviously to toss it toward them, committed to self-sacrifice as he kills or maims at least some of the soldiers. The sniper receives permission to fire based on his own judgment. He fires, and the boy collapses dead—as if his garments were but a balloon out of which the air escapes in an instant. All his targets will fall like that, including the woman who picks up the grenade and attempts to carry out the same intention. Shooting the boy is the sniper's first kill in his deployment to battle. He is calmly methodical, neither hesitant nor exultant in the success of his shooting. His companion wants to exult, but the sniper rejects that angrily—"Get your hand off me." His sense of professionalism masks the unspoken remorse at the unspeakable deed that his professional devotion to duty has demanded of him.

The enemy commander known as the Butcher extracts a boy from a house and commences to inflict horrible punishment on him for the sins of his father, who is held helpless by two soldiers. The father had agreed, under pressure, to collaborate with the sniper and his squad when they had visited him the day before, promising them to identify and locate the Butcher for a significant sum of money. But the man is terrified. He had striven immediately on that prior visit to impress on the sniper how the soldiers' very presence in his house already put him in danger, indicating the Butcher's inhumane use of a drill and bringing out a daughter who had already been victimized with the loss of most of an arm. When the Butcher exacts his punishment on the man and boy, the sniper and his squad are pinned down in position in a building nearby. They are held there by the determined skill of the sniper's enemy counterpart—a sniper, Mustafa, with a formidable reputation. The Butcher dispatches the boy gruesomely with an electric hand drill. He imposes the absolute will of resistance and ruthless retribution that arises in a nation overrun by an invading army. The father breaks free from the two men holding him and is immediately gunned down. The sniper and his squad can do nothing. They withdraw. It will not reflect well on the depiction of a nation that a man such as the Butcher could exist. His is a role invented for the film. It may not be surprising that a nation where such a level of heinous antipathy could hardly seem likely ever to arise will, nevertheless, see candidates for the highest elected leadership in the nation espouse that adversaries be tortured for pure retribution's sake, that innocent family members of adversaries be targeted for the full force of warfare, and that elements of the nation's own citizenry be policed just because of the vaguest association with the nation's enemies active on the other side of the world (LoBianco; Whitesides). Under similar national distress, the Butcher would show up in any nation.

At another time, the sniper once again sees a boy in his scope. The boy has rushed forward to pick up the rocket-propelled grenade launcher from where a man dropped it. The sniper has killed that man. The boy struggles with the RPG, trying to lift it and aim it at the soldiers not far away, mimicking what the man had intended. The sniper whispers his wishes to the boy—that he not pick it up, that he drop it. Allowing the boy more opportunity, possibly dangerously more time than he would have a combatant-aged adversary, he holds his fire. The boy finally drops the weapon and runs away. The sniper's anguish releases with his breath. He catches his breath slowly, sobbing. The boy is not that much older than his own son.

The sniper as a boy defends his younger brother when he is bullied. He pulls the bully off and pummels him mercilessly. The father explains what it means to be sheep, those who are in need of protection; wolves, those who attack the weak; and sheepdogs, those who protect sheep from wolves. The boy acted like a sheepdog, attacking the wolf who had preyed upon a sheep. Did he finish it? Yes. The boy knew this lesson instinctively.

The sniper, retired, takes his boy hunting. It's a hard thing, he explains, to stop an animal's beating heart. It's a different, and more difficult, lesson from the one his own father had instilled. On his last day at home—prior to being assassinated by a soldier who has not recovered from the horrors, stress, and violence of war—the retired sniper tells his boy, upon leaving the house, that he is now in charge of protecting the house, his mother, and his sister. Is he ready for it? He thus asks his own boy whether he is ready for what he wishes the boy struggling with the RPG launcher to please, please, please not do.

Distracted, the boy sitting with his parents and brother eyeballs the compact Bible tucked into the bracket at the back of the pew in front of them. He takes it and stores it away in his clothing. Only the brother notices the theft but says nothing. The sniper still carries the Bible with him, something like a talisman. A comrade remarks that the sniper never reads from the Bible, never quotes it, and ostensibly is unaffected by its spirituality. Confronted with this exposure, the sniper bristles at the implication of hypocrisy but does not defend himself.

We see the sniper's eye in the inverted view of the scope—enlarged, flattened by the lens's distortion, remote, detached from a physical body, perceptive, dispassionate. The role of the sniper is to *overwatch*—assume a hidden position where he can see over a terrain where soldiers are engaged and watch for armed adversaries that the soldiers cannot see. Neither the soldiers nor the adversaries can see the sniper; his deeds come as a surprise to both. He is a combatant in repose—watching from a hidden, safe, elevated position, comfortably cradling the long rifle, which is softly nestled against his cheek resting on the rifle's stock. It is as much about seeing, watching, and breathing as it is about aiming and shooting. The rifle is an extension of the eye.

The preacher talks about God's vision, how we cannot see what God sees nor comprehend how He understands what He sees. It's then that the boy takes the small Bible from the bracket at the back of the pew in front of him. His brother doesn't comprehend the mixed moral status of stealing a Bible from a church. Maybe the wisdom of how He sees will be in the book; maybe just carrying it will bring the wisdom and vision closer. The sniper needs to see as God sees—unseen and seeing all that those below do not see. Having the Bible tucked away in his uniform close to his heart invokes the vision he aspires to more than reading it will.

Mustafa fights where he lives, and the sniper fights on the opposite side of the world from where his wife and young child live. Like the sniper, Mustafa has a wife and small child. Mustafa shoots foreign soldiers, who are the wolves in his land. They fall back against a wall behind them, held upright for an instant as we see the impact on the person—more salient than the impact on the body. Mustafa shoots from an elevated hidden position; he lies in repose cradled against his weapon, and he watches for targets through his rifle's scope. He is clever in his positioning and in his tactics. He is swift and graceful in traversing along rooftops. He seeks out the chance to target his adversary, the foreign sniper with legendary efficacy. The sniper seeks out Mustafa, who reputedly competed at the Olympics. The two of them could have been competitors challenging their skills at the quadrennial global gathering for pure sport. Sportsmanship could have made them friends. In the ancient Greek tradition of Olympics, states at war would participate in the competitions, leaving their animosities and aggressions behind. In their ultimate confrontation, Mustafa is looking for the sniper, and the sniper is looking for him. The sniper believes he sees where Mustafa lies hidden, and believes he can shoot accurately from an impossible distance. Both beliefs are preposterous, and yet he fires even though the gun's report will draw attention to the squad's position in the midst of a large number of adversaries. He adjusts his sight for estimated distance, steadies his gun, breathes out gently, closes that one eye, and pulls the trigger at that moment in between breaths, in between heartbeats, and thus at that corresponding ever-present moment of stopping a heart. We see that the bullet traverses the impossible distance and hits its mark perfectly.

The man in the service training to be a SEAL, still prior to sniper training, engages in compatible, jovial conversation with a woman at a bar. She is not easily impressed and has reason, which turns out to be justifiable, not to find the supervirile bravura of exclusive SEALs alluring. But she is taken with his genuineness, his gentleness, his openness, his attentiveness, his lack of gratuitous masculinity. He calls her the next day, solicitous regarding her recovery from excessive alcohol the night before, which had resulted in humiliating vomiting outside the bar. He calls repeatedly—gentle, affable, solicitous, endearing—cueing readiness for devotion to her. She believes it; she relents. His devotion will be unwavering, so far as his devotion to being a soldier protecting soldiers will allow.

At the wedding reception while they dance, a call comes from base, and his grooms relate it to him—they will be deployed to Iraq. They celebrate; she doesn't oppose his enthusiasm, but she is wary. He calls from Iraq at a moment that seems quiet and safe—though while on an operation in harm's way. A firefight ensues; he drops the phone, not realizing that the connection hasn't been broken. She hears the horrifying noises, calls out for him, but he doesn't respond. Not till later, when he calls, will her anguish subside. He calls her during the firefight that ensues after the shot that killed Mustafa. His squad isn't yet overrun but soon will be. They are running out of ammunition, and the onslaught hasn't been reduced. However many they kill, more rush in. He tells her, more reduced in spirit from the accumulated toll of his experiences than from his current dire predicament, that he is ready now to come home. His resolution has finality to it. That he wants just to be with her and their children expresses his feelings now, regardless of the predicament. That she should know that is paramount, particularly in this circumstance.

Returned from his last deployment, the sniper sits at a bar, nursing a beer. He is sullen. No one sits near him. At one end of the bar a few men talk quietly. At the other end, the American sanitized nonlethal accommodation of militarism—professional basketball—plays on a TV mounted above the bar. The sniper glances at the game. How lame this ritualized, modified, rugged competition with only make-believe importance and consequence must seem. He sits alone in the middle of the vast expanse of the bar. His phone rings. He looks at the number but hesitates. Finally, he picks up and responds without feeling. It is his wife, who does not yet know that he is stateside. She seems hurt by his negligence and also senses his distance and depression, of which he hardly has perspective himself. Her voice warms him, consoling immediately. He promises, nearly in tears, to come home.

The sniper has his calling originally, instinctually, prior to having it inculcated by his father, who imparts the lesson of sheep, sheepdog, and wolf at the dinner table. The mother recoils as he removes his belt to underscore his reaction lest either of the two sons should ever be a wolf. The boy who will become the sniper is buoyed by this emphasis. It aligns with his innate sensibilities, which guided him to attack the bigger boy who had bullied his brother. His purpose builds on valorized sensibility—protective overwatch of the soldiers thrust into danger in his immanent presence, and that protectiveness extends to country and family, even as obscure as the connection might be. The calling would keep him there forever, gung ho about battle, not so much for its own sake but mainly so that he could be the protective one who watches over. That he should be the sheepdog comes without needing to think about it. That he could be the wolf simultaneously is beyond his cognizance.

The sniper understands his job as protecting soldiers. He is careful to stay within designated rules of engagement, which are carefully administered in real-time communication by his commanding officers. They monitor the hazardous task of seeking out combatants who are interchangeable with noncombatant civilians in the urban terrain. The sniper is confident of his ability to identify combatants. He defends his actions somewhat abrasively to his superiors, playing on how his effectiveness in his role should grant him leeway and credibility. His cognizance of the purpose of the intrusion into the foreign country is as vague as his grasp of the Bible that he carries with him always. He explains to a fellow soldier that either we stop their opposition here or in New York or San Diego. This invocation of old-time fears about national security falling like dominoes leaves the soldier confounded. Does the sniper truly believe something that simplistic?

The sniper trains with weights. He is big and very strong. That casual swagger and natural confidence builds from his core strength, even in the relaxed prone position of the sniper. The massive weights on either side of him attach to bars that extend around in front and back of him. He strains as he pulls the weights up, and he releases the grimace as he drops them back down. It is the unique moment when the confidence and casual calm leave him—when there is some indication of the weight he carries always, but always without showing it.

Carrying the weight shows in his instinctive reflex to the moments that demand quick response lest he succumb or endanger soldiers. Like his strengths, the reflexes go with him when he returns to home, wife, and family. A drill, a lawn mower, a saw—all bring out the quick intense attention and readiness for action. It detracts from his ability to listen to his wife, to be present to her. He is at the ready while driving a vehicle to swerve suddenly out of the designated lanes of traffic. He sees a vehicle identical to one carrying adversaries in combat, and he cannot absorb any other information until it passes. His blood pressure stays at a constant high level. He blithely avers to Taya, unconvincingly, that nothing is the matter. He watches footage of battle posted online by Mustafa. He watches a war film on TV, though the screen is blank. It is a boy screaming that he hears in the soundtrack of the imagined war scene. As his newborn daughter cries in her crib in the hospital nursery, Chris bangs on the thick plexiglass window, insistent that the attending nurse attend to his child rather than to the one she is holding. At a party in his own backyard, the family dog, a sheepdog, plays rough with the children. When the dog seems to attack, the sniper rushes over, pulls his belt loose, and holds it folded and high above, ready to pummel the dog, until his wife cries out, snapping him out of the violent trance. Ready to mete out punitive intervention, such as his father had prescribed, he takes the sheepdog for a wolf, just as had been his assumption regarding his enemies in war. The sniper has come to map his war world view so that he can now not avoid seeing and understanding his home world view.

A VA psychologist asks whether he has seen or done things that he regrets. The sniper blithely avers no, that he can account morally for every shot he took, for every combatant he killed. He regrets only not being able to save more soldiers, not being even more protective. He refers to enemy combatants as "savages." His encounters are mostly from a distance from which his targets do not see him. What he sees of them is intimate, which encumbers his reaction in spite of himself when the target is a boy or a woman. His antipathy for the Butcher is emotionally laden, but for Mustafa it is simply a matter of duty and strategic purpose—Mustafa kills soldiers. Twice he leads a squad into the home of a family. Each time, the sniper forcefully extracts—more by threat than by physical effect—complicity. He needs the civilian to provide information. Alternately, he is a civil guest. In the one case the father of the family urges the sniper to understand his family's precariousness just by virtue of the soldiers' presence in his house. The man and his family are caught between the violent potential of the foreign soldiers and the equally violent retribution of his own country's resistance. The sniper understands this not well enough. That one incident exemplifies the sniper's military's presence as foreign invaders in this country, which places noncombatants in danger of intentional and unintentional violence from either side. The man asks for a large sum of money, which will not be of use where he is but will be sufficient to extract him and his family out of the country where he can expect no longer to survive the wrath of those the sniper wants him to betray.

In another family's home, the sniper and his squad are hosted to a holiday meal. The sniper watches as the father guides his young son's school lessons. When the man bends down to pick up the pencil that the boy has let drop, the sniper sees the man's reddened elbow, a telltale sign of time spent prone manning a sniper's rifle. When the sniper finds the cache of arms in the home and drags the man into the next room to account for it, the boy screams in terror. That man, too, also positioned between two unforgiving military forces, will die as a result.

The sniper constructs an internal wall that keeps thoughts of failure, and of loss, at bay. He cannot comprehend his own brother's miserable rejection of the country in which they have done battle. His jovial devotion to soldier buddies blocks out causality. A man he saved who had suffered loss of limb urges him to visit maimed survivors at the VA hospital. The sniper isn't inclined to do that. There will be those physically maimed, and those spiritually damaged, like his brother, or like Marc Lee, whose doubts about the mission the sniper believes to be that genuine cause for getting killed. His wife is distraught at his increasingly dark distance. She urges him not to return to the battles, which he says he must do out of devotion to her as well as to country. She is aghast at the equation because it does not make a lick of sense. He talks of perhaps not surviving and how she would find someone else, which ignites her anguish beyond what she can endure.

That moment training with the weights surrounding him, alone and unobserved but in the midst of the safe region of the armed base, the strain and grimace showing and then falling—this is the sniper as he is by himself. It's what's underneath the steady, calm, jovial, purposive demeanor the rest of the time. The moment, again alone, when he doesn't strive to choke a sob after it's clear that he won't need, once more, to shoot a young boy again shows that hidden vulnerability. When he sits hunkered over a beer and tells his wife, voice broken, that he needs, wants, to come home now, he shows that vulnerability. The hidden weight will sustain long after it seems past—when his wife can no longer sense it, when he seems happily restored to life away from war, with children to play with, and newly committed to a devotion to soldiers transposed beyond battle into the realm of recovery.

The talisman of vision, the compact Bible the sniper carries with him, assuages doubt. The more it's suppressed, the more it plays on him nevertheless. He doesn't doubt himself when he decides, against standing orders for his role, to abandon his sniper position to accompany instead the squad of soldiers searching houses. He doesn't doubt when he positions himself in the street, firing at the fleeing vehicle with the Butcher inside. He doesn't doubt himself when he says he can see where Mustafa has taken a completely hidden position over a mile away, and he doesn't doubt himself when he takes aim and fires—in between breaths and with eyes closed. And he doesn't doubt that he hits his target, still beyond visual range. He doesn't doubt himself when he takes the marine veteran with PTSD, more severe than his, out to the make-do firing range where the man will kill him. The sniper takes cover, but bullets do come his way and miss. He doesn't doubt—except for that one moment when he shares it with his wife—that the bullets will always miss.

A squad of marines searches houses in the streets below. The sniper is in overwatch position as usual. But he sees the marines in danger inside, not on the street. One of them is shot and brought back outside. So he resolves to join them, expecting to teach them tactics that their short training and experience has not provided them. He finds the man who knows the identity of the Butcher and agrees to locate where he is for a large sum. The sniper is chastised upon return to base for leaving his overwatch post, which he does not dispute nor excuse. When he returns with a motorized squad with the payment, he, again, is out of position. So when the man's boy is horrifically tortured and killed, and the man killed, the sniper is pinned down by Mustafa, unable to intervene as would have been easy had he been in secured sniper position. The sniper, threatening detention and the Iraqi judicial system, forces the man who served his squad dinner to lead them into the building where the Butcher hides with his soldiers. Though the sniper escapes intact after killing many of the Butcher's soldiers and the Butcher too, a fierce firefight ensues, and every member of the squad is caught in momentary danger.

When his closest buddy is mortally wounded by Mustafa, the sniper's squad retreats hastily to get the man to urgent care. He does survive for now but not ultimately. The squad, though, expects the worst at that moment. They resolve, with the pride of their status as ultimate warriors, to get payback. Following what turns out to be treacherous information by a source they take to be trustworthy, they walk into a clearly planned trap. Another soldier is killed, and they retreat hastily again.

In his last battle, the sniper is the centerpiece in a squad secreted in enemy territory in the city, but he is in a position to see and target Mustafa, who has killed soldiers erecting a wall to partition part of the city. Mustafa has outfoxed him again, finding a position in what is for him enemy territory and ostensibly out of range from the sniper. The squad realizes that they are in the midst of larger enemy forces, as confirmed by a surveillance drone flying above. The sniper repositions himself and insists he sees where Mustafa lies hidden, even though Mustafa can find targets among nearby marines. The sniper is ordered not to fire lest it reveal their position to the enemy soldiers surrounding them, but he does, with hardly anything but hope that he will hit the target. The shot brings on the anticipated attack. The squad kills many, but many more descend on their position. They are out of ammunition and anticipate being overrun and annihilated. They call in an aerial attack on their own position, which is the only tactic left. The sniper calls his wife, to tell her that he is ready to come home now. He doesn't reveal anything about the situation. It is what he would want to leave for her as his last message. The aerial attack misses its target, buffeted by the turbulence of the sandstorm flowing into the locale. The squad, aided by the very thick fog of war that the sandstorm provides, manages to get out to the street just as the armored convoy arrives to extract them. The sniper is the last one aboard, almost forgotten. A bullet hits his side with a force that knocks him down, but it does not penetrate his body armor. He rises, leaving on the ground his gun, binoculars, and helmet, hastens to catch up with the personnel vehicle, and clasps the hand extended to pull him aboard. Father's rule of never leaving a weapon on the ground no longer has relevance.

Anti-War War Films

The film corroborates what Ralph Waldo Emerson says about heroism:

The hero is of a mind of such balance that no disturbances can shake his will, but pleasantly and as it were merrily he advances to his own

music, alike in frightful alarms and in the tipsy mirth of universal dis-
soluteness. There is somewhat not philosophical in heroism; there is
somewhat not holy in it; it seems not to know that other souls are of
one texture with it; it hath pride; it is the extreme of individual nature.
. . . Heroism works in contradiction to the voice of mankind and in
contradiction, for a time, to the voice of the great and good. Heroism is
an obedience to a secret impulse of an individual's character. (177)

Everything in this passage fits Chris Kyle in *American Sniper* perfectly.
But if a nation sends its soldiers to war, this is the hero it wants—unphilo-
sophical, unholy, "merrily" unshakable, contrary to humanity and to what
is good, and obedient to a wholly individual impulse that is nevertheless
consistent with the military goal. For the sake of how spectacularly Chris
Kyle (film character or the real soldier) fits that role, one has to recognize
that there is something magnificent in that individual—even with his
skewed political world view. Even in perfection, though, the hero too will
suffer immeasurably, in spite of a hardened spiritual core of self-assurance
and denial. To send soldiers to war is to countenance the consequences to
them. If a nation decides to send its soldiers to war, this is the soldier it
wants, replete with what would count as defects in character in civil society,
and replete as well with immense suffering that endures beyond survival.

Showing the experience of soldiers in war for what it is—this is what an
anti-war war movie can do while, specifically, not glamorizing that experience. Other sorts of films that can accomplish an anti-war perspective can
do other things, though mostly this will be a project for documentary cinema. Other films can explore and challenge the purposes and strategies that
a nation embraces in executing a war. This, too, is more easily the project of
documentary cinema.

Though I hadn't told Josie—because I wanted her thoughtful reaction
unfiltered by anything I might reveal about my own expectations—I had
published an essay about "Anti-War War Films." It's gotten me some communication, including inquiries about my reaction to *American Sniper*,
requests for advice about anti-war films, and an invitation to speak at a festival featuring anti-war films. In that essay, I delineate thirteen anti-war
war-film strategies. These are not criteria but just the strategies that I detected
employed in four exemplary films: Lewis Milestone's *All Quiet on the Western Front* (1930), Stanley Kubrick's *Paths of Glory* (1957), Kubrick's *Full Metal
Jacket* (1987), and Terrence Malick's *The Thin Red Line* (1998). Other films

will register some of these strategies, and there could be other such strategies. Like *American Sniper*, these films are not didactic. They show us what we need to see: what soldiers experience, what they suffer, how they kill and die, and how their suffering continues after release from the military. If you want for your nation to go to war, this is the fate that you consign to the soldiers who will fight it.

American Sniper shows war for how soldiers endure fear, horror, doubt, terror, panic, loss, horrific injury, and particularly confrontation with death. It broaches the thin line between heroic bravery and pointless sacrifice. It shows how random victimization is inherent to warfare. It shows how the brutal logic and tactics that a soldier must necessarily follow are serendipitously unmasked through confrontation with an enemy-soldier representative of his own self. It shows how soldiers object to the logic imposed by hierarchical command but then acquiesce to implementing that logic. It shows how soldiers lose or never have a clear, realistic sense of purpose in the conduct of the war that engulfs them. It shows how the culture of the nation contributes to the eagerness that young men exhibit for war and warlike virtues. It shows how soldiers suffer moral degradation as a result of conditioning in training and as an insuppressible response to horror and loss. It shows how soldiers become alienated from the world where they may live in peace, and from the world shared with women. It shows the debilitating forces of horror and terror. It eschews audience emotional investment in single characters glorified or vilified to elicit calculated positive emotional responses to brutality and violence exacted by heroes on villains. It avoids fixing blame or hate-worthiness on individuals, nations, or institutions. It broaches the meaning of war independent of the historical context of particular wars, as an arena of behavior that affords us a sobering contemplation on human existence.

That essay and this one come from someone who learned lessons of how to live with peace from his father, as much in accordance with his sensitivity and instincts as Chris Kyle with his father's lessons. Kyle is one I can have sympathy with, without needing to revere or revile him, being able to respect this individual without needing to idolize or to demonize. It strikes me as painfully and not at all profoundly obvious what Admiral Gene LaRocque said:

I hate it when they say, "He gave his life for his country." Nobody gives their life for anything. We steal the lives of these kids. We take it away from them. They don't die for the honor and glory of their country. We kill them. . . .

Note

1. I am indebted to Josiane Lismay for having shared conversation and thoughts in the development of this essay.

Works Cited

All Quiet on the Western Front. Directed by Lewis Milestone, performances by Lew Ayres, Louis Wolheim, and John Wray, Universal, 1930.

American Sniper. Directed by Clint Eastwood, performances by Bradley Cooper and Sienna Miller, Warner Bros., 2014.

Anderson, Jon R. "*American Sniper* Widow Says the Film Gets It Right." *Military Times*, Dec. 16, 2014.

August: Osage County. Directed by John Wells, performances by Meryl Streep, Julia Roberts, and Chris Cooper, Weinstein Company, 2013.

Baker, K. C. "*American Sniper* Screenwriter Nixed Chris Kyle's Death in Script for the Sake of Kyle's Kids." *People*, Feb. 17, 2015.

Baxter, Joseph. "How Steven Spielberg's Version of *American Sniper* Would Have Been Different." *CinemaBlend*, www.cinemablend.com/new/How-Steven-Spielberg-Version-American-Sniper-Would-Have-Been-Different-69281.html. Accessed 15 May 2017.

Carnage. Directed by Roman Polanski, performances by Jodie Foster, Kate Winslet, and Christoph Waltz, SBS Productions, 2011.

Cooper, Bradley, and Taya Kyle. "Bradley Cooper and *American Sniper* Widow Team Up to Tell SEAL's Story." *NPR*, Dec. 21, 2014, tpr.org/post/bradley-cooper-and-american-sniper-widow-team-tell-seals-story#stream/0. Accessed 15 May 2017.

Dawson, Jeff. "Dirty Harry Comes Clean: Clint Eastwood Talks to Jeff Dawson." *Guardian*, June 6, 2008.

Deleuze, Gilles. "Literature and Life." *Essays Critical and Clinical*, translated by Daniel W. Smith and Michael A. Greco, U of Minnesota P, 1997, 1–5.

Dockterman, Eliana. "Clint Eastwood Says *American Sniper* is Anti-War." *Time*, Mar. 1, 2015.

Eastwood, Clint. "1974 *Playboy* Interview." *Playboy Magazine*, Feb. 1974.

———. "Transcript: Clint Eastwood's Convention Remarks." *NPR*, Aug. 30, 2012, www.npr.org/2012/08/30/160358091/transcript-clint-eastwoods-convention-remarks. Accessed 15 May 2017.

Emerson, Ralph Waldo. *Emerson's Essays: First and Second Series Complete in One Volume*. Harper & Row, 1951.

Feinberg, Scott. "Clint Eastwood: 'I Was Against Going into the War in Iraq.'" *Hollywood Reporter*, Dec. 8, 2014.

Flags of Our Fathers. Directed by Clint Eastwood, performances by Ryan Phillippe, Barry Pepper, and Joseph Cross, DreamWorks, 2006.

Full Metal Jacket. Directed by Stanley Kubrick, performances by Matthew Modine, R. Lee Ermey, and Vincent D'Onofrio, Natant / Harrier Films, 1987.

Galloway, Stephen. "Clint Eastwood Describes His Near-Death Experience, Says *American Sniper* Is Anti-War (Exclusive)." *Hollywood Reporter*, Mar. 16, 2015.

Hainey, Michael. "Clint and Scott Eastwood: No Holds Barred in Their First Interview Together." *Esquire*, 3 Aug. 2016.

Hall, Jason. *American Sniper*. Screenplay. Unpublished manuscript, Mar. 18, 2014

Hausam, Michael. "'I'd Unleash Hell': *American Sniper*'s Dad Put Clint Eastwood and Bradley Cooper in Their Place before Filming." *Independent Journal*, Dec. 2014.

High Plains Drifter. Directed by Clint Eastwood, performances by Eastwood and Verna Bloom, Universal, 1973.

Howell, Peter. "Think Before You Shoot, Clint Eastwood Says of War: Interview." *The Star.com*, Jan. 13, 2015, www.thestar.com/entertainment/movies/2015/01/13/think_before_you_shoot_clint_eastwood_says_of_war_interview.html. Accessed 15 May 2017.

Inglourious Basterds. Directed by Quentin Tarantino, performances by Brad Pitt, Christoph Waltz, and Mélanie Laurent, Universal, 2009.

Ito, Robert. "The Book Ends, and the Story Begins: *American Sniper* Script Looks for the Human behind the Hero." *New York Times*, Jan. 28, 2015.

Johnson, Ted. "PopPolitics: Screenwriter Jason Hall on Why *American Sniper* Is Anti-War." *Variety*, Jan. 10, 2015.

Kapsis, Robert E., and Kathie Coblentz, editors. *Clint Eastwood: Interviews*. UP of Mississippi, 1999.

Kyle, Chris, with Scott McEwen and Jim DeFelice. *American Sniper: The Autobiography of the Most Lethal Sniper in U. S. Military History*. HarperCollins, 2012.

LaRocque, Gene. Interview by Studs Terkel. *"The Good War": An Oral History of World War Two*, The New Press, 1997, pp. 189–93.

LaSalle, Mick. "Ask Mick LaSalle: *Carnage* Wasn't Funny." *San Francisco Chronicle*, Jan. 19, 2014.

———. "Clint Eastwood Aims for a Little Nuance." Review of *American Sniper*. *San Francisco Chronicle*, Jan. 15, 2015.

———. *Letters from Iwo Jima*. Directed by Clint Eastwood, performance by Ken Watanabe, DreamWorks, 2006.

Lisi, Jon. "The Pro-War Versus Anti-War Debate on *American Sniper* Misses the Point." *PopMatters*, May 18, 2015. Accessed 22 Feb. 2016.

LoBianco, Tom. "Donald Trump on Terrorists: 'Take Out Their Families.'" *CNN*, Dec. 3, 2015, www.cnn.com/2015/12/02/politics/donald-trump-terrorists-families/. Accessed 16 Jan. 2017.

Murphy, Audie. *To Hell and Back*. 2nd ed., Henry Holt, 2002.

Murphy, Mekado. "Anatomy of a Scene: *American Sniper*." *New York Times*, Jan. 15, 2015, www.nytimes.com/video/movies/100000003453108/anatomy-of-a-scene-american-sniper.html. Accessed 15 May 2017.

Myers, Meghann. "Bradley Cooper on Portraying Famed Navy SEAL Chris Kyle." *Navy Times*, Jan. 16, 2016.

The Outlaw Josey Wales. Directed by Clint Eastwood, performances by Eastwood, Sondra Locke, and Chief Dan George, Warner Bros., 1976.

Page, Clarence. "Anti-War, Pro-Troops in Film and in Life." *Chicago Tribune*, Jan. 30, 2015.

Pale Rider. Directed by Clint Eastwood, performances by Eastwood, Michael Moriarty, and Carrie Snodgress, The Malpaso Company, 1985.

Paths of Glory. Directed by Stanley Kubrick, performances by Kirk Douglas, Ralph Meeker, and Adolphe Menjou, Bryna Productions, 1957.

Powers, John. "Full of Complexity and Ambivalence, *American Sniper* Shows the Cost of War." *NPR*, Jan. 28, 2015, www.npr.org/2015/01/28/382157425/full-of-complexity-and-ambivalence-american-sniper-shows-the-cost-of-war. Accessed 15 May 2017.

Rich, Frank. "*American Sniper* Proves Obama's Politics Beat Cheney's." *New York Magazine*, Jan. 30, 2015.

Rogen, Seth. "Seth Rogen Apologizes for *American Sniper* Tweets." *CBS News*, Jan. 22, 2015, www.cbsnews.com/news/seth-rogen-apologizes-for-american-sniper-tweets/. Accessed 15 May 2017.

Rothermel, Dennis. "Anti-War War Films." *Resisting War, Educating for Peace*, edited by Andrew Fitz-Gibbon, Rodopi, 2010, pp. 75–105.

———. "Eastwood's Treatment of the Life of Creativity and Performance in *Bronco Billy, Honkytonk Man, White Hunter Black Heart*, and *Bird*." *New Essays on Clint Eastwood*, edited by Leonard Engel, U of Utah P, 2012, pp. 90–120.

———. "Mystical Moral Miasma in *Mystic River*." *Clint Eastwood, Actor and Director: New Perspectives*, edited by Leonard Engel, U of Utah P, 2007, pp. 218–41.

Saving Private Ryan. Directed by Steven Spielberg, performances by Tom Hanks, Matt Damon, and Tom Sizemore, DreamWorks, 1998.

Shane. Directed by George Stevens, performances by Alan Ladd, Jean Arthur, and Van Heflin, Paramount, 1953.

Smith, Ronald. "*American Sniper* as Apple Pie." *Commentary*, Mar. 1, 2015.

Sudden Impact. Directed by Clint Eastwood, performances by Eastwood, Sondra Locke, and Pat Hingle, Warner Bros., 1983.

Suebsaeng, Asawin. "Oscar-Nominated *American Sniper* Made Joe Biden Cry." *Daily Beast*, Jan. 14, 2015.

The Thin Red Line. Directed by Terrence Malick, performances by Jim Caviezel, Sean Penn, and Nick Nolte, Fox 2000, 1998.

White Hunter Black Heart. Directed by Clint Eastwood, performances by Eastwood, Jeff Fahey, and Charlotte Cornwell, Malpaso Productions, 1990.

Whitesides, John. "Trump Backs Waterboarding and 'a Lot More' after Brussels Attacks." *Reuters*, 22 Mar. 2016, www.reuters.com/article/us-usa-election-idUSKCN0WO11J. Accessed 16 Jan. 2017.

Wilson, Michael Henry, editor. *Eastwood on Eastwood*. Revised English ed., 2010. Cahiers du Cinéma.

13

American Sniper and the Critics
A Note on the Art of Interpretation

Leonard Engel

How important are reviews in determining a film's quality? *A very good question requiring much research!* In determining ticket sales, how important are reviews, especially those that use volatile language and harangue about patriotism? *Very important!* And the more heated the controversy, the more tickets sold. Clint Eastwood may understand this better than anyone else in Hollywood because his films are often at the center of controversy and usually produce substantial box-office returns. While many of his films have received critical, often sharply conflicting, commentary, none has elicited more diverse criticism than *American Sniper* (2014). Among other things, the divisive uproar caused a virtual stampede to see the film. It may, ultimately, exceed all his other films in producing revenue. For most reviewers the key issue is the film's bias: Is it pro-war or anti-war? Does it support patriotism or undermine it? Does it present the marksman Chris Kyle as a hero or a wanton killer? Controversy also attended the book on which the film is based—*American Sniper: The Autobiography of the Most Lethal Sniper in U. S. Military History* (2012), a memoir by Chris Kyle (written with Scott McEwen and Jim DeFelice). The book's bias, however, is transparent—it is highly favorable to Kyle; after all, he is the main author. In no uncertain terms, the book celebrates his shooting skill and the many American lives that skill saved. His patriotism is unquestioned, and to many readers he is a hero. But the film tells a different story.

First, here is a brief sample of the diverse comments on the film. David Denby succinctly articulates the irony of the controversy in the opening sentence of his *New Yorker* review: "Clint Eastwood's *American Sniper* is both a devastating war movie and a devastating antiwar movie, a subdued celebration of a warrior's skill and a sorrowful lament over his alienation and misery" (151). Michael Phillips weighs in on the ambiguity of the film's message: "People will take what they want to take from *American Sniper*, Clint Eastwood's latest film. Already it has turned into an ideological war to be won or lost, rather than a fictionalized biopic to be debated" (par. 1). And Kyle Smith renders a brief summary of some of the more outrageous comments from reviewers: Canadian actor/comedian and sometime critic Seth Rogen claims that

> *American Sniper* reminded him of Nazi propaganda. Michael Moore dubbed snipers "cowards" and called our Iraq war enemies "brave." MSNBC's Ayman Mohyeldin called [Chris] Kyle a "racist" who went on "killing sprees." A. O. Scott of the *New York Times* scolded the film for being "an expression of nostalgia for [George W. Bush's] Manichaean approach to foreign policy." In a *Guardian* piece by American feminist Lindy West, a headline read: "Chris Kyle was a hate-filled killer. Why are simplistic patriots treating him as a hero?" Writer Rania Khalek dubbed Kyle "an American Psycho." Alternet writer Max Blumenthal compared Kyle to Beltway sniper "John Lee Malvo" (sic: the long-range murderers were John Allen Muhammad and Lee Boyd Malvo). (Smith 51)

Smith's own view is revealing: "*American Sniper* . . . caught critics unaware. It came as a kind of gut punch to the cultural gatekeepers who had no idea [it] was coming and were genuinely gobsmacked at the overwhelming national response to it. It hit them right where it hurts" (50–51). So the film and the "overwhelming national response" to it "gobsmacked" the reviewers and critics! What to make of this once raging controversy? And what is Eastwood's role in it? One is reminded of an anecdote about the almost nonchalant remark Clint made when an earnest associate asked him what the audience would think (about the meaning of one of the scenes they were shooting in an earlier film): "The audience can think whatever it wants to think" was Eastwood's curt response.

American Sniper's tumultuous reception also brings to mind the commentary (often sharply divergent) that earlier Eastwood films provoked: *High Plains Drifter*, *Pale Rider*, *Unforgiven*, *Million Dollar Baby*, *Mystic River*, and even *J. Edgar*; all had reviewers in various stages of apoplexy. However, none of those reviews revealed the volatility of the remarks about *Sniper*. So the question must be asked: how can experienced reviewers, whose profession is viewing films and then writing about them, propound such conflicting views about the same film? Film viewers who occasionally read reviews might legitimately ask: is there a path through this thicket, this dizzying maze of diverse criticism? Is it possible to assemble a reasonable approach to *American Sniper*—to engage the film, as Michael Phillips asks above, as a "fictionalized biopic to be debated"?

I believe there is, but attentive viewing is necessary, for there are subtle clues in the film that distinguish it from the book. Some of the more perceptive critiques zero in on carefully selected details that are not in the book or in the interviews Chris Kyle gave. Attention to these details may help one get beyond the pro-war/anti-war issue and the heated subject of patriotism. In the book Kyle's commitment to the rightness of his duty and to his patriotism is never questioned; his only regret (stated in interviews after the book was published) is that he didn't kill *more* enemies in order to save *more* of his fellow Americans' lives.

However, Bradley Cooper's Kyle is less confident, and as the film moves toward its tragic conclusion, his self-assurance fades. He says the same things in the film as the real Kyle says in the book, but his tone of voice, his facial expression, and his body language show a lack of conviction. Through these small but important details, especially Cooper's unsure, fading voice and his occasional staring into space, Eastwood reveals subtle changes in Kyle's character. Clearly, Cooper's demeanor and attitude depict a different person from the one in the book or even from the one going through basic training. In an early scene depicting that training, Kyle and his fellow trainees, in full combat attire, are lying on their backs on a beach with ocean surf breaking over them while aggressive drill sergeants bark orders and shout questions at them. Provoked by one sergeant who keeps asking, "How do you feel?" Kyle responds: "Dangerous. I feel dangerous."

In a later scene when he meets Taya (Sienna Miller) in a bar, this "dangerous" Chris Kyle, recently graduated from sniper school, is a confident Navy SEAL. Taya is not overwhelmed; she is sarcastic and flippant at first but is soon captivated by his quiet self-assurance. They begin dating, have a speedy courtship, marry, and soon afterward he is sent to Iraq. Nevertheless, from this optimal moment in his life, we witness the stress he endures, and then—gradually at first—his breakdown: the slow, inevitable movement toward his sad end. The distance from the two early scenes—depicting a pumped-up Kyle shouting macho phrases in that wild ocean surf and an in-charge Kyle tenderly courting Taya—to the tentative, almost disoriented Kyle that we see toward the end of the film is a measure of the heavy toll the war and his unique part in it have taken on him.

Two critics, Thomas Powers in the *New York Review of Books* and Kyle Smith (quoted earlier) in *Commentary*, have pointed to the power of Eastwood's version of Kyle's downward spiral. I want to focus on some of the scenes that they mention and, perhaps, push their implications toward a deeper understanding of this subtle and complex film. In his provocative critique of both the film and the book, Powers claims that Eastwood and writer Jason Hall produce a film of "disciplined art and moral complexity. Part of the magic is the acting of Bradley Cooper when delivering the half-dozen lines, lifted more or less intact from the book, that capture the serene confidence of Kyle at the beginning of his military career, and the strain bringing him close to collapse at the end" (8). When told by a navy recruiter that ninety percent of those who sign up to be SEALs can't take it and quit, Kyle responds: "I'm not one of those men, sir, I don't quit." "The simplicity of these lines," Powers argues, "gives them strength but Cooper without effort pushes them further, conveying absolute conviction. I'd have signed up Cooper on the spot, just as the recruiter did" (8).

This quiet self-assurance and strength are also evident in Kyle's first major test in battle. Positioned on a rooftop overlooking a bombed-out portion of Fallujah as a line of US trucks carrying soldiers approach on a nearby road, Kyle sees a woman and a young boy emerge from one of the buildings. He thinks she is concealing something under her clothes because she's not swinging her arms freely, and he asks for confirmation (he's wearing a headset) from an outside contact point that she might be carrying a weapon. The responding voice says it cannot confirm and tells him it's his "call." With his finger poised on the trigger, Kyle watches and waits as the woman and boy move toward the trucks. Then, abruptly, Eastwood and writer Jason Hall interrupt the narrative with an extended flashback showing a young Kyle receiving high praise from his father for his accurate shooting when he kills his first deer—then his meeting and marrying Taya; and his recruitment and boot camp—before returning to Fallujah where the woman and boy approach the advancing soldiers. Suddenly the woman stops, pulls out a grenade, hands it to the boy, and points toward the approaching vehicles. The boy starts running toward them, getting ready to throw the grenade, and Kyle squeezes the trigger. The boy falls, dropping the grenade; not far behind, the woman picks it up and is about to throw it when Kyle squeezes the trigger again. She falls, and the grenade explodes nowhere near the intended target. The armed SEAL next to Kyle, assigned to protect him from rear attacks, exuberantly expresses his admiration, but Kyle dismisses the praise. Later, with his buddies, who are teasing him about his hesitation before shooting the woman and young boy, he quietly admits it wasn't how he thought his first kill would "go down." However, he has little time for further reflection because, almost immediately, we see him atop another roof, scanning the buildings and nearby rooftops for enemy snipers.

Kyle completes four tours of duty, and between tours, while he's home, we see his passivity and inattention, resulting in an increasing distance between him and Taya. In one scene, he is sitting absolutely still, in a dream-like daze, staring at a blank TV screen; in another, he is uncommunicative and listlessly moving from one room to another. Finally, a frustrated Taya exclaims, "You're here, but you're not here! The war is changing you!" Almost immediately after these depressing times at home, he is back in the battle zone and seems to come alive again, at one point even joining ground troops as they move from building to building, kicking in doors and searching for al-Qaeda operatives. In one of the buildings, Kyle and his men discover what appears to be a friendly family and are treated to a meal, but while eating Kyle senses something amiss and starts looking around. In an adjoining room, he discovers a trapdoor in the floor, revealing a hidden cache of weapons and ammunition. His acuity in this incident, along with his growing reputation as an expert marksman, leads his buddies to nickname him "the Legend."

However, as his kills mount up, signs of stress and battle fatigue increase. They are especially evident in a later scene when Kyle must make another life/death decision about a child. This boy, younger than the earlier one, perhaps reminding Kyle of his own son, emerges from a door and starts running. He sees a weapon lying on the ground next to a dead insurgent and stops. With the boy focused in the crosshairs of his gun and his finger on the trigger, Kyle whispers, "Don't pick it up. Don't pick it up." The boy picks it up and looks around. "Put it down," Kyle whispers again, his voice hoarse with anguish, "put it down." The boy hesitates, still holding it, while Kyle's face is contorted with emotion. The boy finally throws it down and runs off. Nearly devastated, breathing heavily, almost in tears, Kyle rests his head on the gun. His stress is palpable.

Shortly after, Kyle is again perched on a rooftop, surveying a broad swath of the city, but this time his mind is on the enemy marksman Mustafa who has been picking off American soldiers. Kyle locates him on a rooftop over a mile away and fixes his sight on him. Most of his buddies don't think he should risk taking the shot—the distance is too great and the shot will disclose their position to the enemy. Watching Kyle prepare for the shot, however, convinces them that he should take the risk and try to kill the enemy sniper. Kyle does shoot, killing Mustafa but also revealing their location to the advancing enemy troops. Almost immediately, he calls Taya, telling her that he's been thinking about what she said during his last time at home and that he is now coming home for good. But he and his buddies first have to escape from the insurgents who are aware of their position and are almost on top of them. In addition, a blinding sandstorm has come up.

They do escape, barely, and Kyle is the last to be hauled aboard an escaping vehicle. It's a chaotic scene: the sand swirling and the SEALs, with little visibility, feeling their way, amid enemy gunfire, from the rooftop down to the street and the waiting truck. It's a nightmarish underworld—the "fog of war," one of the SEALs calls it, and the terror that the men must feel prompts this response from Powers to reviewers who have criticized the film for pandering to the warmongers: "I do not see how this final scene of blind confusion can possibly be interpreted as a statement of Eastwood's support for the wisdom or necessity of the war" (8).

When he leaves Iraq for good and returns to the States, Kyle doesn't immediately go home. We see him drinking alone in a bar, expressionless, staring into space, his cell phone near his hand. He picks it up, dials, and Taya answers, thinking he's still overseas. "Where are you?" she asks, trying to make sense of the call. In tears, he tells her that he's stateside, that he needed "some time," but now he's coming home. She has no idea what's going on with this behavior, but it seems to fit his apathy, revealed earlier, and the increasing distance between him and the family. After he returns, she pressures him to get help, and we next see him talking to a psychiatrist in a VA hospital. When asked if he has any regrets about what he's done in

Iraq, Kyle responds in a quiet voice, "No sir. That's not me. I'm ready to meet my maker and account for everybody I killed." His only regret is that he hadn't killed enough; if he had more kills, he claims, he might have saved more American lives. However, his facial expression, body language, and, especially, his voice belie his true feelings, suggesting a disconnection between his surface appearance and what's going on inside.

As Kyle Smith astutely observes, Chris Kyle in his *Autobiography*—unlike Bradley Cooper's character in the film—

> comes across as something of a swaggerer, and he has been revealed to have fabricated some of his stories, but it's critical to Eastwood's film that Kyle is not the one telling the story. Stouthearted, determined, professional, immensely skilled, and an emissary of moral order . . . Cooper's Chris Kyle is one of the great military heroes in cinematic history. . . . but in Bradley Cooper's eyes we can see the toll of duty. He says his soul is at rest. We know it isn't. (Smith 51–52)

Clearly, Cooper's Kyle is a different person from Kyle's portrayal of himself in the book. In the film, Kyle is anything but a bragging "swaggerer," as evidenced in an earlier scene when he's home on leave. He's in a tire shop with his son having new tires put on his truck and is approached by another vet who was in Iraq when Kyle was and claims that Kyle saved his life. The soldier's effusive expression of thanks clearly embarrasses Kyle, and when the vet stoops down and speaks directly to the boy, telling him his dad is a hero, Kyle's discomfort is palpable. He murmurs a dismissive thanks to the vet and can't get away quickly enough.

In the earlier scene at the VA hospital, when the psychiatrist presses Kyle regarding regrets over the many people he's killed and Kyle's response is negative—that his only wish is that he had had more kills in order to save more American lives—the doctor then asks if he's still interested in saving war vets. When Kyle responds positively, the doc walks him through the halls of the hospital to see soldiers who are severely damaged, both physically and emotionally, and need help.

What we see in the next scene is not pretty. Kyle is in a room conversing with injured vets in wheelchairs who have lost hands, arms, feet, and, in some cases, both legs (mostly from roadside bombs). They are doing their best to cope with their condition and have a positive attitude; one is even joking while telling the story of how he lost his left hand but saved his right by reaching for a cigarette the instant the bomb exploded. Asked if he still smokes, he laughingly admits that he does. The humor only serves to deepen the loss these men face every day. This scene alone should be more than enough to convince the most doubting viewer that this is *not* a pro-war film. The hospital experience deeply affects Kyle, and he begins to make regular visits. We then see him accompanying other vets to a rifle range, aiding them in their practice shooting. We see him having fun with his kids, and we see his relationship with Taya improve. But at this point the tragedy strikes a final blow: after saying goodbye to his kids and promising them he'll be back in a little while to play a game with them, he kisses Taya and joins another vet, whom he is trying to help, and they leave for target practice. For a long moment as she slowly closes the door, Taya watches as Kyle greets the other vet, climbs in the truck, and drives away—her gradual closing of the door is the closing of Kyle's life for he is shot by the same vet he is trying to help, shortly after they arrive at the shooting range.[1]

What we see next is a long and stately funeral procession intermixed with photos of the real Kyle with his family. These final scenes are overwhelming and have an unforgettable dramatic poignancy. They powerfully reinforce what earlier scenes have suggested: this film is anything but a pro-war movie! What it is, is an abiding tribute to the men and women who have fought and died for this country. Incisively, Kyle Smith articulates what I believe to be Eastwood's overriding concern:

> Eastwood is the first director . . . inclined to salute the millions of grunts and sailors and flyboys and leathernecks standing in formation in a line back to Omaha Beach and Vicksburg and Valley Forge . . . the entire parade, including those still in uniform today, and [Eastwood is] skilled enough to summon the full force of Hollywood emotional imagery to provide a stricken but grateful nation a long-needed moment to pay respect to our troops and their sacrifices in Iraq. (52)

Like a rhymed couplet at the end of a Shakespearean sonnet, which succinctly summarizes the meaning of the previous twelve lines, this concluding sequence of *American Sniper*—the slow, solemn procession of vehicles and troops—encapsulates the core of the film. It is a dynamic tribute to the men and women who have given their lives and are still willing to make that supreme sacrifice for their country, even when the war is wrong.

Note

1. Chris Kyle and Chad Littlefield, a thirty-five-year-old friend, were shot and killed at a rifle range in Texas in February 2013 by another Iraq veteran whom they were trying to help.

Works Cited

American Sniper. Directed by Clint Eastwood, performances by Bradley Cooper and Sienna Miller, Warner Bros., 2014.

Denby, David. "Living History: *Selma* and *American Sniper*." Review. *New Yorker*, vol. 90, no. 41, 22–29 Dec. 2014, pp. 150–51.

Hughes, Mark. "*American Sniper* Says Much More Than You Think." *Arts & Entertainment*, 16 Jan. 2015.

Kain, Erik. "*American Sniper* Isn't Pro-War Propaganda." *Forbes*, 29 Jan. 2015.

Kyle, Chris, with Scott McEwen and Jim DeFelice. *American Sniper: The Autobiography of the Most Lethal Sniper in U. S. Military History*. HarperCollins, 2012.

Norris, Chris. "Review: *American Sniper*." *Film Comment*, vol. 51, no. 1, Jan. / Feb. 2015, 68–71.

Phillips, Michael. "*American Sniper* (Two Stars): The Eastwood Brand; Reverent Script, Approach Flatten Messy, Popular Autobiography." *Baltimore Sun*, 16 Jan. 2015, p. T17.

Powers, Thomas. "The American Hero." *New York Review of Books*, 2 Apr. 2015. 6–8.

Smith, Kyle. "*American Sniper* as Apple Pie." *Commentary*, vol. 139, no. 3, Mar. 2015, 50–52.

14

"The First Cut Is the Most Important Cut"
An Interview with Joel Cox

Paul Seydor

J oel Cox is what Hollywood trade papers often refer to as an industry veteran. This means that he's a craftsman who came up through the ranks, paying his dues and honing his skills long and patiently as apprentice, assistant, associate, and coeditor before being promoted to editor, after which, through a combination of extraordinary talent, fierce drive, and hard work, he carved out a distinguished career for himself. Born Joel Edward Cox in Los Angeles, California, on April 2, 1942, he's been in the film industry quite literally from the cradle. The son of a stand-in (i.e., the person who stands in for the star while a scene is being lighted or otherwise prepped), Joel at six months old appeared in Mervyn LeRoy's *Random Harvest*, starring Ronald Colman and Greer Garson. He continued playing in movies and also appeared on television shows, including the *Eddie Cantor Show*, until around the age of twelve when—long since bored by life on the set, which consisted mostly of long hours between his scenes—he told his parents that he wanted to finish his education. "I didn't know what I wanted to do," he said, "but I did know I was more of a hands-on person, and I always had a creative streak." His parents bent to his wishes, and he finished high school.

After graduation he went to work in the mail room at Warner Brothers, uncertain what he wanted to do apart from a keen interest in the sound department. What happened instead is that he was sent over as a substitute for a film messenger who was out sick a few days—this involved nothing glamorous, just carting film around the lot from the editing rooms to the coding rooms, the screening rooms, and the labs. When Rudi Fehr, the head of the studio's editing department, asked Joel what he thought about editing, Joel told him, "Three days ago I knew nothing about it, but now I'm extremely interested." So Fehr promised him a position when one became available. "It took me three years in the mail room before I got my first opportunity," he recalled.

Joel had been an apprentice for a few years when the legendary editor Sam O'Steen took him under his wing and showed him how to cut. From there he assisted several distinguished editors including Barry Malkin (with Francis Ford Coppola on *The Rain People*), Walter Thompson (on two films), and finally Ferris Webster on Clint Eastwood's *The Outlaw Josey Wales*, where he so impressed the director that when postproduction was over Eastwood told Joel he wanted him on all his films. He was Webster's coeditor after that, and, when Webster retired in 1983, Joel flew solo on Eastwood's *Sudden Impact*, a collaboration that would number over thirty films and make film history. He won the Academy Award for Best Film Editing for *Unforgiven*, for which he also received an American Cinema Editors Award. The Academy twice more nominated him, for *Million Dollar Baby* and *American Sniper*, while his editing of *Changeling* garnered a BAFTA nomination. Calling himself one of the luckiest men in the world, Joel considers it a privilege that early in his career a number of distinguished editors allowed him to sit in their cutting rooms and observe them at work. Equally generous, Joel accorded his assistant Gary D. Roach the same advantage, Roach becoming his coeditor on several films and now launched on a successful career of his own.

An editor of great versatility, Joel has cut crime, police, and detective pictures, as well as Westerns, comedies, thrillers, romances, musical films, biographical films, art films, war films, and documentaries. His current project, from which he took the time for this interview in March 2016, is *All Eyez on Me*, a biography of Tupac Shakur, one of six features he's edited without Eastwood as director.

Among Joel's many distinctions are two that, so far as I have been able to determine, make him unique among film editors. The first is that he is the only person who ever worked in the Warner Brothers mail room to have received an Oscar. The second is that after he and his wife, Judy, relocated to Paso Robles, California, they planted a vineyard on their property and created a five-varietal Bordeaux blend that they christened "Unforgiven." Brought to market in 2014, it has collected two gold medals, including one from the prestigious San Francisco Chronicle Wine Competition, and their subsequent blends have garnered awards as well. From Oscar winner to wine gold medalist, Joel Cox goes from strength to strength.

PS: *I'm often amazed by how few people, including even many who work in the business, know what we film editors actually do. When I'm introduced, people often say, "Oh, you cut out all the bad parts," as if we do nothing more than choose takes without blown lines and assemble them in the right order. The reality is that we are the first people who get to see the film as a film. Before it goes through our hands, it's a collection of pieces, of individual takes from various angles and of various sizes, but it has at best only a potential shape or structure. Would you like to offer some thoughts on this?*

JC: Well, the first cut I think is the most important cut—because the editor goes through all the material and comes up with what he believes is a footprint for the movie. I say "footprint" because my belief is that the editor's job is to put together a first cut that is his best determination of what the director was aiming for. Now we're not going to hit all the points because he's going to have a take he likes, he's going to have moments he likes, and he may not even tell you about them. In fact, it's not like the old days before digital when we used to watch the dailies together every night after shooting. You don't do that any longer.

PS: *Ever since films started being edited on computers, watching dailies with directors has gone the way of Moviolas and flatbeds. Many times I've had scenes in the first cut and run them for the directors before they've even had time to look at the dailies.*

JC: And now there's so much footage and the directors are so busy that it's left up to you to view the footage and make the decisions on your own. Now you may hit it and you may not, but it rarely takes very long to discover how you differ. Then you make the appropriate changes, and, if you've done your job right, you should be very close. Now if you're not, well, that's typically a lack of experience.

PS: *But another explanation is editors' relationships with the directors. It's a cliché that director-editor relationships are like marriages, but they are, at least in the sense that when a director finds an editor that he or she clicks with, then, as in your case with Clint Eastwood or mine with Ron Shelton, we eventually reach the point where, cinematically speaking, we can virtually complete each other's sentences. You and Eastwood have been together since the midseventies.*

JC: That's true. In my forty-year relationship with Clint, he usually just leaves it up to me. After watching the first cut, Clint stops at a certain point—he's almost never fussy—and says not to worry about this or that, and soon enough, in a remarkably short period of time, sometimes as little as four or five days, we get from my first cut to his director's cut. Right off the bat, I would be that close to—that in sync with—what he was after.

PS: *A director I work with, who was himself a distinguished editor before he became a director, used to say that often the takes the director chooses initially are not the takes that wind up in the completed film. This makes sense if you consider that if the dailies you're watching today are a love scene, but the scene the director worked on that day is an action sequence, he might not be in the best frame of mind to pick the takes from a love scene.*

JC: Very true. Also, when you're watching dailies at the end of a long day of shooting and picking the so-called best takes, that's kind of an isolated process that has very little to do with immersing yourself in the whole scene the way we do when we begin editing it. Most good directors know this and are respectful of the editing process. I've been fortunate enough that I've been pretty much left to my own for that first cut. Clint will say, "Put it together and we'll see what you see."

PS: *Peckinpah, who shot massive amounts of coverage, used to say, "I know what I see in the dailies. I want to see what my editors see in them."*

JC: Again, true, but you have to earn that confidence. I had been working as an assistant editor/coeditor with Ferris Webster on quite a few films with Clint. So by the time Ferris retired and Clint promoted me, he and I already had such a relationship, and I had already gained his confidence. It's like the marriage idea you mentioned—you have to become comfortable with each other so that you can build that trust.

PS: *People often think that in editing a film, the director is there right at your side, selecting the takes, telling you where to cut, and so forth. But it's not like that at all—for one thing, we start editing a film from the moment we get a full set of dailies, so we're editing while the director is on the set or on location shooting the film. And since films are rarely shot in sequence, you're not editing the scenes in script order—you're editing them according to the demands of the production schedule.*

JC: Absolutely. It takes a lot of experience to learn how to get yourself into a proper frame of mind from, say, scene 34 in morning to scene 88 in the afternoon, or to cut the climax of a movie early in the shoot, and the opening at the end. Yet you have to make each sequence be as good a version as you're able to of what it is. Don't worry whether it's too long. Think instead about what the particular scene is saying and is meant to do, what is going on in it, and make it the best scene you can. You worry about the transitions and the pacing of the film as a whole later on. The transitions from scene to scene are vitally important, but first you've got to get each scene together and working as its best—

PS: *In other words, you make each scene play as best you can and you don't get overly concerned about cutting it too tight or eliminating lines at this point—*

JC: Exactly. In my opinion, the best gift an editor can give his director is to show him the entire film as he shot it, edited together, before you start cutting it down. It's a disservice to the director and, more important, the film to take it upon yourself to start cutting lines, scripted business, scenes, or even manipulating the order of the scenes before that first cut, because you might find those lines you took out are important and you didn't realize it because you didn't give them a chance to be seen in the context of the whole film.

PS: *Not only that, but I find that it's more efficient to put it all in when I'm first cutting a scene because my mind is already in the material of the scene, its rhythms, its emotions, so it's much faster to edit the scene together at its full length then and tighten it later after watching it in the film where you have a clearer idea of how it's working within the context of the whole. Tightening is a relatively quick process, but having to open a scene up and put stuff in is a much more time-consuming process—*

JC: Because your rhythms get all messed up. Editing the first cut of a film is so important because you're setting up a rhythm that your director can now see and, yes, as you said, it's easy to take it down later. But if you start taking stuff out at the beginning and then start putting it back in later, you lose that fundamental rhythm from scene to scene because you didn't give yourself or the film a chance to develop it in the first place.

PS: *But so that this is not misunderstood, when you talk about putting everything in the first cut, it's not that the first cut is a pudding or that it's a mere assembly—rather, it's a true cut in which the film is made to play as a real film. It's long but not loose or flabby—*

JC: Exactly right. It's *not* a rough cut, it's not something just thrown together and we'll see where you want to change it. It's a true cut. It's long because it has everything in it, which is as it should be because the director should see his film with everything he shot in it. And the great advantage is that you and the director watch the picture he shot and then you're both beginning on the same page for the next stage in the process, which is the director's cut and after that the fine cut. Only now you will get there much faster and more efficiently because you've shown him, properly cut and edited, everything he shot.

PS: *Editors' first cuts are also very sophisticated cuts in other ways. I would never show any director a first that wasn't fully tracked with temporary sound effects and music.*

JC: And now that we are editing digitally, that is, on computers, we've got multiple layers of tracks, so we've put sound effects in, temporary music, temporary visual effects—we're really *driving* those first cuts in a very complete way. Directors today want and expect all that in the first cut. In other words, the first cut of a film, the editor's cut as it tends to be called, is, as you said at the beginning, a real movie in all senses of the word. Earlier I used the word "footprint" to describe the first cut, but in the digital age it's much more than that, more like the blueprint.

PS: *Mention of music and sound effects reminds me—the first time you cut something for Eastwood himself involved music and it was on* Josey Wales, *wasn't it?*

JC: I was Ferris Webster's assistant, it was my first film with Clint, and he just watched me like a hawk. At some point when Ferris had to go into the hospital for a short while, Clint comes into the cutting rooms and says, "Can we go ahead, make some changes?" The first thing he wanted was to cut down the piece of music in the campfire scene where they're dancing. He wanted to cut the scene in half. I said, "Sure, okay. But I need a few minutes so I can do it right." So he went out to his office, and I cut it. Now because I had a background in sound effects and music—I worked for two years on the *F.B.I.* series, and Kenny Wilhoit showed me how to cut music—I made the music cuts perfectly. Clint comes back and runs it and says, "What did you take out?" I said, "I took out a hundred feet, a little over a minute," and he says, "Where?" And I said, "Right here." And he said, "How did you do that?" Because every time Ferris shortened a scene with music in it, you could hear the music cuts because he didn't bother to finesse them so that they were inaudible. A lot of editors from the old days could only work with one track and all they cut was dialogue, not music or effects, and you often had to live with these awful music edits until the music editor came along. So that was the beginning of how Clint and I formulated our relationship. And when we finished the film, he said to me, "I don't know what your plans are, but my plan is to have you here on all my films."

PS: *For at least the last quarter century, if not longer, no picture editor could get by without being at least minimally proficient in cutting sound effects and editing music. Most people are also surprised when they hear how much of our work is taken up with the performances by the actors. Many people think we just pick a good take and move on to the next. But it's much more complicated than that—we typically have to do a lot of orchestrating of performances, weighing the implications of playing the master shots, the over-the-shoulders, the close-ups, the medium shots, et cetera. It's not just a simple matter of picking the best line readings.*

JC: Years ago I was at a symposium and they were asking the different editors how they worked and what they did. And one editor said that he stacks lines—that is, he has his assistant string all the takes with good line readings together and that's what he cuts from. And another editor said he puts every take in and then takes out what didn't work and then he tries to make a decision. Well, that's trial and error editing. I'm from the school where you learn to structure a scene and you figure out where you want to go, where you want to end up, and then you get the best line readings that work for the effects you're after. It's impossible to pick the best line reading in the absence of context, of what the scene is about, its place in the structure, or at least what you're trying to make it accomplish.

PS: *Once very early in my career I was talking with an editor who told me, "I just put in all the best takes," by which she meant the best line readings. And I thought to myself, but didn't say to her because I didn't want to appear disrespectful, "Well, what does that mean? If the best line reading is in a close-up, but it's not right to be in the close-up at that point, then how is it the best take?" Further, you can't just pick line readings in isolation because the line reading you choose will be determined in part by the line readings by other actors in the scene.*

JC: A lot of the time there's an overuse of close-ups—the close-up, the close-up, the close-up. Let's say the actor's line reading in the wide shot isn't as good as the reading in the close-up—are you going to cut to the close-up just because the line is read better? But what if the effect of a close-up is wrong for the scene as a whole for that line reading? When you make a cut like that, just for a line reading, you're doing a disservice to the film and a disservice to the sequence. Everything should be so smooth that you don't even see the edits. This is one place where experience really tells. A lot of young editors and directors just go for the best line readings regardless of anything else, and that can result in a lot of jumpy, awkward editing. We start doing cuts that jump here or there and audiences are very, very savvy about this stuff. If you force them to be aware of your editing, the next thing you know they're thinking consciously about what you meant—they're out of the film—when what you really want is for them to be sucked *into* the film and flowing with the film.

PS: *They're thinking* about *the film rather than responding* to *the film—*

JC: And then you've lost them.

PS: *One of the things I like about several of Eastwood's films—it's the same thing that I like about a lot of Peckinpah's and what makes working on Ron Shelton's films so rewarding—is that they contain a lot of long scenes that have peaks and valleys, emotional and psychological rises and falls, and sometimes go through a variety of moods, which require that you have to modulate the performances, you can't just play everything in close-ups or in master shots.*

JC: If you use a close-up too early for a line reading, how can you punctuate the scene later? But if you hold that close-up back until there's a real reason for it, then the audience realizes this is important, that it's saying something.

PS: *I always tell my students that they have to think of close-ups, especially tight close-ups, as exclamation points, italics, underlinings, or bold face—whatever—it's going to make a* big *point.*

JC: It's going to make it *very* big. And sometimes in scenes you mean to do just that. Clint often says, and he's right, "You've got a forty-foot screen, use it."

PS: *You hear these stories from actors who say, "Save it for the close-up."*

Which has to be one of the stupidest things I've ever heard because look at our bodies. What are our heads and faces, about a tenth or twelfth of our bodies, something like that?—so they're reducing their expressive resources by ninety percent or more.

JC: There was an actor I showed a scene to—I won't tell you who this is, only it was not on one of Clint's films—anyhow, I showed him the scene and the guy says, "You know, back there I read that in the close-up much better." I said, "Well if that's the case, we would be cutting the film all over the place chasing close-ups instead of creating a moment that's more important to the story. Only you and the director and myself—maybe—know that there might be better line readings, but in the context of the scene it's better this way." And he didn't say another word. Listen, I'm going to tell you what was one of the greatest compliments of my work. It was from Hilary Swank after she won the Academy Award for *Million Dollar Baby*. She did this interview the day after the awards ceremony. I happened to be there, and she saw me and came over to me, started crying, and said, "You and I know that you cut my performance, and you're the reason I have this." And it doesn't mean she doesn't think she did a good job or that I "saved" her. Not at all—she did a fabulous job! But it was the honing, the molding, the shaping that we have to do as editors from all the takes and angles and sizes that were shot, which can so alter the impression a performance makes. Pauses and beats are another thing. Sometimes a look is more powerful than any words, and knowing where and how to place those looks and how long to sit in the moment for an extra beat or two—

PS: *It's where the art comes in. Didn't Meryl Streep also say something similar after she first saw* The Bridges of Madison County?

JC: We ran it for her in this obscure theater out in Lenox, Massachusetts, because she was shooting a film there. It was just her and her assistant in this thousand-seat theater. When the film ends and we're all there waiting for her to say something, she just walks off away from us. Finally her assistant comes up and he says how great the film is and then *she herself* comes up—I'd never met her before—and she says, "How did you do this? I was there for every line. I know what I did, I don't know how you pulled it all together . . . but it's magnificent." Wow, I mean like that's quite a statement.

PS: *And from one of the world's greatest actresses. It's so rare to have actors appreciate how much we do for and with their performances. If I were to hold up any single example of your work as editing that completely serves the actors and the performances, Joel, I think* Bridges *would be the one—*

JC: Well I would too because I love that film. I think their performances are just riveting. It was so real—about real people you could identify with.

PS: *Let me tell you what my favorite moment is. It may strike you as an odd one—it's when they first meet. He's this free agent of a professional photographer and she's this Iowa housewife whose whole life is responsibilities and obligations. He tells her about coming across this town during one of his travels that he found interesting, so he just stopped and stayed there for a few days to enjoy it. This leaves her absolutely incredulous, so much so she almost becomes angry because she simply can't grasp the idea of a person whose life consists in the kind of freedom that allows him to set aside what he's doing just to explore a whim, a feeling, for the sheer pleasure of enjoying it. It's a great moment—*

JC: And she nailed it, and of course he did too.

PS: *Yes, he did. Moviegoers would, I think, be surprised to learn that when film editors talk shop they talk mostly about editing performances.*

JC: I believe it is harder to cut an emotional drama than an action film. And when people ask me how I do it, how do you know when to cut, I can't tell them because . . . well, because it's in my—it's in me. It's not written into a textbook, you have to feel your way through it—you hold here and you move it along there—it's feeling, it's emotion. And again I go back to that term—it comes from experience.

PS: *But to be clear about this, I am assuming that what you mean by experience is the experience of watching a lot performances and of working with a lot of different actors with different styles—*

JC: Absolutely. I see a lot of films, all kinds of films, and I'm always learning. Plus, I'm a people watcher. I love to go shopping with my wife, and often I will go outside of the store at a mall or somewhere and I will observe how people behave. You never know when you are going to have a scene that you've seen actually happen. And I think that's been an advantage that I've had for a long time.

PS: *You said something in one of your interviews that brought a smile to my face because I've said it myself so many times: once you start editing a film, you never read the script again.*

JC: That is the truth. Even up until today, I only read the script once. I'll look at the dailies, I'll run all the takes and make detailed notes of what is in them. That puts it in my mind. The script was written to go a certain way, but the director and the actors have changed it, and I have to be available to that change. I can't try to shoehorn it back to the script. And when I edit the scene, then I'm reasonably confident it'll be the scene that was *shot*.

PS: *By that point the script is effectively gone because all you've got is the footage that was exposed and printed.*

JC: Right. Once it's directed, acted, and shot, that is the scene. It may be completely different, it may be matching it, but whatever it is, it's what was shot, not necessarily what was "intended," whatever that may mean. We can't, you know, twist the film around, force it to become something else, because it's what it is.

PS: *Joel, can you give some specific instances of what happens when you and Clint don't agree on how a scene should go? When Ron Shelton and I disagree, it's never an argument—instead, he'll say, "Can we try it this way?" He goes off while I make the changes, then we run it and he'll say, "Okay, I like it" or "No, go back to what you had," or if we like them both, often I can find a way to combine them.*

JC: That's exactly right. Listen, over the years Clint and I have never had a disagreement in the sense of an argument. He would allow me to say anything, and if he liked the idea we would pursue it. But he always wanted me to tell him the truth. "You do me no good," he always says, "if you're just a head bobber." Now you don't have to be hard about it, you must be diplomatic—I tend to just, let's say, softly suggest things. It's all in the way you present it. But we never had a disagreement. I may have disagreed *with* him, that is, his preference for one take over another or how a scene should be played, but he is the director, and it's my job to make whatever he wants done work as best I can. But if you don't tell the truth, then you're doing the director a disservice and you're definitely doing the film a disservice.

PS: *Several of your films with Eastwood have been based on true stories or are what we'd call basically realistic stories, and have eschewed digital effects. But one notable exception, that is, one that has lots of effects, is* Flags of Our Fathers, *which I watched twice preparing this interview. It wasn't until I watched the ancillary materials on the second disc in the Blu-ray set that I became aware of how many CGI shots—computer graphics effects— were used. I was bowled over by how convincing the digital effects are and by how completely unaware of them I was while watching the film.*

JC: One reason I think you were so little aware of the CGI is that we used it to *complete* the scenes, not to *make* the scenes. In other words, the background is used to situate the film in time, but it's supporting what's in front of the background; it's supporting scenes that were otherwise completely staged and acted out by the actors. That makes all the difference.

PS: *There are three films of yours with Eastwood that I've felt have never quite gotten their due compared to some of his other, let's say, more "awarded" films, and yet that I think are even better than some of those. One of them is* Flags of Our Fathers, *which seemed to me to have gotten lost to some extent in* Letters from Iwo Jima. *Yet I actually prefer* Flags *because I think it's a richer, more complex experience, and it certainly filled me with greater emotion. Then there's* Changeling, *a film that a critic friend of mine feels is virtually an epic vision of America at a certain time and place in our history. And for me, it was* A Perfect World *that marked a big turning point in Eastwood's career as a serious director because of how it reflected changes in his attitudes and thinking—at least as they are manifested in his films—toward women and toward men of action, in many respects more so even than* Unforgiven.

JC: Well, let's take *Flags* first. Paramount expected the film to make fifty million dollars and it only made ten or twelve its opening weekend. So instead of supporting the film, they let it drop off. This is often what happens in today's world. The publicity people have got a certain number in their minds that a film has to hit, and if it doesn't then they regard it as a disaster and move on. Same thing happened to *Changeling* with Universal. It didn't get the big box office initially, that huge opening weekend, and since they have no concept how to work a film into a long run and make the money it deserves to make, they just let it go.

PS: *You've alluded here to one of the most frustrating rituals in current American filmmaking. When I first got started in this business in the mideighties, previews actually served a useful and even worthwhile purpose inasmuch as they gave you a chance to watch your film in front of an audience that had no other investment in it than enjoying themselves at a movie. And you could take the data of their responses and use it to fine-tune the film, clarify points of exposition or plot, address certain issues of performance and pacing and timing and theme and narrative that do not come out fully until you run the film in front of an audience and observe how it's playing. The marketers then figured out how best to promote the film. But what has happened in the years since then is that now it's no longer the studio's marketing people asking, "How can we best promote this movie?" Rather, now it's, "This is how you have to change your movie in order to make it easier for us to market it."*

JC: Yes! *Changeling* is a sensitive film but a hard one to watch because of its subject matter—a mother's child is taken and is the victim of a serial murderer who is a pedophile. It opened to ten or twelve million, and Universal immediately regarded it as a disaster. Well, they should have stuck with the film because Angelina Jolie gave her best performance to date, I think—absolutely riveting and bone-crush cold. She was so perfect. I can't imagine anybody else doing that performance.

PS: *I agree. I went back and read some of the reviews of* Changeling. *Even from some critics who are pretty good and really like Eastwood's work, there was the oddest set of reactions: it's not exciting, there isn't much romance here—a ridiculous thing to say about a film like this—it's not as dramatic as it might be. And I'm thinking to myself—I saw* Changeling *before it opened and thus before the reviews appeared—that either I was, or they were, in a psychotic state, and I don't think it was me. Precisely what they were carping about were some of the very things I liked about it and respected it for—the ironclad integrity in the telling of the story in refusing to push things too hard, a refusal to be lurid and gross and sensational, and at the same time to stay close to the character of the mother and her anguish and desperation. And you never forced the contemporary parallels—for examples, the place of women in American society, the power of men, especially men in law enforcement, and other themes. These are there for us to notice if we care to, but they never overwhelm or detract from the mother's refusal to abandon hope she will find her son someday.*

JC: We told the story.

PS: *I wanted to ask you about editing the battle scenes in* Flags of Our Fathers. *Some years ago you mentioned the thirty thousand feet of film shot for the landing in* Heartbreak Ridge, *a scene that was about ten minutes long in your first cut and that wound up being only about a minute and a half in the final film. That is often the case with battle scenes and other big action sequences—there's only a certain amount that can be planned and carried out in the shooting. The director gets as much material as he can, but it's inevitably left to the editor to sort through, shape, and structure it.*

JC: Fortunately Clint shot both tremendous material and a tremendous *amount* of material, so I had a lot of freedom to go to different places and structure the scene for maximum effect. And as with all my first cuts, I put in everything I thought we might use, including the kitchen sink. Then eventually I cut it down, but only after Clint had the opportunity to see it all *work*. And that's important because he gets to see everything he's got, and then it makes it so easy to cut it down.

PS: *I have a specific question about the big beach-landing scene in* Flags. *Most of the early part, the landing itself, is confined entirely to the marines' point of view. Yet as they're walking across the open stretch toward the mountain, you cut to the Japanese soldiers' point of view to show us the trap doors opening from the ground or from inside the bunkers, past their shoulders and their machine guns as the marines approach them. Spielberg does the same thing at the beginning of* Saving Private Ryan. *But I was wondering if there were ever any talk of holding us completely to marines' point of view, at least until after the Japanese open fire. Did you break the point of view for reasons of drama, suspense, and tension?*

JC: Well, it was in the script that way—the idea was to give a perspective of what the enemy is doing. And it was the only way we could dramatize how vulnerable the marines were, how much danger they were in, deadly danger, and how effectively the Japanese had managed to lull them into thinking there would be no resistance, which was part of their plan from the outset, as we showed in *Iwo Jima*. We wanted to make that danger seem as threatening as possible to the audience, which of course it was.

PS: *Eastwood is famous for shooting relatively few takes and eschewing too much rehearsal—*

JC: No rehearsal!

PS: *He seems really to value the kind of spontaneity that comes early, and he seems to think that something is lost with too much rehearsal, too much study, too much thinking or rather overthinking. I recollect an interview with you on one of the documentaries that came with a set—I believe it was* Flags—*where you said that he told you, "Look, get the first cut together but don't agonize over it." In other words, he was suggesting to you that he'd almost like to see a first cut that is akin to a* performance, *rather than something too worked over, or am I misreading him?*

JC: No, you're reading him right. He believes there's an energy, conviction, and truth that comes out early on and that doesn't necessarily survive if you try to do it over and over, when it might become self-conscious.

Also, he just believes in his people. Now that's not only me, that's everybody on the crew. He has a team he works with from film to film, and the reason for that is they know his style and they know what he wants, and we just show up and make a film. There's no dancing, there's no hair pulling. There's only one ego on the film and that's his, and he doesn't have much of an ego himself, so it's very much a collaborative effort.

PS: *When I first told you that* A Perfect World *was one of Eastwood's films that I especially like, you seemed to agree that you do too. Can you elaborate?*

JC: Well, for an audience it was a difficult film to watch because anytime you have any kind of child endangerment people get a little nervous. Same with *Changeling*. But Kevin [Costner] was great; in fact, it's one of his best performances. And one of Clint's too. It was a kind of turning point for both those guys as actors—they both made major changes from previous performances and the kinds of characters they usually played.

PS: *Yes, Eastwood actually allowed the Laura Dern character—another wonderful performance—to be smarter, more capable and competent than his character, who is filled with doubts about the whole enterprise. And in those days, Kevin always seemed to want to be appealing. And the story could so easily have become the bad guy with the heart of gold, but the film doesn't go there. In the end, however sympathetic he may be, Costner's criminal really is a killer, and the scene where he pulls the gun in the family's house near the end shows that in some fundamental way—sociopathic may be too strong a word, but he is surely different from us.*

JC: It's very strong.

PS: *The boy has a big part. It can often be, let's say, challenging to edit child actors.*

JC: Well, it certainly was on this film. It was extremely difficult to put together inasmuch as the little boy didn't have much experience. But Clint loved his look, and Clint knows how to work with kids very well. What he does is he turns the camera on and he starts talking to the kid and he says, "Well try it this way. Do this. See if you can do that." And he lets the boy do that line, and then he stops and gets set up again. Then Clint signals for the camera to start running but without telling the kid. And he talks to him, and that's how he gets all the pieces I need to edit the performance together. But it was very much a performance that had to be painstakingly put together piece by piece in the cutting room.

PS: *I know what you mean. I once had a movie where a distinguished stage actress was going through a very bad period in her life, and I swear to you she did not get through one line reading without tripping over it. I remember that in putting together the first cut of her scenes, I sometimes had to disregard the visuals and just construct the line readings so that they worked, and then I figured out how to get around the visual jumps with properly motivated cutaways or over-the-shoulders.*

JC: Sometimes that's all you can do. But that's our job as editors. It isn't just cut the heads and the tails off takes and splice them together. It's a lot of mining and manipulating the material.

PS: *Joel, you've been doing this job in one capacity or another for well over fifty years now, and you've got close to that many films under your belt, if not more. What keeps the work fresh and fulfilling?*

JC: I've been lucky to work almost exclusively on really good films my entire career and with some of the best people. But I don't know if I would ever say one film is harder or better or that I'm prouder of it than the others. Each film is a separate entity and I like them in their own ways. As for what keeps me going, it's something I alluded to earlier: I'm always learning. Every film is different, every scene is different, every performance is different, and I learn something from all of them. I'll stop working the day I stop learning, and I've not stopped learning.

Afterword

Drucilla Cornell

In my 2009 book, *Clint Eastwood and Issues of American Masculinity*, I argued that throughout his work as a director Eastwood has been profoundly engaged with the issue of what it means to be a good man. Of course, to even think about what it means to be a good man you are inevitably confronted with the question of how men treat women, not only in sexual and erotic relationships but in all aspects of life. One of Eastwood's constantly recurring themes is the attempt of a father to reconcile with the daughter whom he has alienated because of failure to give her the love and attention she needed in early childhood. We live in a culture and society in which men all too frequently desert their children or downgrade the importance of their female children. This is one of Eastwood's most interesting themes because it turns on two important points in his films: the possibility of psychic repair and the capacity of men to learn over time the importance of being a good father. Although Eastwood did not direct *Trouble with the Curve*, he produced it, and this movie certainly continues with the theme that a good man and the struggle to become one cannot be separated from the effort to be a father who both respects and seeks the flourishing of his female children. In another film, parenting is not only viewed from the standpoint of the alienated father but also from the standpoint of a woman who, for corrupt political reasons, is actually given a child that is not her own after her own son goes missing. I am, of course, writing here of *Changeling*, based on a true story in which a serial killer kidnaps, tortures, and ultimately murders young boys. The main character's son was more than likely murdered, but, since some boys escaped,

Christine Collins spends the rest of her life looking for her son and never finds him. But the movie is not primarily about maternal devotion, although that is unquestionably one of its themes. Here Eastwood portrays, with great sympathy for the female character, how a sexist and misogynistic society denies women their voice even on the primordial issue of whom they have mothered. The woman, played by Angelina Jolie, is actually institutionalized for her insistence that this is not her child, and the inability for her to be heard against the self-interest of the Los Angeles Police Department is portrayed in its full tragedy.

Eastwood, as we know, has been a lifelong Republican, but I have suggested that despite his libertarian politics Eastwood not only portrays the horror of war but also shows us how the very meaning of masculinity is tied into our fantasies about what it means to be a hero. And yet, in his later works, there seems to be much more ambivalence about the connection between heroism and masculinity. We sometimes forget that Nelson Mandela was the leader of the Spear of the Nation, the armed wing of the African National Congress. In a sense, the early Mandela was hailed a revolutionary hero as a general of a revolutionary army. I say this because *Invictus*—a movie about Mandela's famous insistence that rugby be respected and that sports could be an important tool in the reconciliation of a country torn apart by race—returns us to the theme of masculinity and heroism but not because of Mandela's role in the armed struggle. Here we turn, of course, to the examination of a different kind of hero, Mandela, and the theme is not one of war; yet the question of reconciliation and the role of male leadership in it is certainly at the heart of the film. Indeed, the title of the film, based as it is in a famous poem, seems to be one that celebrates the way in which men can live up to the calling associated with an almost macho view of masculinity. Does this go against what I've earlier written—that in the movies he directs Eastwood is struggling against that very notion of macho masculinity? I think we could read the movie in that way, but, because it is grappling with Mandela and reconciliation, *Invictus* is a complex movie indeed.

The theme of intergenerational friendship and war is certainly at the heart of *Gran Torino*, where an aging autoworker, Walt Kowalski, befriends a young neighbor who is part of the Hmong people. At first, Walt is openly racist and suspicious of his neighbors, but their warmth and hospitality win him over. Here, in some of Eastwood's most humorous scenes, we see Walt teaching the young Hmong teenager how to be a man. Their friendship begins as Walt intervenes to protect Thao from harassment by a gang that is trying to recruit him. Walt first uses traditional masculine means to stand up against the gang, literally putting a gun to the head of one of the leaders. Tragically, the revenge of the gang is to rape Thao's sister. Here again we have Eastwood coming to terms with the limits of a macho view of masculinity as his character is eaten up with guilt about how his attempt to scare the gang led to such a brutal revenge. *Gran Torino* is one of Eastwood's most moving films in that Walt decides to sacrifice himself in order to expose the gang, confronting them in a way that will make them think he has a gun and so shoot him down in front of neighboring witnesses; the police, therefore, will finally be able to arrest the gang members. Walt is suffering from some kind of serious lung disease, but it is left ambiguous as to whether or not he makes the decision he does because he knows that he is perhaps terminally ill. He literally locks Thao up in the basement of his house because Thao thinks that Walt is going to confront the gang with traditional revenge—that is, in a gun battle. As Walt does so, he makes it clear to Thao that he is protecting him from the kind of male violence that can only lead to an endless cycle of revenge. Certainly, in *Gran Torino*, Eastwood seems to be continuing with his themes of reconciliation—in this film, reconciliation that involves overcoming racism—intergenerational friendship, and "instruction" on what it means to be a good man. I would interpret *Gran Torino*, in line with *Flags of Our Fathers* and *Letters from Iwo Jima*, as an anti-war film.

In this short afterword I cannot review all of Eastwood's films since *Letters from Iwo Jima*, but I do want to address his controversial new work, *American Sniper*. *American Sniper* has been attacked by many, including the filmmaker Michael Moore, as celebrating US imperialism and the worst kind of male violence. But perhaps that critique of *American Sniper* is too simple. On the one hand, Chris Kyle is certainly celebrated for his commitment to his country and for his saving of comrades in battle. Certainly the Iraqi people are portrayed in an insensitive or outright racist manner. The insurgents are purportedly brutal to their own people, the leader using an electric drill to kill those who even speak to Americans. This seems to be a long way from the portrayal of the Hmong people in *Gran Torino* and Walt's overcoming of his own racism. There certainly is no critique of the role of the United States for engaging in an unjust war that completely destroyed the infrastructure of Iraq. We see a destroyed city, but its destruction is taken for granted. The critics write that this is nothing but a warmongering film that celebrates US imperialism. A number of the essays in this book address the complexity of this film. I simply want to note for now that despite the difference between *American Sniper* and some of Eastwood's other films when it comes to war and race, the film continues to expose the horrors of war. The damage done to Chris Kyle himself and his estrangement from his wife are central to the development of the film's narrative. In the end, Chris Kyle works with soldiers who have been either physically or psychically wounded by the war. He remains, however, unapologetic for his role as a sniper, and Eastwood clearly portrays him as a hero.

There are subtleties in two of Eastwood's most important films after *Letters from Iwo Jima*—*J. Edgar* and *Hereafter*—which both continue and enrich Eastwood's engagement with questions of masculinity. J. Edgar Hoover is, of course, often remembered as a hero, but the film shows him as a closeted gay man who is constantly making up stories about himself to promote his own heroism because he feels that he is in some profound way failing as a man. It can be interpreted as a brutal critique of Hoover, but I would rather read it through the lens of Eastwood's struggle to show how stereotypes of masculinity can often lead men to promote visions of themselves so as to compensate for their sense that they can never live up to what a man is supposed to be. *Hereafter* is one of Eastwood's most daring films, exploring the question of whether there is life after death and whether psychics can actually speak to the dead. It is also a heterosexual love story in which a news reporter, Cécile de France, puts herself on the line, after surviving a tsunami, by writing a book about her own experience of life after death. The main character, George Lonegan, a psychic burdened by his gift, is unable to carry on normal relations because he can see into people in a way that makes those around him feel exposed and unable to protect their privacy. This kind of profound empathy, the ability to see into others, is often associated—certainly in Hollywood films—with women. But here Eastwood gives this "talent" to a man.

Eastwood has been extremely productive since *Letters from Iwo Jima*, and this book is most welcome in continuing to critically engage with a director who is unquestionably one of the most important directors we have ever seen in this country.

Filmography

Thunderbolt and Lightfoot (1974)
The Eiger Sanction (1975)
The Outlaw Josie Wales (1976)
The Enforcer (1976)
The Gauntlet (1977)
Every Which Way but Loose (1978)
Escape from Alcatraz (1979)
Bronco Billy (1980)
Any Which Way You Can (1980)
Firefox (1982)
Honkytonk Man (1982)
Sudden Impact (1983)
City Heat (1984)
Tightrope (1984)
Pale Rider (1985)
Heartbreak Ridge (1986)
The Dead Pool (1988)
Pink Cadillac (1989)
White Hunter Black Heart (1990)
The Rookie (1990)
Unforgiven (1992)
In the Line of Fire (1993)
A Perfect World (1993)
The Bridges of Madison County (1995)
Absolute Power (1997)
True Crime (1999)
Space Cowboys (2000)
Blood Work (2002)
Million Dollar Baby (2004)
Gran Torino (2008)
Trouble with the Curve (2012)

Eastwood as Director (1971–2017)

Play Misty for Me (1971)
High Plains Drifter (1973)
Breezy (1973)
The Eiger Sanction (1975)
The Outlaw Josey Wales (1976)
The Gauntlet (1977)
Bronco Billy (1980)
Firefox (1982)
Honkytonk Man (1982)
Sudden Impact (1983)
Pale Rider (1985)

"Vanessa in the Garden" (*Amazing Stories* [TV series], season 1, episode 12, 1985)

Heartbreak Ridge (1986)

Bird (1988)

The Rookie (1990)

White Hunter Black Heart (1990)

Unforgiven (1992)

A Perfect World (1993)

The Bridges of Madison County (1995)

Absolute Power (1997)

Midnight in the Garden of Good and Evil (1997)

True Crime (1999)

Space Cowboys (2000)

Blood Work (2002)

Mystic River (2003)

"Piano Blues" (*The Blues* [TV miniseries], episode 7, 2003)

Million Dollar Baby (2004)

Flags of Our Fathers (2006)

Letters from Iwo Jima (2006)

Changeling (2008)

Gran Torino (2008)

Invictus (2009)

Hereafter (2010)

J. Edgar (2011)

Jersey Boys (2014)

American Sniper (2014)

Sully (2016)

The editors are indebted to Richard Schickel's *Clint Eastwood: A Biography* (Knopf, 1996) for much of the information about Eastwood as an actor. For details on each film, see pages 505–15 of his biography. We are also indebted to Raymond Foery for sharing the information about Eastwood as a director.

Contributors

Kathleen A. Brown is an associate professor of history at St. Edward's University in Austin, Texas. Her teaching includes courses on war and film, film history, and movements for social change. She has contributed cowritten chapters—on cinematic depictions of war, history, and sexuality—to studies of film and television. Her own work has appeared in *Film & History*, *Peace & Change*, and *Southern California Quarterly*.

David Buchanan is an associate professor in the English and Fine Arts Department at the United States Air Force Academy in Colorado Springs, Colorado, where he also serves as an instructor pilot in the Powered Flight Program. His research and teaching interests include Native American literature, the literature of war and violence, and the work of the rhetorician Kenneth Burke. His monograph *Going Scapegoat: Post-9/11 War Literature, Language and Culture* appeared in 2016.

Drucilla Cornell is a professor of political science, women's studies, and comparative literature at Rutgers University, and also a visiting professor at Birkbeck University of London and at the University of Pretoria in South Africa. She has a JD from UCLA School of Law, and, prior to her life as an academic, she was a union organizer, working for the UAW, the UE, and the IUE in California, New Jersey, and New York. She was a National Research Foundation Chair in Customary Law, Indigenous Values, and the Dignity Jurisprudence at the University of Cape Town, Faculty of Law. Her books include *Moral Images of Freedom: A Future for Critical Theory* and *Clint Eastwood and Issues of American Masculinity*. Her latest book, coauthored with Kenneth Michael Panfilio, *Symbolic Forms for a New Humanity: Cultural and Racial Reconfigurations of Critical Theory*, was published in spring 2010. Cornell is also a playwright whose plays have been produced nationally and internationally.

Film editor **Joel Cox** was nominated twice for Academy Awards *(American Sniper* and *Million Dollar Baby)* and won the Oscar for Best Film Editing for *Unforgiven* (1992). He has also been nominated for eighteen other awards, winning three of them. He started working with Clint Eastwood on *The Outlaw Josey Wales* (1976) and has continued to the present, serving as film editor for thirty Eastwood films.

Leonard Engel, professor emeritus of English at Quinnipiac University, was selected Outstanding Faculty of the Year in 1989, and in 2013 he received Quinnipiac's Excellence in Teaching Award. His edited collections include *The Big Empty: Essays on the Land as Narrative* (University of New Mexico Press, 1994); *Sam Peckinpah's West* (University of Utah Press, 2003); *Clint Eastwood, Actor and Director* (University of Utah Press, 2007); *A Violent Conscience: Essays on the Fiction of James Lee Burke* (McFarland Press, 2010); and *New Essays on Clint Eastwood* (University of Utah Press, 2012). With Matt Wanat, he has edited *Breaking Down* Breaking Bad*: Critical Perspectives* (University of New Mexico Press, 2016).

Raymond Foery is a senior professor in the Department of Film, Television, and Media Arts at Quinnipiac University. He has contributed chapters to studies on the work of Clint Eastwood, and Rowman and Littlefield published his *Alfred Hitchcock's* Frenzy: *The Last Masterpiece* in 2012. He is currently working on "Restructuring the Auteur Theory for the Twenty-First Century."

John M. Gourlie, professor emeritus of communications at Quinnipiac University, teaches film and media studies and has a special interest in the Western. He has written numerous articles on American fiction and film and has collaborated with Leonard Engel on the introductions in *The Big Empty*, *Sam Peckinpah's West* (he also has chapters on Peckinpah in each book), and *Clint Eastwood, Actor and Director* (with a chapter by him on

Million Dollar Baby). He has a chapter on James Lee Burke in *A Violent Conscience*, and a chapter on Eastwood in *New Essays on Clint Eastwood* (2012).

Edward Lamberti received his PhD from King's College London in 2016 for his thesis on Levinasian ethics and performativity in the films of the Dardenne brothers, Barbet Schroeder and Paul Schrader. He is a teaching assistant in the Department of Film Studies at King's College London. He is also operations manager at the British Board of Film Classification and the editor of *Behind the Scenes at the BBFC: Film Classification from the Silver Screen to the Digital Age* (BFI/Palgrave, 2012; longlisted for the 2013 Kraszna-Krausz Book Award for Best Moving Image Book).

Landon Lutrick is a PhD candidate in the Department of English at the University of Nevada, Reno. His current research focuses on twentieth-century and contemporary American literature and film, addressing the intersections of genre and critical regionalism in the American West.

Mark Maynard is an English instructor at Truckee Meadows Community College in Reno, Nevada. He is also a freelance journalist and scholar of Western American literature and culture. His linked short-story collection *Grind*, published in 2012 by Torrey House Press, was the winner of the 2015 Nevada Writers Hall of Fame Silver Pen Award, and was the Nevada State Library's 2016 Nevada Reads selection.

Wyatt D. Phillips is an assistant professor of film and media studies in the Department of English at Texas Tech University. He specializes in the political-economic and industrial histories of American screens, with a special focus on the development of genre. He has published articles in the journal *Film History* and in collections on early cinema, adaptation, and the transnational Western.

Glenda Pritchett is an associate professor of English, the coordinator of the First-Year Writing Program, and the editor of *Double Helix*—a journal of critical thinking and writing—at Quinnipiac University, Hamden, Connecticut. She received her MA and PhD from the University of Chicago in medieval English language and literature. Her interests recently have broadened into conference presentations and publications on popular-culture film

1264   Contributors

and television. Her chapter *"Breaking Bad* and *Django Unchained*: Strange Bedfellows" appeared in *Breaking Down* Breaking Bad: *Critical Perspectives* (University of New Mexico Press, 2016).

Craig Rinne teaches business communications at Florida Atlantic University, but, when a new frontier opens, he writes about Western-related topics. His dissertation at the University of Florida analyzed the 1990s post–Cold War Western film cycle.

Dennis Rothermel is a professor emeritus in philosophy at California State University, Chico. His research lies in the intersection of continental philosophy and cinema studies. His recent publications include "Slow Food, Slow Film" and "Heroic Endurance" in the *Quarterly Review of Film and Video*; and book chapters on Joel and Ethan Coen, Clint Eastwood, John Ford, Bertrand Tavernier, Julie Taymor, "Anti-War War Films," "Grievability and Precariousness," "Workerist Film Humor," and *True Blood*. He has coedited a collection of theoretical essays in film and media theory, *A Critique of Judgment in Film and Television* (Palgrave Macmillan, 2014), which includes his chapter "The Tones of Judgment in Local Evening News." He is working on a monograph on Westerns, and another on Gilles Deleuze's cinema books.

Paul Seydor was an academic before he began his career as a film editor in the mideighties. With over twenty-five feature and television films to his credit—including *White Men Can't Jump, Turner and Hooch, Cobb, Tin Cup, The Program, Play It to the Bone, Dark Blue, The Wall, Guess Who,* and *Obsessed*—he was nominated for both an Academy Award and an American Cinema Editors Award for his short documentary *The Wild Bunch: Album in Montage* (1997), and he was the winner of an American Cinema Editors Award for Best Edited Motion Picture for Non-Commercial Television for *The Day Reagan Was Shot* (2002). He is the author of *Peckinpah: The Western Films—A Reconsideration* (1980, 1997), widely regarded as the finest critical study of the director's work. In 2005 he prepared a special edition that restored several cut scenes to the theatrical version of Peckinpah's *Pat Garrett and Billy the Kid*, an experience that served as the basis for his most recent book, *The Authentic Death and Contentious Afterlife of Pat Garrett and Billy the Kid: The Untold Story of Peckinpah's Last Western Film* (2015). He is a professor of cinema at Chapman University's Dodge College of Film and

Media Arts, where he teaches advanced editing, and is still active as a film editor. His most recent credit is *The Young Messiah* (2015), the screen adaptation of Anne Rice's *Christ the Lord: Out of Egypt*, and he is currently completing *Villa Capri*, written and directed by Ron Shelton and starring Morgan Freeman, Tommy Lee Jones, and Rene Russo.

John Streamas is an associate professor in Washington State University's Department of Critical Culture, Gender, and Race Studies; he teaches courses in multicultural literature, Asian American studies, and theories of race and ethnicity. His research into racial and narrative implications of time and space has led to publication in several anthologies. He also writes poems, stories, informal essays, and bad puns.

Matt Wanat is an associate professor of English at Ohio University, Lancaster, where he teaches writing, literature, and literary and cultural theory. His scholarship examines intersections of narrative, genre, and culture in the areas of American literature and cinema studies. With Leonard Engel, he edited *Breaking Down* Breaking Bad*: Critical Perspectives* (University of New Mexico Press, 2016), and he has published articles on film and literature, including essays on the work of Sam Peckinpah, Jack Schaefer, and Clint Eastwood. Matt continues to explore the Western, along with questions concerning narrative rhetoric and the agrarian.

Brett Westbrook is an independent scholar who lives and writes in Austin, Texas. Areas of research and publication include masculinity studies, film adaptation, and the Hollywood Western.

Index

267